ASTOUNDING
DAYS

A SCIENCE FICTIONAL
AUTOBIOGRAPHY

Books by Arthur C. Clarke

ARTHUR C. CLARKE

ASTOUNDING DAYS:

A SCIENCE FICTIONAL AUTOBIOGRAPHY

BANTAM BOOKS

NEW YORK · TORONTO · LONDON · SYDNEY · AUCKLAND

ASTOUNDING DAYS A SCIENCE FICTIONAL AUTOBIOGRAPHY

A Bantam Spectra Book / March 1990

PRINTING HISTORY
First published in Great Britain 1989 by Victor Gollancz Ltd.

Library of Congress Cataloging-in-Publication Data
Clarke, Arthur Charles, 1917—
     Astounding days: a science fictional autobiography   /   Arthur C. Clarke.
        p.   cm.—(A Bantam spectra book)
     "First published in Great Britain 1989 by Victor Gollancz Ltd."—T.p. verso.
     Includes bibliographical references.
     ISBN 0-553-34822-1
     1. Clarke, Arthur Charles, 1917- . 2. Science fiction—Authorship. 3.
Authors, English—20th century—Biography.
I. Title
PR6005.L36Z464   1990
823'.914—dcB —dc20   *89-18053*
                                                              CIP

230-8741

Published simultaneously in the United States and Canada

Bantam Books are published by Bantam Books, a division of Bantam Doubleday
Dell Publishing Group, Inc. Its trademark, consisting of the words "Bantam
Books" and the portrayal of a rooster, is Registered in U.S. Patent and
Trademark Office and in other countries. Marca Registrada. Bantam Books,
666 Fifth Avenue, New York, New York 10103.

PRINTED IN THE UNITED STATES OF AMERICA

OPM   0   9   8   7   6   5   4   3   2   1

Gratefully and affectionately dedicated to the memories of

Harry Bates
F. Orlin Tremaine
John W. Campbell

CONTENTS

I
BATES

II
TREMAINE

III
CAMPBELL

IV
EPILOGUE . . . *ANALOG*

APPENDIX

BATES

(1 9 3 0 – 1 9 3 3)

1
FIRST
CONTACT

Sometime towards the end of 1930, in my thirteenth year, I acquired my first science fiction magazine—and my life was irrevocably changed.

The March 1930 issue of *Astounding Stories*—or, to give its full title, *Astounding Stories of Super-Science*—was not, however, the first sf* magazine I had ever seen. My initiation to the genre had been provided two years earlier by the November 1928 *Amazing Stories*, so I must digress slightly to explain just how amazing that issue really was. I had forgotten it for almost five decades, when the realities of the Space Age caught up with it in a manner so uncanny that it still sends a *frisson* down my spine.

The magnificent cover of this large-format magazine (25 cents—which is pretty amazing in itself) was by the most famous of all sf artists, Frank R. Paul (1884–1963). It showed Jupiter looming over the improbably tropical landscape of one of its inner moons, and being admired by visitors from Earth as they streamed out of their silo-shaped spaceship.

---

*For years there has been a running feud between the old-timers who insist on this abbreviation, and the newcomers who think that sci-fi is more sophisticated. Perhaps it's time to call a truce; at least sci-fi has the advantage of being instantly understandable to everyone. And either is better than "scientifiction," now mercifully extinct.

The disc of the giant planet is dominated by the oval of the Great Red Spot, and by bands of clouds sculpted into loops and swirls by storms the size of Earth. The fine details of these atmospheric disturbances could not possibly have been observed by terrestrial telescopes in 1928—yet they are precisely the same as those revealed by the Voyager space-probes almost half a century later! Paul's cover is one of the best—because indisputably documented—examples of precognition I've ever encountered: I wish I had thought of including it in my *Strange Powers* TV series. . . .

This issue of *Amazing Stories* was the property of the first sf "fan" I ever met, an elderly gentleman (he must have been at least thirty) named Larry Kille, who lived a few doors away from the house where I was born in the West Country seaside town of Minehead. The building—and indeed the whole terrace of which it is a part—is still almost unchanged, and must now be at least a hundred years old.*

I recall nothing of Larry except his magazines, but am happy to pay this belated tribute to his memory. A far greater impression was made on me by his grandmother, always referred to as "Old" Mrs. Kille.

She lived in a small room surrounded by some of the most hitech machinery of the early twenties. There can be no doubt that my own interest in science owes much to the fascinating hardware that Mrs. Kille operated with effortless skill, and for which I was sometimes allowed to provide power. Electric motors were not then commonplace, and everything was hand (or foot) driven.

I can still hear the clicking of the hundreds of needles, and the whir of the well-oiled gearwheels, as Mrs. Kille's knitting machines churned out stockings and sweaters by the yard. They were, I realize now, another branch of the family tree which includes the word-processor on which I am entering this

---

*On my 70th birthday—December 16, 1987—the Minehead Town Council installed a plaque at "Sunnyside," 13 Blenheim Road, commemorating this event. I appreciate the gesture: but it does make me feel slightly posthumous.

text. Sixty years later I was to win a bottle of champagne from the London *Sunday Times* for suggesting the alternative name "word-loom" (see Chapter 40); I must use it to drink a toast to Mrs. Kille, who so patiently tolerated a small boy's questions.

She also stimulated my curiosity by lending me such books as Ignatius Donnelly's 1882 masterpiece of spurious scholarship, *Atlantis: The Antediluvian World*—the veracity of which I did not doubt for a moment, never imagining at that tender age that printed books could possibly contain anything but the truth.

Donnelly should be the patron saint of the peddlers of UFO/ Parapsychology mind-rot; not only did he claim that all the ancient civilizations were descended from Atlantis, but in his spare time (he was also a Philadelphia lawyer, lieutenant governor of Minnesota—and twice a congressman) he "proved" that Bacon wrote Shakespeare, Marlowe—and Montaigne's essays!

He also argued (in *Ragnarok: The Age of Fire and Gravel*) that the earth had once been hit by a comet—and here he was almost certainly correct. However, he deserves little credit for this "discovery," since his timing was off by tens of millions of years. Like his successor Velikovsky, he was occasionally right— but for completely wrong reasons.*

The Kille family, as you will have gathered, was a hive of off-beat intellectual activity, and I have warm but fading memories of other members who helped me expand my mental horizons beyond those of a small provincial town. Curiously enough, I do not believe that Larry's 1928 *Amazing Stories* made such a great impression on me at the time; after all, I was only eleven. But at the ripe age of thirteen, I was ready for its considerably less sophisticated—believe it or not—rival. For whereas Hugo Gernsback's† *Amazing* had some pretension to scientific accuracy

*In, perhaps, an unconscious demonstration of the power of mind over matter, Donnelly—who had written science-fiction placed in the Twentieth Century—managed to reach it with a few hours to spare. He died on January 1, 1901.

†Hugo Gernsback (1884–1967). The father of magazine sf, despite some claims to the contrary. He started publishing *Amazing* in 1926, and with characteristic resilience bounced back with *Wonder Stories* after the 1929 bankruptcy of his company.

(it boasted Ph.D.s on its editorial board), *Astounding* was the quintessence of pulpdom, pure and unashamed.

The story of its almost accidental birth has been told by its first editor, Harry Bates, writing in Alva Rogers's *A Requiem for Astounding* (Chicago: Advent, 1964)—an invaluable reference which I expect to be consulting frequently in the course of this memoir.

The 1920–30 period, just before the Depression, was the heyday of the pulp magazines—the popular fiction of the barely literate masses who have now irrevocably defected to TV. One of the biggest of the pulp empires was that presided over by William Clayton, who deserves to be remembered kindly as a publisher who paid *on acceptance* (and not, as was all too often the case, on newsstand appearance—or even threat of lawsuit). He also paid one of the highest rates in the field—two cents a word. Very generous, at a time when a sentence of this length could buy a pound of steak.

Now, the pulps depended upon their garish covers for their newsstand sales (their subscription lists, I imagine, were minuscule). At the end of 1929, Clayton owned a stable of thirteen magazines, and this was an unlucky number for a very practical reason.

The glossy covers were the most expensive part of the magazine, and they were printed on a single large sheet of paper. One does not have to be a mathematical genius to appreciate the problem that this involved with 13 magazines. . . .

To quote from Harry Bates's reminiscent "Editorial" in Alva Rogers's *Requiem:* "Now, there were blank places on this sheet. The proofs occupied places arranged in four rows of four columns each, only thirteen of the sixteen places being filled. This meant that month after month three of the sixteen places would stare empty at Clayton, in effect reproving him for not having three *more* magazines so they need *not* be empty. . . . Clayton on looking at this sheet would often have these particular money-lustful thoughts: 'If I had sixteen magazines I'd get the three additional covers cheap . . . the paper now wasted would be free . . . there would be very little added charge for press time. . . .' If the sales of an additional magazine reached only break-even point, there would still be a profit from its absorption of the overhead—and there would not be any editorial cost, for he'd just toss it to Bates, who would merely work double."

So Harry Bates was summoned to the great man's office, and told to invent a new magazine. He had seen the three-year-old *Amazing* on the newsstands with "covers chock-full of preposterous machinery and colored rays and monstrous or monstrously dressed creatures doing things. What awful stuff! Cluttered with trivia! Packed with puerilities. Written by unimaginables! But now I wondered if there might be a market for a well-written* magazine on the *Amazing* themes. . . ."

Clayton accepted the idea instantly—but he never achieved the magic 4 × 4 total. Because it gives so vividly the flavor of those times, here is the honor roll of the long-since-fallen in the newsstand wars—the companion magazines listed on the first (January 1930) issue of *Astounding Stories of Super-Science:*

Ace High Magazine
Ranch Romances
Cowboy Stories
Clues
Five Novels Monthly
Wide World Adventures
All Star Detective Stories
Flyers
Rangeland Love Story Magazine
Western Novel Magazine
Big Story Magazine
Miss 1930
Forest and Stream

---

*Most informed critics would agree that this prodigy did not arrive on the sf scene until twenty years later, with Anthony Boucher and J. Francis McComas's *Magazine of Fantasy* (later *Fantasy and Science Fiction*), which published reprints from James Thurber, P.G. Wodehouse, Robert Graves and *original* material from C. S. Lewis and Kingsley Amis. If you think this could ever happen in *Astounding*, read on.

And I cannot resist quoting from Harry Bates's hopes for his newborn. Here, in full, is the Editorial from issue Number 1.

Introducing
ASTOUNDING STORIES

What are "astounding" stories?

Well, if you lived in Europe in 1490, and someone told you the earth was round and moved around the sun—that would have been an "astounding" story.

Or if you lived in 1840, and were told that some day men a thousand miles apart would be able to talk to each other through a little wire—or without any wire at all—that would have been another.

Or if, in 1900, they predicted ocean-crossing airplanes and submarines, world-girdling Zeppelins, sixty-story buildings, radio, metal that can be made to resist gravity and float in the air—these would have been other "astounding" stories.

To-day, time has gone by, and all these things are commonplace. *That* is the only real difference between the astounding and the commonplace—Time.

To-morrow, more astounding things are going to happen. Your children—or their children—are going to take a trip to the moon. They will be able to render themselves invisible— a problem that has already been partly solved. They will be able to disintegrate their bodies in New York, and reintegrate them in China—and in a matter of seconds.

Astounding? Indeed, yes.

Impossible? Well—television would have been impossible, almost unthinkable, ten years ago.

Now you will see the kind of magazine that it is our pleasure to offer you beginning with this, the first number of ASTOUNDING STORIES.

It is a magazine whose stories will anticipate the super-scientific achievements of To-morrow *(sic)*—whose stories will not only be strictly accurate in their science but will be vividly, dramatically and thrillingly told.

Already we have secured stories by some of the finest

writers of fantasy in the world—men such as Ray Cummings, Murray Leinster, Captain S. P. Meek, Harl Vincent, R. F. Starzl and Victor Rousseau.

So—order your next month's copy of ASTOUNDING STORIES in advance!

—The Editor

Optimistic words, which we may now read with a certain amount of cynical amusement, for they expressed aspirations rather than achievements. It's been a long wait for gravity-defying metal and invisibility—not to mention matter-transmission—but the most important prediction was triumphantly fulfilled. The children of 1930 did indeed walk on the moon.

When *Astounding* was launched, to help fill that annoying blank space in the Clayton proof-sheets, there were not enough sf writers in the English-speaking world to fill a monthly magazine with good fiction. So Harry Bates had to train them, and even became one himself. Besides some typical wild-and-woolly space adventures (the "Hawk Carse" series, which I still remember fondly) he wrote two novelettes of distinction. "Alas, All Thinking" (published in June 1935, under the editorship of his successor, F. Orlin Tremaine) must have one of the most enigmatic titles ever to baffle a pulp magazine's readership.

Much more famous is "Farewell to the Master" (October 1940), because this was the basis of the classic movie *The Day the Earth Stood Still.* Typically, Hollywood changed the ending—which, as we shall see in due course, was the whole point of the story.

It is indeed sad to report that Harry Bates died almost destitute: a well-known sf writer saw him in his last days standing blankly on a street corner, wearing Salvation Army cast-offs, while passersby tried not to notice him. Today, the first issue of the 20-cent magazine he founded would, if in mint condition, leave very little change from a thousand dollars.

Now to return to that March 1930 issue, and the manner in which I acquired it. . . .

Two years earlier, at the age of eleven or twelve, I had

graduated from the elementary school* which still stands virtually unchanged in the center of Bishop's Lydeard, the small Somerset village where my father (like many other demobilized officers) had rented a farm after the end of the First World War. Unfortunately, he had little talent for business or agriculture; his previous occupation had been a Post Office engineer, and I have sometimes wondered if his background in telecommunications could have influenced my future career. (Any genetic component could just as well have come from my mother's side: to the end of her life she could still read the high-speed Morse she had learned as a telegraph operator.)

After Father's death in 1931, Mother continued to run the farm, augmenting its income (or neutralizing its losses) by riding lessons, breeding Cairn terriers, and taking paying guests. By efforts whose heroism I only later appreciated, she managed to bring up the four of us—in order of age after myself, Fred, Mary, and Michael. Though she must always have been short of money, I do not recall any real hardship, and a diet of food that could not possibly have been *more* organically grown, heavily laced with clotted cream, ensured our physical well-being.

The farm, which bears the odd name "Ballifants" (derived from that of an old English family; "Bullivant" is another version), is still run by my brother Michael and his wife Joyce. A few years ago I was able to use my ill-gotten gains to purchase it for the Clarke family, and I am always happy to inspect the latest improvements on my increasingly rare visits to the UK.

Mike's innovations are not always successful; his Manure-Spreading Hovercraft never got off the ground and is now an ignominiously rusting pile of junk. But the secondhand church organ he assembled piece by piece in a large back room of the house—bending the longest pipe to avoid going through the roof—works magnificently. Joyce is a first-class musician, between milking cows, and many a poacher has been scared off

---

*My infants'-school teacher has just died a few days short of her hundredth birthday. Thank you, Maud Hanks, for tolerating a grubby little eight-year-old farmboy.

the Clarke estate by the legend of the Mad Monk and his midnight recitals.

But back in the hard times of 1928, all these embellishments were inconceivable, and it was only with great difficulty that Mother was able to send me to Huish's Grammar School (now Richard Huish College) in the country town of Taunton, five miles away. Here I received my secondary education until I joined the Civil Service in 1936.

The old Huish's—of typically Victorian scholastic-cum-ecclesiastic architecture—no longer exists; it was, alas, demolished some years ago to make way for a more important facility—a carpark. Somewhere beneath that expanse of tarmac—though doubtless filled in with rubble, otherwise there will one day be a nasty accident—must lie the room once aptly known as "The Dungeon."

It was intended as a place of study for senior pupils (and precocious "swots" like Arthur Clarke) but I recall at least one time when it became an arena for conflict. There is still a faint scar on my right wrist, resulting from a tug-of-war that could have turned out fatally. I was at one end of a metre-ruler, my opponent at the other. It was a friendly enough contest—but we were foolish enough to conduct it on opposite sides of a broken window. I was pulled onto the shattered glass, and donated some pints of blood to the Dungeon floor before I was bandaged up.

As might be expected, in addition to our assigned textbooks there was a lot of non-curricular reading matter lying around the place, and one day my eyes lit upon an extraordinary magazine. Its garish cover showed something that looked like a cross between a submarine and a glass-domed conservatory, driving towards a pockmarked globe resembling no celestial body familiar to me. (I already knew the moon better than my native Somerset, thanks to a succession of homemade telescopes.) However, there was no doubt that it was *supposed* to be our satellite, because the cover bore the legend "*Brigands of the Moon*—A Thrilling Interplanetary Novel of Intrigue and Adventure—by Ray Cummings."

In a curious parallel to Frank Paul's Jupiter illustration, artist

"Wesso's" portrait of the moon looks very much like the shattered face of Callisto, now revealed by the Voyager mission to be covered with overlapping craters from pole to pole. But Wesso (Hans Waldemar Wessolowski) deserves no credit for this, and his cover takes other liberties with the Solar System. What is clearly Mars has been moved close enough to show considerable surface detail—and the even more unmistakable Saturn flaunts its rings in the lower right-hand corner. Most remarkable, though, is the Sun—enormous, and apparently eclipsed by a hitherto unknown celestial body, so that the streamers of the corona are visible. . . .

But all this is nit-picking. It's a gorgeous cover, and still sets the back of my neck tingling even today. It epitomizes the "sense of wonder" we sought—and found—in the old pulps.

They don't make spaceships like that any more.

I read that March 1930 *Astounding* from cover to cover, doubtless when I should have been doing geometry or algebra or (ugh) Latin, then returned it to the literary debris of the Dungeon. A few days later, I noticed that it was still lying around, and that no one had claimed ownership. I quickly rectified that deplorable oversight, and so started my collection. Today, that magazine, although not as valuable as the first issue, would nevertheless be worth several hundred dollars. It's not even listed in the latest dealer's catalogue I have.

Over the next few years, I acquired many of its brethren by a process which was very much a matter of chance. According to legend—and I have no reason to doubt its accuracy—all these "Yank pulps" invaded the United Kingdom as ballast in returning cargo ships. Presumably it was worth disposing of unsold issues in this way, rather than recycling the paper. (If you can call it paper: such a feat of transmutation might well have been beyond the chemical technology of the time.)

These magazines—the Westerns, the True Confessions, the *Thrilling Detectives*—eventually ended up in Woolworth's at three pence apiece. Every day I would sacrifice part of my lunch hour to sift through the piles of non-sf dross in search of the occasional gem. It was what we would now call a "random access" process; there were entire issues that never reached the shores of the United Kingdom (or at any rate the Taunton Woolworth's), so there were heartbreaking gaps in my collection. Sometimes it took me years to assemble all the installments of a serial. . . .

To see what I was missing, I started an index, listing all issues and filling in their contents from the "Coming Next Month" box (not always reliable!) and from subsequent readers' comments. (I also did this for *Amazing, Wonder,* and their *Quarterlies,* of which more—perhaps—at some future time.) Later still, when the correspondence columns had put me in touch with other British "fans," I was able to buy—or swap—missing issues. By the outbreak of war in 1939, I had acquired a complete run.

It was a red-letter day when a whole box full of magazines (at a few pennies each) arrived at the local post office, where I was the night telephone operator and so had plenty of time for reading before I bicycled off to school, five miles away. And once I received a complete set of *covers* only, from a fan who had discarded them when he had his copies bound. I was very glad to have them—they looked marvelous, carpeting the floor in a display that would have put Clayton's 4 × 4 array completely to shame—but I could not understand the psychology of anyone who could deprive my precious magazines of their chief glory through so savage a mutilation. Perhaps he was colorblind.

With the outbreak of war, the supply of surplus magazines quickly dried up; ships bound for the United Kingdom had more valuable cargoes to carry. But by this time I had made many contacts in the U.S., and one of them was Willy Ley, the science writer and a founder of the German "Society for Space Travel." All through the war, Willy conscientiously mailed me the (now large format) *Astoundings* as soon as they rolled off the press. I shall always be grateful to him; like all his many friends I was not only saddened but angry when he died only a few weeks before the Apollo 11 mission—the event he had spent much of his life promoting. There is now a crater named after him on the new maps of the moon.

At its peak, my collection of sf magazines must have totaled several hundred issues, and I don't like to think what it would be worth today. It probably reached its maximum extent at the London flat I shared in 1937–40 with the writer William F. Temple and the late Maurice Hanson—and which, for a while, served as the unofficial headquarters of the British Interplanetary Society. It still stands at 88 Gray's Inn Road, apparently unchanged, though a Luftwaffe bomb neatly excised the pub at the end of the block where we entertained so many of our friends.

But when we were dispersed during the war, so was most of my library. Today, I have exactly one magazine from the pulp Era—a 1930's *Amazing Stories,* presented to me many years ago after one of my lectures on a U.S. campus. From time to time I tenderly unwrap it, to let the musty odor trigger Remembrance of Times Past.

For a decade or so I used to dream wistfully that I was still rummaging at Woolworth's, or had discovered a hidden hoard of those magic volumes. In my more lucid moments, however, I realized that Sturgeon's Law—90% of *everything* is trash—was perhaps generous if applied to my favorite adolescent reading.

And there were practical problems. Through the 1950s and 1960s I was continually on the move (the Great Barrier Reef, the Indian Ocean, Stanley Kubrick, Apollo . . .) and a thousand or so magazines would have been a considerable encumbrance. They would also—and this really breaks my heart—have been virtually unreadable, not only for literary reasons, but material ones.

Those old pulp magazine publishers invented biodegradability long before it became popular. Pick up one of their products today, and as often as not it literally disintegrates in your hands. You are also liable to get instant tetanus from the rusty staples.

Sour grapes, perhaps—but this knowledge had quite reconciled me to the fact that I would never again have a complete run of *Astounding* on my shelves. I had, in fact, ceased to read it (or any of its rivals)* some time in the 1970s. This was partly

*The only exception: *Isaac Asimov's Science Fiction Magazine,* which Isaac kindly sends me every month. At a minimum I always read his editorials, if only to see what cracks he's made at me.

due to the ever-increasing demands on my time, partly because the best fiction of the year would later be more conveniently encapsulated in book form (The Hugo and Nebula Award collections, the *Best of 19—* etc). Unfortunately, I now no longer have time to read even these. . . .

As is so often the case in our all-too-exciting century, the advance of technology suddenly changed the situation. A few years ago, the complete run of *Astounding*—now renamed *Analog*— from 1930 through 1984(!) was issued on microfiche (by Micro Information Concepts, of Dallas), each issue taking one six-by-four inch fiche. Though my reading backlog was several yards high, I could not resist the temptation; was it not Freud who once said that "Happiness is a childhood dream achieved in adult life"?

So now, in six small plastic boxes, I have the virtually imperishable equivalent of several bookcases of disintegrating pulp; I can easily carry a ten-year run of the magazine in one hand. The cost works out at a dollar per issue, instead of up to a hundred times as much—at least for the earlier volumes, which to me are still the ones of greatest interest. Perhaps best of all, every decade's covers are shown in their full polychromatic garishness on a single fiche. . . .

This embarrassment of riches would be almost useless without an index, which is also provided on microfiche (up to 1980). However, the large-format book version on which this is based *(The Complete Index to Astounding/Analog,* compiled by Mike Ashley—Robert Weinberg Publications, 15145 Oxford Drive, Oak Forest, IL 60452) is very much handier to consult, and I have found it absolutely invaluable.

Mike Ashley must have spent years on his far grander version of the project I had started half a century earlier at the other end of England. I had merely listed the stories and authors, in each magazine as it appeared; such a chronological sequence is only the first half of Ashley's book. The remainder is a real index, in which all stories, articles, authors and artists are listed alphabetically, so that it is possible to see at a glance everything that any given writer had contributed during the entire history of the magazine. There is also a good deal of statistical information—and, as an indispensable bonus, a "Letter Index" listing all the vast correspondence *Astounding* ever printed from its devoted readership. I was surprised to learn from this that my first "Letter to the Editor" had appeared in May 1938, with ten others in the years up to 1971. (See the Appendix for a complete listing.)

With Ashley's *Index* as my roadmap to the more than half a thousand fiches, I needed only one thing to complete my happiness—a reader. Micro Information Concepts supplied me with a little slide-projection device (sitting beside my word-processor right now) which throws a bright, sharp image on a small screen. Later, I bought a professional microfiche viewer in Hong Kong and carried it back to Colombo in my cabin on the floating campus, the good ship SS *Universe*.

So now I can revisit days I had once thought lost beyond recall, when, to quote Tennyson:

Here about the beach I wandered, nourishing a youth sublime
With the fairy tales of science, and the long result of Time.

My patient teachers at Huish's Grammar School might query that "sublime," but the rest of the poem is right on target.

2

"PHANTOMS OF REALITY"

The very first issue of *Astounding* (January 1930) has a cover which neatly combines all the clichés of pulp science fiction. In the foreground, an intrepid aviator who has crashed near the South Pole is battling with an unusual species of beetle; an entomologist might be more amazed—or should one say astounded—by the fact that it has a fine set of needle-sharp teeth, rather than the minor detail that it is man-sized.

And you will not be surprised to learn that there is a damsel in distress—and a very skimpy fur coat, especially for the Antarctic—cowering behind the hero as he confronts *The Beetle Horde*.

Such was the title of the two-part serial which opened Volume 1, Number 1. (Every editor of a new magazine always wonders if there will be a Volume 2—or even a number 2.) Let me list the contents of this pioneering issue: *The Beetle Horde* (Victor Rousseau); "The Cave of Horror" (Captain S. P. Meek); "Phantoms of Reality" (Ray Cummings); "The Stolen Mind" (M. L. Staley); "Compensation" (C. V. Tench); "Tanks" (Murray Leinster); "Invisible Death" (Anthony Pelcher). Though a couple of the titles are noncommittal, no one glancing at this menu would be under the impression that he had picked up *Cowboy Stories* or *All Star Detective*.

Who Messrs. Staley, Tench, and Pelcher were I have no idea;

the first two never appeared again, and the last sounds suspiciously like one of the pseudonyms that abounded in those days—if only to avoid an all-too-prolific writer appearing twice on the same contents list.

The remaining authors, however, are all worthy of at least brief notice. Although "Victor Rousseau" (Victor Rousseau Emanuel, 1879–1960) only contributed four more stories to *Astounding* (all in its initial year) he achieved a distinction many writers would envy today—lengthy reviews in *The Times Literary Supplement*. The only novel of his that is now remembered is *The Messiah of the Cylinder* (1917), an anti-Utopia written in reply to H. G. Wells's *When the Sleeper Wakes*. (Wells is mentioned many times in the text.) It seems very likely that George Orwell must have read Rousseau/Emanuel's novel—the theme would certainly have appealed to him—because it contains several quite striking anticipations of *1984*.*

You will see from this that there is more to *Astounding*'s opening contributor than one might guess from the synopsis of *The Beetle Horde*:

Tommy Travers and James Dodd, of the Travers Antarctic Expedition, crash in their plane somewhere near the South Pole. They are seized by a swarm of man-sized beetles† and carried down to Submundia, a world under the Earth's crust, where the beetles have developed their civilization to an amazing point, using a wretched race of degenerated humans, whom they breed as cattle, for food. The beetles are ruled by a human from the outside world, a drug-doped madman. Dodd recognizes this man as Bram, the archaeologist, who had been lost years before at the Pole and given up for dead by a world he had hated because it refused to accept his radical scientific theories. His fiendish mind now plans a horrible revenge by lead-

---

*For this information I am indebted to Richard D. Mullen's essay, "H.G. Wells and Victor Rousseau Emanuel: *When the Sleeper Wakes* and *The Messiah of the Cylinder*." (*Extrapolation*, May 1967, Vol. VIII, No. 2.)

†I can't imagine why I accidentally typed "beetles" when copying this.

ing his unconquerable horde of monster insects to ravage the world, destroy the human race, and establish a new era—the era of the insect . . .

Dr. Bram's reaction to the referees of *Nature* seems somewhat excessive, but you will not be surprised to learn that his "unconquerable" horde is disposed of rather easily by incendiary bombs. However, he has a terrifying back-up in case the beetles let him down. Was Rousseau having some fun at the expense of his credulous readers? Judge for yourself:

Bram was going, but he pulled himself together with a supreme effort.

"Invasion by—new species of—monotremes," he croaked. "Deep down in the—Earth. Monotremes—egg-laying platypus as big as an elephant—existing long before the Pleistocene Epoch. . . ."

Well, I suppose anything is scary if it's big enough; but a giant *platypus*?

We will meet Victor Rousseau again, you will be glad to hear; meanwhile let me introduce you to Captain S. P. Meek (1894–1972), an Army Ordnance officer who wrote sixteen short stories for *Astounding*, all but four involving the adventures of his "scientific detective," Dr. Bird.

Captain Meek clearly knew a great deal of science, and it shows in his stories—but after half a century I've still not forgiven him for one crime. An sf writer is allowed to invent not-yet-existing technologies, as long as they are plausible, but he must *not* state as a scientific fact something that is flatly untrue. Of course, many writers do this accidentally; but Capt. Meek deserves a posthumous court-martial for doing it deliberately in "Cold Light" (see Chapter 6).

"The Cave of Horror" is simply ridiculous; it concerns an invisible monster—one of the favorite themes of early sf, of which the first example is perhaps Fitz-James O'Brien's 1859 short story "What Was It? A Mystery." Dr. Bird meets—and of course routs—something in the Mammoth Cave of Kentucky which should have been protected as a major tourist attraction:

> The monster stood about twenty feet tall, and its frame was surmounted by a head resembling an overgrown frog. Enormous jaws were open to seize the sheep. . . . The body was long and snakelike, and was borne on long heavy legs ending in feet with three toes, armed with vicious claws. The crowning horror of the creature was its forelegs; they were of enormous length, thin and attenuated, and ended in huge misshapen hands, knobby and blotched . . .

If the monster was invisible, how did Dr. Bird see it? I'm glad you asked me that. . . .

He argued that though the creature could not be seen by human eyes, it would be visible in ultraviolet. So he used a powerful source of UV, and a camera with quartz lenses—carefully (and correctly) explaining that ordinary glass would block the shorter light waves.

The scheme worked; but why a creature living in total darkness (though for some reason it did have eyes as large as saucers) should bother to be invisible is rather hard to explain on any evolutionary theory.

We will meet Dr. Bird again; now a few words about Ray Cummings (1887–1957).

I can just remember meeting him, in the last year of his life, at the 1956 World Science Fiction Convention in New York. Although he had published little for years, he was still celebrated in sf circles for "The Girl in the Golden Atom"—a story about a size-diminishing drug that permitted submicroscopic adventures. One could write volumes on the truly mind-blowing scientific absurdities this concept involves,* but Cummings used many variations of the theme through his career.

The best thing about "Phantoms of Reality" is its haunting

---

*Though I have no doubt that my ingenious friend Isaac Asimov managed to legitimize some of them in his "novelization" of *Fantastic Voyage*. I flatly refused to do the same for a sequel.

title; the story is a trivial adventure in a "parallel world" occupying the same space as New York City, but imperceptible—and impalpable—because of its different vibration rate. The heroes manage to tune into it, but unfortunately fail to use this marvelous discovery to solve the city's housing problems.

Far and away the most important writer in this first issue was Murray Leinster, and his story "Tanks" was all too prophetic. It opens with the flat statement: "The deciding battle of the War of 1932 was the first in which the use of infantry was practically discontinued . . . *History of the U.S., 1920–1945*."

Murray Leinster (William Fitzgerald Jenkins, 1896–1975) had an enormous output of fiction—much of it run-of-the-mill, but some of excellent quality. He developed many original ideas, and patented at least one of great ingenuity and commercial value. It was the "front-projection" system which enabled Stanley Kubrick to shoot *2001*'s "Dawn of Man" sequence in a genuine African location—without leaving London. (The article "Applied Science Fiction" in the November 1967 *Analog* is Will Jenkins's own account of his remarkable invention.)

I can still recall my amazement when Stanley first showed me the principle of front-projection in the MGM Studio at Elstree, just north of London. We stood at one end of the set, facing the huge screen of retro-reflective ("cat's-eye") material covering the far wall. Stanley lit a match—and its image came straight back at us, its brilliance apparently undiminished after a journey of more than a hundred feet.

Next time you watch Moonwatcher and his friends cavorting in the African dawn, see if you can detect the illusion. You will get a hint of the principle involved, when the feasting leopard turns its head towards you, from the zebra it has just killed.

We will meet Leinster again; for the moment I would like to quote from his entry in Peter Nicholls's invaluable *Encyclopedia of Science Fiction*, which I find myself consulting almost as often as Mike Ashley's *Index:*

"For nearly half a century Murray Leinster wrote to the heart of magazine sf with craftsmanship and consistency, and will be remembered for that."

Hear, hear. . . .

3

THE
HARD STUFF

I would not like anyone to think that my boyhood reading consisted entirely of pulp magazines, so perhaps it's time to back away a little from *Astounding*. I devoured "real" books as well; but I must confess that they, too, were almost all science fiction.*

My first encounter with the master, H. G. Wells, was slightly discreditable. Browsing through the shelves of W. H. Smith's Taunton branch during my lunch hour I discovered *The War of the Worlds*—but its price of several shillings was beyond me.

No problem; I was (as you may have gathered) a fast reader. Day after day I returned to the shelf, and after a week or so I had finished the now dog-eared volume.

I still recall, with gratitude, the manager of the bookshop, who knew exactly what I was doing. Even if he had to mark down *The War of the Worlds* as second-hand, it was a good investment for W. H. Smith. They must have sold a fair number of my own books over the last forty years.

My principal source of hardcover books was the Taunton

---

*I was also an avid reader of various British boys' magazines, such as *Magnet, Boy's Own Paper,* and *Meccano Magazine,* which often printed sf—frequently from American sources, so that more than once I was annoyed and disappointed to encounter stories that were already familiar.

Public Library; though I now find this almost incredible, I seem to remember borrowing a minimum of a book a day, before I made the five-mile bicycle ride back to Ballifants to do my evening's homework. No one will ever be able to do as much reading as my generation did in its youth: TV has put an end to that.

At about the same time, I must have discovered Jules Verne; I still have my sixty-year-old copy of *A Journey into the Interior of the Earth*—a much more sensible title than the more usual *Journey to the Center* . . . ! Oddly enough, I do not remember my first encounter with *From the Earth to the Moon* or *Twenty Thousand Leagues Under the Sea*, the two books which relate most closely to my own interests.

Rider Haggard *(When the World Shook)* and Conan Doyle *(The Lost World*—still my candidate for the perfect specimen of its genre) had also swum into my ken. And occasionally—perhaps once or twice a year!—I ran across other hardcover sf. The only title which now remains in my memory is a lost civilization/ suspended animation novel by an Australian writer, Erle Cox, *Out of the Silence* (1925). I can still recall how his hero entered the subterranean time-capsule, triggering one lethal death-trap after another—much like Indiana Jones at the opening of *Raiders of the Lost Ark*.

Soon after it was published in 1930, I discovered W. Olaf Stapledon's *Last and First Men;* I can still visualize the very shelf on which I found it in the Minehead Public Library. That such an imaginative work would be purchased by a provincial librarian was doubtless due to the reviews it had received. "As original as the solar system," said Hugh Walpole (how did he know?) while Arnold Bennett praised the author's "tremendous and beautiful imagination." Similar compliments came from a failed politician, then living by his wits—one Winston Churchill.

Though its opening chapters have been completely dated by events which make some of their political ideas seem naive, no book before or since has had such an impact on my imagination; the Stapledonian vistas of millions and *hundreds* of millions of years, the rise and fall of civilizations and entire races of Man, changed my whole outlook on the Universe and has influenced much of my writing ever since. Twenty years later, as Chairman of the British Interplanetary Society, I persuaded Stapledon to give us an address on the social and biological aspects of space exploration, which he entitled "Interplanetary Man?"* His was one of the noblest and most civilized minds I have ever encountered: I am delighted to see a revival of interest in his life and work.

Ironically, Stapledon had never heard the phrase "science fiction"—or even seen an sf magazine!—when he was writing what he called his "story of the near and far future." He was ultimately introduced to the transatlantic pulps by the Liverpool author Eric Frank Russell, to whose help and guidance I shall pay tribute later in these memoirs. Stapledon expressed polite amazement, as well he might, when he discovered this flourishing literary culture.

Not until years later did I discover how many so-called mainstream writers have tried their hand at science fiction at least once in their career. Kipling ("With the Night Mail" and "As Easy as ABC") is perhaps the most distinguished British—or should one say Anglo-Indian?—example. And writing on *Astounding*'s own turf, H. Bruce Franklin goes so far as to claim, "There was no major l9th-Century American writer of fiction, and indeed few in the second rank, who did not write some science fiction or at least one utopian romance" *(Future Perfect,* NY: Oxford University Press, 1966). His examples include Poe, James Fenimore Cooper, Twain, Melville ("one of the first robot stories in English")—and, most surprising of all, Henry James.

I wish I had known, forty years ago, that James left "in hundreds of pages of manuscript the unfinished *The Sense of the Past,* a tale of time travel." It would be most interesting to see how James handled this theme, especially in view of his famous disagreement with the author of *The Time Machine.* (See *H. G. Wells: Desperately Mortal,* David C. Smith, Yale Uni-

*Published in the *Journal of the British Interplanetary Society,* Vol. 7, No. 6; November 1948.

versity Press, 1986.) At the very least, it could be used to trounce the mandarins who still scoff at the genre, despite the hundreds of university courses and Ph.D. theses it has now generated.

Yet there are times when those of us who were reared on the pulps feel a little uncomfortable with this new respectability, fearing that academic acceptance may be the kiss of death. Sf was more fun when it didn't take itself so seriously: one of its best practitioners was only half joking when he remarked: "Science fiction should go back to the gutter, where it belongs."

Time to get down there again. . . .

4

"BRIGANDS OF THE MOON"

With a brief shudder at the threat of giant platypuses (platypusi?) in the concluding installment of *The Beetle Horde,* I will pass over *Astounding*'s second issue and concentrate on the third, indelibly burned into my memory by Wesso's splendid cover for Ray Cummings's *Brigands of the Moon.*

Perhaps getting bored with his repeated atomic explorations, Cummings had now chosen a larger canvas where, in the blurb-writer's breathless and oddly capitalized words: "Black Mutiny and Brigandage Stalk the space-ship Planetara as She Speeds to the Moon, to Pick Up a Fabulously Rich Cache of Radium-ore."

The story—and this at once places *Astounding* above the ordinary run of pulps—is preceded by a foreword by the author which is well worth quoting, even today. Ray Cummings had a real appreciation of science and technology, and their impact upon society, which he had acquired from the best possible source—as a member of Thomas Edison's staff.

Here is Ray Cummings, talking directly to his American reader in 1930—yet also to us:

I have been thinking that if, during one of those long winter evenings at Valley Forge, someone had placed in George Washington's hands one of our present day best sellers, the illustrious Father of our Country would have read it with considerable emotion. I do not mean what we call a story of science, or fantasy—just a novel of action, adventure and romance. The sort of thing you and I like to read, but do not find amazing in any way at all. But I fancy that George Washington would have found it amazing. Don't you? It might picture, for instance, a factory girl at a sewing machine. George Washington would be amazed at a sewing machine. And the girl journeying in a subway to and from her work! Stealing an opportunity to telephone her lover at the noon hour; going to the movies in the evening, or listening to a radio. And there might be a climax, perhaps, with the girl and villain in a transcontinental railway Pullman, and the hero sending frantic telegrams, or telephoning the train, and then chasing it in his airplane.

George Washington would have found it amazing!

And I am wondering how you and I would feel if someone were to give us now a book of ordinary adventure of the sort which will be published a hundred and fifty years hence. I have been trying to imagine such a book and the nature of its contents.

Let us imagine it together. Suppose we walk down Fifth Avenue, a pleasant spring morning of May, 2080. Fifth Avenue, no doubt, will be there. I don't know whether the New York Public Library will be there or not. We'll assume that it is, and that it has some sort of books, printed, or in whatever fashion you care to imagine.

The young man library attendant is surprised at our curiously antiquated aspect. We look as though we were dressed for some historical costume ball. We talk old-fashioned English like actors in an historical play of 1930 period.

But we get the book. The attendant assures us it is a good average story of action and adventure. Nothing remarkable, but he read it himself, and found it interesting.

We thank him and take the book. But we find that the language in which it is written is too strange for comfortable reading. And it names so many extraordinary things so casually! As though we knew all about them, which we certainly do not!

So we take it to the kind-hearted librarian in the language division. He modifies it to old-fashioned English of 1930, and he puts occasional footnotes to help explain some of the things we might not understand. Why he should bother to do this for us I don't know; but let us assume that he does.

And now we take the book home—in the pneumatic tube, or aerial moving sidewalk, or airship, or whatever it is we take to get home.

And now that we are home, let's read the book. It ought to be interesting. . . .

And *Brigands of the Moon* is indeed interesting, almost sixty years later, though not always for reasons that Cummings would appreciate. The hero of *Brigands* (and its sequel, *Wandl, the Invader*) is Gregg Haljan, the twenty-five-year-old Third Officer on the "Space-Ship *Planetara.*" Note the hyphen; it would be an interesting project for some philologist to find at what point in this century space-ship became spaceship. (Presumably airship underwent the same metamorphosis.)

Gregg Haljan speaks to us in the first person through the "disc version" of his adventures. Presumably it is a video disc because he modestly deplores what "the commercial sellers of my pictured version were pleased to blare as my handsome face. . . . That I am 'tall as a Viking of old'—and 'handsome as a young Norse God'—is very pretty talk in the selling of my product. But I deplore its intrusion into the personality of this, my recorded narrative." Objection noted, Gregg, but not quite believed.

The good ship *Planetara* operated by "Martel Magnetic Levitation," and here I am sorry to say that Cummings introduces some fictitious science with the footnote: "As early as 1910 it was discovered that an object magnetized under certain conditions was subject to a loss of weight, its gravity partially nullified."

Without access to the files of *Physics Abstracts* (long since recovered, I trust, from my efforts as Assistant Editor in the late 1940s) I cannot tell whether Cummings was making this up, or was reporting some real—though mistaken—experiments. Certainly, attempts to modify gravity go back at least to Michael Faraday, who first linked electricity and magnetism, and later tried to extend the connection to other natural phenomena. He succeeded with light—but failed with gravity.

So has everyone else since Faraday (including Einstein) though experiments have continued to this day. Some of the more absurd, I regret to say, were publicized in the pages of *Astounding* by its brilliant but eccentric editor, John W. Campbell; fortunately, his sponsorship of the "Dean Drive" comes outside the time frame of this memoir. (And so, even more fortunately, does his infatuation with ESP and "Dianetics". . . .)

I have long ago forgotten the plot of *Brigands* (Martian agents attempt to hijack *Planetara,* in order to get control of the Moon's radioactive wealth etc., etc.) but I am glad to say that Haljan is no Terran chauvinist, and does his best not to exacerbate interplanetary relations ("My words need give no offense to any Martian who comes upon them. . . .").

I am less happy with the fact that Cummings's extensive cast of Bad Guys includes one "Sir Arthur Coniston"; I had rather hoped to identify with an "English lecturer, adventurer and sky-trotter."

What I do recall vividly, after more than fifty years, is the magical name of the Martian capital, Ferrok-Shahn, as well as some of Cummings's ingenious technology. Perhaps my favorite gadget is the "Benson Curve-light," that allowed one to look around corners. The Curve-light, it seems to me, is a long-felt want; I know TV crews who would kill for it.

And here is a passage that is *really* Astounding for 1930:

> . . . We were at this time no more than some sixty-five thousand miles from the moon's surface. The *Planetara* presently would swing upon her direct course for Mars. There was nothing that would cause passenger comment in this close passing of the moon; normally we used the satellite's attraction to give us additional starting speed.

My jaw literally dropped when I read that last sentence. To the best of my knowledge, the concept of "gravity assist"—which is not at all obvious, and at first sight seems to violate conservation principles—was not discovered until some twenty years later.* In the 1970s and 1980s it became an essential technique for the exploration of the outer planets, the *Voyager* space probes using the gravity fields of Jupiter and Saturn in a kind of cosmic billiards. And in 1983 it had its most brilliant application to date, when the space probe International Cometary Explorer was vectored to within less than a hundred miles of the moon, to give it enough velocity to intercept Giacobini–Zinner (see Chapter 10).

Was this a lucky guess on Ray Cummings's part? I have no idea; in any event, I salute him across the decades.

And here is another uncanny prediction. The spaceship (sorry, space-ship) *Planetara* used gamma-ray detectors to locate sources of lunar radioactivity from orbit, so Cummings would have been fascinated by a diagram in *Lunar Science: A Post-Apollo View* (Pergamon, 1975) which bears the caption: "A relief map of the radioactivity of the regions of the moon overflown by the Apollo 15 and 16 Command Modules." It shows the concentrations of thorium, uranium, and potassium—as deduced from their gamma-ray flux!

Alas, after this auspicious beginning Cummings makes a real astronomical howler. Outward bound towards Mars, *Planetara* encounters an unknown asteroid, no less than eight hundred miles in diameter! Now Ceres, the largest of the minor planets, has a diameter of barely six hundred miles, and after more than a century of photographic surveying it is now quite certain that all asteroids with a diameter of more than a few miles were discovered long ago.

Cummings was probably aware of this, because he tries to cover himself by remarking that the asteroid was travelling in "a narrow ellipse. No wonder we had never encountered this fair little world before. It had come from the

*The first reference I know is "Perturbation Manoeuvres" by Derek F. Lawden (*Journal of the British Interplanetary Society*, Vol. 13, No. 5; September 1954).

outer region beyond Neptune.* At perihelion it would reach inside Mercury, round the Sun, and head outward again."

That would give it an orbital period of about a century, and ample opportunities for discovery during its passage through the inner solar system. And what a discovery it would have been:

> A little sea was now beneath us . . . deep purple in the night. Occasional green-verdured islands showed, with the lines of white surf marking them. Beyond the sea, a curving coastline was visible. . . . We slid gently downwards. Thirty thousand feet now, above a sparkling blue ocean. The coastline was just ahead; green with a lush, tropical vegetation. Giant trees, huge-leaved. Long, dangling vines; air plants, with giant pods and vivid orchidlike blossoms. . . . A fair little world, yet obviously uninhabited.

All this, on a body less than half the size of the Moon—which is, of course, already far too small to retain an atmosphere! Luckily for *Planetara*'s passengers, this miraculous celestial apparition turned up in the nick of time. The leader of the brigands was not particularly bloodthirsty—for a Martian—and he gladly took advantage of the encounter. Gregg Haljan, now a prisoner of the mutineers, draws the obvious parallel: "My vagrant thought flung back into Earth's history. Like this, ancient travellers of the surface of the sea were . . . put ashore, marooned upon some fair desert island of the tropic Spanish main."

Alas, desert asteroids do not exist outside the pages of fantasy (*vide* also Saint-Exupéry's *The Little Prince*). But perhaps the landscape gardeners of the future, with the help of tech-

---

*Had Cummings been writing a little later, he might well have used Pluto—discovered by Clyde Tombaugh in the very month that *Brigands* started appearing on the newsstands! The worldwide public interest that this evoked must have given the sf magazines quite a boost, and Stanton A. Coblentz wasted no time in writing "Into Plutonian Depths" (*Wonder Stories Quarterly*, 1931).

nologies as yet unborn, will correct this oversight on the part of Nature.

The remainder of *Brigands* is very much routine pulp adventure—*Planetara* crashes on the moon, and there are endless fights before the villains are routed. (Sir Arthur falls to his death after a hand-to-hand struggle with Gregg; too bad—I would like to have known more about him.) Yet it has its moments; there are some excellent descriptions of the Archimedes-Imbrium region, which prove that Cummings knew his way about the Moon.

Forty years later, *Apollo* 15's Dave Scott and Jim Irwin were to drive over this very same territory in their electric "moonbuggy," while Al Worden waited for them in the orbiting Command Module.*

Gregg Haljan was to have another four-part adventure *(Wandl, the Invader,* February–May 1932) involving "a weird planet, a fifth the size of the moon" that had unaccountably arrived in the solar system and parked itself between Mars and Jupiter. (The universe was a much busier and more crowded place in the good old pulp days.)

The first illustration of *Wandl* is so repulsive that I don't have the heart to read past it. A grim-looking circle of vaguely military types is gathered round a terrified naked *brain,* cowering on spindly legs. It is about two feet across, with eyes, nostrils, and a tiny mouth puckered into a scream. The caption reads like a bulletin from Gestapo Headquarters: "Here it is, gentlemen. And this time, if we can make it speak. . . ."

What a way to treat visitors from the stars!

Altogether, Ray Cummings wrote ten stories—including two

---

*One of my most prized possessions is the relief map of the landing site (Hadley Rille) bearing the autographed message: "To Arthur Clarke with best personal regards from the crew of Apollo 15 and many thanks for your visions in space." On their second EVA they drove along the rim of a small (300-meter diameter) crater which the mapmakers had named after my early (1955) novel *Earthlight*—now dedicated to the three astronauts.

DATE	BORROWER'S NAME	

BX
1406.2 Day, Thomas
D38
1993 Where have you
gone, Michelange-
lo?

other novels—for *Astounding* during the years 1930–39. In one ("Beyond the Vanishing Point," March 1931) he returned to his patented theme of submicroscopic adventure in an atom of gold.

This forgotten novel contains, unless I am quite mistaken, one element of some historical and psychological interest. Here is Cummings's villain, Franz Polter:

> He was a foreigner, born, I understood, in one of the Balkan Protectorates; and he was here, employed by Dr. Kent as a laboratory assistant. . . . In aspect he was, to us, repulsive. A hunchback, with a short thick body, dangling arms that suggested a gorilla; barrel chest; a lump set askew on his left shoulder, and his massive head planted down with almost no neck . . . above the face, a great shock of wavy black hair. It was an intelligent face; in itself, not repulsive.

Apart from the last redeeming sentence, this could describe one of the hunchback assistants who hover incompetently around the mad scientists of Grade B horror movies ("You fool! You brought the wrong brain!"). But "Franz Polter" has reminded me of a very great man who actually lived—and whom Ray Cummings must have known, perhaps personally, as a major opponent of his one-time employer, Thomas Edison!

Everyone remembers Edison's greatest achievement—the invention not merely of the incandescent lamp but of the entire system of electrical generation and distribution. It was a *direct current* system; what is now almost forgotten is that Edison fought desperately, unscrupulously—and unsuccessfully—against the alternating current system which is now universal.

The man who made it possible to design alternating current circuits and machinery, using complex numbers that doubtless baffled Edison (even today, many "practical" engineers are terrified by the square root of minus one), was the General

Electric Company's mathematical genius Charles Proteus Steinmetz (1865–1923).*

And Steinmetz was perhaps the most famous hunchback of his day. Whether Cummings helped Edison in his ill-advised contest, I have no idea. But it seems inconceivable to me that he was not—at least subconsciously—thinking of the deformed genius when he created "Franz Polter." The name itself is suggestive; it reminds one of the German word *poltergeist* which means (among other things: *vide* Steven Spielberg) a hobgoblin. And Steinmetz came from Germany—not a "Balkan protectorate."

But enough of this amateur psychoanalysis†; thank you, Ray Cummings, for all the pleasure and stimulus you gave me—and myriads of other readers—in a simpler and more peaceful age. I am glad that, as a young writer at the beginning of his own career, I once had the opportunity of shaking your hand—and thus, vicariously, that of Thomas Alva Edison.

*Equal credit, on the engineering side, must go to Nikola Tesla, whose patents cover most of the basic AC machinery. Tesla (1856–1943) was one of the few *genuine* mad scientists the world has ever seen; fortunately he never showed any interest in conquering it, being more interested in pigeons than in humans.

†Not quite. I have just discovered that the villain of Cummings's four-part serial *The Exile of Time* (April-July) is "a repulsive cripple," which certainly does nothing to allay my suspicions.

5

INTERLUDE
IN THE
REAL WORLD

The chief pleasure of browsing lies in the unexpected discoveries one makes—I would use the word *serendipitous*, if it wasn't so badly overworked, and my Wordstar Dictionary knew how to spell it.

I was just starting to read part two of *Brigands of the Moon* when an item opposite the very first page brought my train of thought to a screeching halt, then shunted it four decades into the past. I am still in a considerable state of shock, for reasons you will shortly appreciate.

Here is a summary of the April 1930 issue's page 59:

SAFE FLYING IN FOGS

The outstanding development in aviation recently was the "blind" flight of Lieutenant James H. Doolittle, daredevil of the Army Air Corps, at Mitchel Field, L.I. which led Harry F. Guggenheim, President of the Daniel Guggenheim Fund for the Promotion of Aeronautics, to announce that the problem of fog-flying had been solved at last. . . . He was able to locate the landing field by means of the direction-finding long-distance radio beacon. In addition, another, smaller radio beacon had been installed . . . which governs the immediate approach to the field. The sensitive altimeter showed Lieut. Doolittle his altitude and made it possible for him to calculate his landing to a distance of within a few feet of the ground.

Probably the strangest device of all that Lieut. Doolittle has been called upon to test . . . against fog is a sort of heat cannon . . . the fog is supposed to curl up and die before the scorching breath of the "hot air artillery."

This brief "filler," doubtless inserted by Harry Bates to plug a gap at the end of a story ("Vampires of Venus"—a title almost as inevitable as "Monsters from Mars"), uncannily intersects my own life in no less than three distinct places.

A dozen years after it appeared, I was a Royal Air Force signals officer helping to run the world's first radar talk-down system, GCA (Ground Controlled Approach), specifically designed to land aircraft in fog and bad weather. It had been invented in 1941 by the brilliant and versatile physicist (and later Nobel laureate) Luis W. Alvarez, now in the news with his theory—he assures me that it is no longer merely a theory—that a giant meteor impact was responsible for the extinction of the dinosaurs.

In 1987 Luie published his account of these matters (and much, much more) in his autobiography *Alvarez: Adventures of a Physicist* (NY: Basic Books, 1987). Breaking an ironclad rule for the first time in years, I wrote a "puff" which duly appeared on its jacket:

Luis seems to have been there at most of the high points of modern physics—and responsible for many of them. His entertaining book covers so much ground that even non-scientists can enjoy it: who else has invented vital radar systems, hunted for magnetic monopoles at the South Pole, shot down UFOs and Kennedy assassination nuts, watched the first two atomic explosions from the air—and proved that (surprisingly) there are *no* hidden chambers or passageways inside Chephren's pyramid?

And now he's engaged on his most spectacular piece of scientific detection, as he unravels the biggest whodunnit of all time—the extinction of the dinosaurs. He and his son Walter are sure they have found the murder weapon in the Crime of the Eons. . . . But I've no idea *what* he'll get up to next.*

My own somewhat lighthearted account of the GCA saga will be found in the essay "You're on the glide-path—I think" (*Ascent to Orbit: A Scientific Autobiography,* Wiley, 1984) as well as in fictional form in *Glide Path* (1963). The closing chapters of this, my only *non*-sf novel, owe nothing to my own imagination, but are straightforward description; I have merely changed "GCA" to "GCD" (D = Descent). The following extracts will show you what the "heat-cannon" of 1930 had grown into by 1944:

The raw, wet day merged imperceptibly into a raw, wet night. The massive GCD trucks formed a tiny, isolated enclave in a world of slowly moving fog—a fog that was saturated with water, yet seemed unable to make the transition to honest-to-goodness rain. Alan was reminded of a description of the planet Venus he had read in one of those farfetched science fiction magazines that Howard used to patronize. He would much rather be on Venus, he decided; apparently it was a good deal warmer there.

It was shortly to become a good deal warmer here. . . .

. . . It seemed as if the sun were rising in the wrong quarter of the sky. The pulsing, yellow light spanned the entire field of vision, and the mounting roar of flames, muffled though it was by rain and fog, was something that could be felt as well as heard. The wall of fire was too far away in the mist for them to make out the individual jets; all that could be seen was the ill-defined curtain of light that marked its presence.

When the second line of burners ignited, it took the visitors completely by surprise. They had lost their orientation

---

*Alas, Luie died on September 1st, 1988, and so never had a chance of reading this tribute.

in the darkness, and had forgotten that the outer burners were *behind* them—and much closer than those in front. There was a sudden "whoomph!" and within seconds the trucks were sandwiched between two sheets of fire. Both sides of the sky were burning; the ground shook with the sheer force of the pounding flames. The night was no longer cold and clammy; it was uncomfortably warm even at this point, eighty feet from the nearest burner.

One of the generals leaned across to Alan and shouted, raising his voice above the roar: "I've just worked it out from the fuel figures you gave me—this thing is generating ten million horsepower of pure heat!"

... There were gaps in the fiery fence where the pipe went underground, and if one did not linger to admire the view, it was possible to run the gauntlet in complete safety. ...

... The hissing roar rose to a crescendo; the heat from the blazing jets battered for a moment with terrifying violence against his exposed skin. Then he was through, and the fire and fury subsided behind him. The open runway was ahead.

Mopping their brows, and looking slightly singed, the generals joined Alan on the vast acreage of concrete: And there they fell silent, beholding a miracle.

Like most miracles, it was a very simple one. Overhead, the stars were shining.

On either side the fog still rolled, moving sluggishly through the night. But here, in a narrow band scarcely more than a hundred yards wide, a swathe had been cut clear from ground level up to the open sky. As long as the burners pumped their millions of gallons into the night, Runway 320—perhaps alone in the whole of England—would have good weather. Alan was witnessing the crude beginnings of meteorological engineering, and the sight was unforgettably impressive.

"It's magnificent," muttered one awe-struck watcher. "But is it *practical*?"

Probably not—except in wartime. In any event FIDO (the acronym stood for Fog, Intensive, Dispersal Of) was superseded by improved blind landing systems which made it unnecessary to have any visual contact with the ground. Installations may still exist at some military airfields.

At the beginning of this chapter, I mentioned that the 1930 news item contained *three* direct references to my own career. I have given you two of them; now I leave you to judge the relevance of the third.

Lieutenant Doolittle was certainly no "daredevil," or he would not have survived to become one of the most famous generals in the Air Force. In his eighty-eighth year, he received the Seventh Lindbergh Award, given "to honor the Lindbergh heritage and advance his belief in the need to have both technological growth and environmental preservation—in balance."

General Doolittle received the Award in 1984; 1987 was the sixtieth anniversary of Lindbergh's historic flight, so the Tenth Award was presented in Paris.

It was an unforgettable experience to watch, that May 20, a perfect replica of the *Spirit of St. Louis* land at Le Bourget— while Concorde took off on an adjacent runway.

And to receive a cable which read:

OUR DEEP APPRECIATION AND PROFOUND ADMIRATION TO 1987 AWARD RECIPIENT ARTHUR C CLARKE FOR A LIFETIME OF EXTRAORDINARY CONTRIBUTION TO BALANCE IN THE SPIRIT OF CHARLES A LINDBERGH
                              ANNE MORROW LINDBERGH AND FAMILY

6
"COLD LIGHT"

After this detour into the real world, the time has come for my promised castigation of Captain S. P. Meek. I remember with particular vividness his "Dr. Bird" adventure in the very first *Astounding* that ever came into my hands, because even at the tender age of fourteen I felt that there was something seriously wrong with his science.

Dr. Bird is called upon to investigate a mysterious plane crash, at which the bodies of the crew had been found "broken into pieces, as if they had been made of glass." He diagnoses that they had been suddenly subjected to "cold beyond any conception you have of cold ... near the absolute zero of temperature, nearly four hundred and fifty degrees below zero on the Fahrenheit scale. At such temperatures, things which are ordinarily quite flexible and elastic, such as rubber or flesh, become as brittle as glass. . . ."

True enough; but then the good Doctor goes on to talk scientific gibberish: "Ordinarily cold is considered to be simply the absence of heat; and yet I have always held it to be a definite negative quantity. All through nature we observe that every force has its opposite or negative force to oppose it. We have positive and negative electric charges, positive and negative, or north and south, magnetic poles. We have gravity and its opposite apergy, and I believe cold is really negative heat."

His Secret Service companion very sensibly—and correctly—

replies: "I always thought that things were cold because heat was taken away from them—not because cold was added. It sounds preposterous."

It is—it is. But worse follows, when Dr. Bird describes a "thought experiment" that does indeed sound plausible . . .

"Consider an ordinary searchlight; it is a source of heat, and if we use a lens to concentrate its beam at one spot, the heat will be concentrated there."

Fair enough: everyone has used a burning glass to concentrate sunlight. But then Dr. Bird continues:

"Suppose that we place at the center of the aperture of the searchlight an opaque disc, in such a manner as to interrupt the central portion of the beam. As a result, the beam will go out in the form of a hollow rod, or pipe, of heat and light with a cold, dark core. . . . If we now pass this beam of light through a lens in order to concentrate the beam, both the pipe of heat and the cold core will focus. . . . *This means that we have focused or concentrated cold.* (My italics) . . . This is experimentally true. It is one of the facts which lead me to consider cold as negative heat."

Experimentally true, indeed!

It turns out, of course, that the all-too-familiar scientific criminal has built a super-weapon, with which he downs aircraft carrying valuable cargoes:

It consisted of a number of huge metallic cylinders, from which lines went to a silvery concave mirror mounted on an elaborate frame which would allow it to be rotated so as to point in any direction.

"Some kind of projector," muttered the doctor. "I never saw one quite like it, but it is meant to project something. I can't make out the curve of that mirror. It isn't a parabola and it isn't an ellipse. It must be a high degree subcatenary or else built on a transcendental function."

Pretty heavy stuff for 1930. I was quite impressed, and it didn't occur to me at the time what fabulous eyesight Dr. Bird must have possessed, to distinguish between high-order mathematical curves at several hundred yards range. But perhaps he operated on the useful principle, "Often wrong, but never uncertain"—for he was certainly wrong in this case.

As he makes his obligatory deathbed confession, the inventor of the "cold light" apparatus proudly tells Dr. Bird that "I could vary the focal point from a few feet to several miles . . . I could throw a beam of negative heat with a focal point which I could adjust at will. . . . Even at two miles I could produce a local temperature of three hundred degrees below zero."

A variable curvature mirror of optical quality is a neat trick, achieved only recently by applying a partial vacuum to one side of an aluminized mylar film. Moreover, a mirror with an adjustable (distant) focal point would have to be an ellipse. I don't know why Captain S. P. Meek brought a catenary* into the act, unless he wanted to show off.

Though it may seem that I have used something of a sledge-hammer to crack a rather small nut, I feel that it is justified in this case because Captain S. P. Meek was much better qualified than most of *Astounding*'s authors, and should not have peddled fictitious science to his innocent readers. *Absurd* science—yes. *False* science—no!

I admit that I myself have used both categories in my collection of allegedly humorous stories, *Tales From the White Hart*, but they are clearly tongue-in-cheek and should mislead no one—though one can never be quite sure of this. Recently I made one of my rare appearances in *Astounding*'s much more sophisticated successor with "The Steam-Powered Word-Processor: a Forgotten Epic of Victorian Engineering" (see Chapter 40). The title itself should have warned any alert reader, and matters got steadily worse from there onwards as I described the misadventures of the Rev. Charles Cabbage, incumbent of St. Simian's in the village of Far Tottering. Nevertheless, one literary agent (neither British nor American, I hasten to add) thought that it was not a spoof, but a "genuine research report."

Well, you can't win them all. In fact, you're lucky to win *any* of them.

---

*The curve taken by a uniform chain or cable hanging between two points. As far as I know, it has no application in mirror design.

7

"OUT OF THE DREADFUL DEPTHS"

One man has two stories in the June 1930 *Astounding*. Of "The Moon Master," under the author's real name Charles Willard Diffin, I remember nothing. The synopsis tells me more than I now want to know about it: "Through infinite deeps of space Jerry Foster hurtles to the Moon—only to be trapped by a barbaric race and offered as a living sacrifice to Oong, their loathsome, hypnotic god." What a narrow escape the Apollo astronauts had!

But "C. D. Willard's" "Out of the Dreadful Depths" has haunted me for more than half a century, largely through the impact of its illustration. This shows a truly impressive monster, like an octopus with a single giant eye (and a slavering, most un-octopus-like mouth) dexterously removing the crew members from an ocean liner only a little larger than itself. To add to the horror of the scene, each enormous tentacle ends in a mini-head with *another* mouth and *another* eye. . . .

I feel fairly sure that this imaginative piece of artwork contributed to my long-standing love affair with the world's largest, and most fascinating, invertebrates. But it did not mark its beginning; I can pinpoint that with absolute accuracy to an illustration in Frank Bullen's classic whaling book, *The Cruise of the Cachalot*, which I probably encountered at about the same time as my first science fiction magazine.

Although I have not seen the book for years, I can still recall that illustration. But let me quote Bullen's description of the encounter he witnessed about a hundred years ago—and less than a thousand kilometers due east of me right now, out in the Indian Ocean:

> . . . A very large sperm whale was locked in deadly conflict with a cuttlefish, or squid, almost as large as himself, whose interminable tentacles seemed to enlace the whole of its great body. The head of the whale especially seemed a perfect net-work of writhing arms—naturally, I suppose, for it appeared as if the whale had the tail part of the mollusc in his jaws, and, in a business-like, methodical way, was sawing through it.
>
> By the side of the black columnar head of the whale appeared the head of the giant squid, as awful an object as one could well imagine even in a fevered dream. Judging as carefully as possible, I estimated it to be at least as large as one of our pipes, which contained three hundred and fifty gallons; but it may have been, and probably was, a good deal larger. The eyes were very remarkable from their size and blackness, which, contrasted with the livid whiteness of the head made their appearance all the more striking. They were, at least, a foot in diameter, and, seen under such conditions, looked decidedly eerie and hobgoblin-like. . . .

Under *any* conditions, I should have thought. And the illustration was, especially for its time, remarkably accurate; I can say so with confidence, because many years later my friends were able to get hold of a giant squid for me. More of that in a moment.

I have introduced these marvelous animals into three of my stories. The first, "Big Game Hunt" (in *Tales From the White Hart*, 1956) should not be taken too seriously, though much of the scientific background is perfectly valid. As the title indicates, it concerns an attempt to capture a living giant squid—something that has not been done to this day. The hunt is disastrously successful.

In my novel about whale-ranching, *The Deep Range* (1957), things work out rather better. My scientists succeed in trapping a 130-foot long specimen in good condition, and I leave them worrying about how much it will cost to feed. We now know that they would have another almost equally serious problem, because giant squids cannot long survive in water much above the freezing point; their blood will not absorb oxygen efficiently at higher temperatures. Any specimens observed on the surface (at least in tropical seas) will thus be dying—even if they are not being chewed up by hungry sperm whales.

This probably explains Melville's observation in the chapter of *Moby Dick*, entitled, simply, "Squid":

> But one transparent blue morning, when a stillness almost preternatural spread over the sea . . . a great white mass lazily rose . . . and at last gleamed before our prow like a snow-slide, new slid from the hills. Thus glistening for a moment, as slowly it subsided, and sank. . . .
>
> . . . Almost forgetting for the moment all thoughts of Moby Dick, we now gazed at the most wondrous phenomenon which the secret seas have hitherto revealed to mankind. A vast pulpy mass, furlongs in length and breadth, of a glancing cream-color, lay floating on the water, innumerable long arms radiating from its centre, and curling and twisting like a nest of anacondas, as if blindly to clutch at any hapless object within reach. No perceptible face or front did it have, no conceivable token of either sensation or instinct; but undulated there on the billows an unearthly, formless, chance-like apparition of life. . . .

As I have remarked elsewhere (*The Treasure of the Great Reef*, Chapter 27) this passage presents a problem. "*Furlongs* in length"? A furlong is an eighth of a mile—660 feet! That would be a slight exaggeration even for the monster in *Astounding*: I can only suppose that Melville meant fathoms.

But how big do squids really get? Though nobody really knows, there have been some attempts to make estimates on the basis of the scars—up to a foot in diameter—their suckers make on the bodies of sperm whales.

When Yorkshire Television was filming my *Mysterious World* series in 1980, we had a stroke of luck. A giant squid was washed ashore at St. John's, Newfoundland, and taken to the local marine laboratory where Dr. Frederick Aldrich displayed it to our cameras. Although it was, as he explained wistfully, only an immature female, a mere twenty feet long, it was still an awe-inspiring beast which I should hate to meet underwater. And Dr. Aldrich estimated that mature specimens might be up to *one hundred and fifty feet* in length.

There is at least one apparently well-authenticated account of a small ship being sunk by a giant squid, after the crew had incautiously fired upon it. The incident occurred within a year or two of Frank Bullen's sighting, and within a few hundred kilometers of it. (Melville's squid was also in the same area, a quarter of a century earlier, and the two accounts bear a striking similarity; both stress the calmness of the sea and the "great mass" rising out of it.)

I have in front of me at the moment a faded photocopy from *The Times* of July 4, 1874, which tells in highly convincing detail how the P&O liner *Strathowen* picked up the survivors from the 150-ton schooner *Pearl* after the squid had "collided and coalesced" with her, and then overturned her with "monstrous arms like trees."

Frank W. Lane, from whose book *The Kingdom of the Octopus* (1957) I first learned of this story, was never able to confirm it from any other source. But my own television program of a quarter century later helps to strengthen Lane's summing-up:

To me, the most convincing evidence of authenticity is the casual remark that the man who warned the master of the *Pearl* not to molest the squid was a Newfoundlander . . . at the time of this incident the one place in the world where men were most likely to know about large squids, and their ferocity if attacked, was Newfoundland. . . .

The biggest squids I have encountered were somewhat smaller, but made an unforgettable impression. In 1963 my late (and sadly missed) friends composer/conductor Artie Wayne and his wife Vida* invited me to sail round Ceylon in their mini-liner, the ex-minesweeper and now floating movie studio *Via Vida*. One night, not far from the east-coast port of Trincomalee:

> The crew hung a powerful electric light over the side, and started netting the scores of squid that came swarming around it, darting through the water like torpedoes. When I handled one, I was most impressed by its beauty, and in particular by the lovely blue glow of the luminescent photophores ringing its eyes.
>
> It seemed such a pretty, harmless creature, its rubbery body only six inches long. But then I remembered the *Pearl*, just 170 miles due east of us, and the *Cachalot*, 600 miles east of *her* (all three of us, oddly enough, on almost the same parallel of latitude) and the *Pequod*, perhaps a thousand miles to our south. I looked at the shadows flitting through the darkness around the bright circle of *Via Vida*'s light; and presently I decided to go down to my cabin, and to secure the porthole lest any "monstrous arms like trees" came crawling hopefully aboard during the night.
>
> (*The Treasure of the Great·Reef*, Chapter 26)

It is now known that the smaller squids (and their close relatives, the cuttlefish) have one of the most complex systems of communication in the animal kingdom; it may be even more fully developed than that of dolphins. They can use their entire bodies as billboards—an even better analogy would be

---

*My genial hosts on many occasions in their beautiful Los Angeles home. At the Dorothy Chandler Pavilion in 1969 Vida helped me dry my tears as I tore up one of the best speeches of thanks never delivered. When I ran into Mel Brooks years later, I snarled: "Mel—you stole my Oscar." (*The Producers* beat *2001*.)

color TVs—writing messages upon them in beautiful, swiftly changing patterns of fluorescence.

I do not know if the giant squid also has this ability, but hinted at it in "The Shining Ones"—the tale of an encounter between a one-man submarine and an unknown species of the great cephalopods in the undersea canyon that leads into Trincomalee. (Written, I am surprised to find, in 1962—the year *before* my own meeting with slightly smaller specimens at the same location.)

In any event, there can be no doubt that the oceans hold other animals, besides the well-publicized cetaceans, with the ability to send and transmit complex messages. Perhaps some day we may be intelligent enough to understand them.

It will be good training, for Close Encounters of another kind.

Until recently, it was believed that the giant squid was by far the largest of the marine (or any other!) invertebrates. There is now considerable—and awesome—evidence that this is not the case; that honor may belong to the octopus.

The octopus has always had a bad press, but is actually a most endearing—even affectionate—creature. I am ashamed to say that I once speared one, off the southwest coast of Australia (you will find the photographic evidence of the crime in *The Coast of Coral,* 1956) and what happened next served me right. When I went back for its mate (which I kept for study, and later released) he/she *bit* me.

The pain was no worse than the prick of a hypodermic needle—but I was scared, because there is a very small Australian octopus, with brilliant blue bands along its three-inch (not feet!) tentacles, which can inject a poison much deadlier than cobra venom. Luckily, the larger varieties have no need of such chemical overkill, and their bites are, at most, mildly anaesthetic —to humans, if not to crabs.

However, this incident has always puzzled me, because of its total violation of the laws of probability. Jacques Cousteau (who has promised me he'll sail his revolutionary windjammer *Alcyone* to Sri Lanka sometime in the next few years) reports that his men have played with octopods hundreds of times—and have *never* been bitten. Yet the only time I played with one—I was!

I have since played *around* them, but have been careful to keep away from their little parrot-beaks. And on one occasion, to my chagrin, a small octopus proved that its intelligence was superior to mine.

I had lured the little creature—all of twelve inches long—out of its lair, and was deliberately chasing it to see if it would react as I expected. Everyone knows that, when frightened, an octopus emits a cloud of ink (sepia); however, this is not a smoke-screen, but a decoy.

I *knew* this—and was determined not to be fooled. Suddenly, the little octopus squirted out its ink, which remained in a small, compact cloud, following the animal's original track. At the same instant, the octopus shot off at right angles. . . .

Like a stage magician, it had tricked my eyes. By the time I had averted my gaze from the decoy, there was no sign of the original. It had found a cavern in the reef, safe from its stupid human tormentor.

I would not care to take such liberties—even inside a research submarine—with the creature that was washed ashore at St. Augustine, Florida, in 1896. The largest known octopus weighs only a few hundred pounds, whereas the mutilated fragments of this monster weighed *six or seven tons*. No wonder that, after some initial dithering, the experts (I don't believe there are any, even now) decided that it must be a piece of decayed whale.

Seventy-five years later, a fragment of the St. Augustine carcass, preserved in the Smithsonian Institution, Washington, was examined by Professor Joseph Gennaro of New York University. A specialist in cellular biology, Professor Gennaro concluded that the creature was *not* a whale—and not even a giant squid, the next obvious candidate. *It was an octopus.*

For my TV series, the professor took the jar containing the surviving fragment back to the beach where it had come ashore, and gave the reasons for his astonishing conclusion. He also tried to convey some idea of the creature's size, by laying a common octopus on the sand—and then pointing to a car parked *two hundred feet away*. It looked a toy at that distance.

So now the Thing from the Dreadful Depths no longer seems quite so absurd. But I still won't believe the mouth and eye at the end of each tentacle.

8

"THE POWER AND THE GLORY"

The July 1930 issue of *Astounding* contains two stories which made a considerable impression on me, though for very different reasons.

"Beyond the Heaviside Layer," by the ubiquitous S.P. Meek, is of such transcendental silliness (to use the adjective he taught me—see "Cold Light") that it leaves me almost at a loss for words. But not quite. . . .

Dr. Bird does not feature in this tale, which concerns the adventures of a scientist who (a) is convinced that the Heaviside* Layer is actually a sea of some gelatinous material enclosing the Earth, (b) burns a hole through it with infrared projectors, and (c) flies through the hole in a rocketship (at a top speed of two hundred miles an hour).

Ionospheric physicists will be astonished to hear that, when they had broken through the breach in the Heaviside Layer, eighty miles up, the scientist and his reporter companion *landed* their ship on "a glistening plain of bluish hue . . . on which lay

---

*Oliver Heaviside (1850–1925) was one of the most original mathematical physicists of the nineteenth century. When I was researching his life for the chapter "The Man Before Einstein" in my long-out-of-print *Voice Across the Sea (1968)*, I was astonished to discover that he had derived the famous equation $E = mc^2$—in 1890!

a huge purple monstrosity of gargantuan dimensions. The thing was a shapeless mass, only the four huge eyes standing out regarding us balefully."

The monster picks up the rocket—then drops it when attacked by something even nastier. The scientist deduces that it must be a "single celled animal of the type of the earthly amoeba," and then makes what must be one of the most brilliant extrapolations of all time: "If an amoeba is that large here, what must an elephant look like?" One would have thought that an elephant, of *any* size, at four hundred thousand feet would be an unlikely phenomenon.

Luckily, our heroes escape, and establish a space patrol to wipe out any intruding amoebae (or elephants) that try to come through before the Hole in the Heaviside Layer closes. . . .

Enough: and the story isn't even original. A far greater writer, Sir Arthur Conan Doyle, did it with "The Horror of the Heights" in 1913—only ten years after the first heavier-than-air machine had staggered off the ground. His intrepid aviator encountered giant jellyfish in the upper atmosphere, with fatal results.* Neither Doyle nor Meek explained how generations of keen-eyed terrestrial astronomers had failed to detect all this zoological activity, practically on top of their telescopes.

I apologize for exhuming this tale, but have three reasons for doing so. It is a reminder that, not so long ago, the Heaviside Layer seemed almost as remote as the moon. In 1930, no man had traveled ten miles from the surface of the Earth: Piccard's first balloon flight, which barely reached that altitude, came just a year later.

And thirty years after that, scientists *did* punch a hole in the Layer—by accident. On the first test flight of the Saturn 1 rocket (October 27, 1961), the dummy payload was a hundred tons of water, which was dumped in the ionosphere at an altitude of eighty-four miles—almost exactly the height where

---

*There are very similar creatures in *2010: Odyssey Two* and the novella "A Meeting with Medusa." And if you think I stole the idea from Doyle or Meek, you are quite wrong. I stole it from Carl Sagan (see *Cosmos*—both book and TV series).

Capt. Meek's characters had their adventure. Though no drowned amoebae were reported, shortwave radio reception was promptly wiped out over a large area of the northern hemisphere, and it took hours for the "hole" to repair itself.

And finally, before we mercifully re-inter "Beyond the Heaviside Layer," it does contain one suggestion which intrigues me. Captain S. P. Meek stresses the point that the layer is an "organic liquid," as is proved when the heat-rays turn it into clouds of soot.

Perhaps the oil companies have been looking in the wrong direction. But before you start laughing—did you know that there are apparently well-authenticated cases of organic material falling out of the clear sky? I cannot help wondering if Captain Meek knew of these reports. However, it seems unlikely, because it was not until several years later that *Astounding* got around to them.

But we'll deal with Charles Fort when we meet him, in 1934.

Charles Willard Diffin's "The Power and the Glory"—less than four pages long—is altogether more intelligent, and naive though it seems today, is even more relevant now than when it was written in 1930.

A young scientist succeeds in releasing atomic energy (from thorium—almost a bull's-eye on Diffin's part) and calls his old professor to come and witness his triumph, which, he is sure, means nothing less than "a new heaven and a new earth—the liberation of mankind from the curse of Adam."

The older man listens sadly, then demonstrates to his ex-pupil that, with a minor modification, the machine can produce a death ray. He had made the identical discovery, years before—and concealed it. For the good of mankind, the other must do the same.

The story is, of course, merely one of the countless variants of the Prometheus—Faust—Frankenstein theme, but even today, I still find Diffin's little parable quite moving, and admire Harry Bates's courage in printing a tale so untypical of the gung-ho pulps.

Yet, on deeper analysis, the story has a fatal flaw. Such a

secret could never be hidden for long, once the time was ripe for it. Next week—or next month—or next year—someone else would follow the same route.

And, indeed, only eight years after "The Power and the Glory" was published, Hahn and Strassmann discovered uranium fission, and set mankind upon the road to Hiroshima.

9

"THE FIFTH DIMENSION CATAPULT"

The first anniversary issue of *Astounding*, January 1931, has a cover which must surely have triggered unseemly speculations even in those far-off days, before Dr. Kinsey and his associates had discovered Sex.

It shows a very impressive robot, advancing towards a gentleman who is trying to halt it with his revolver, while the usual terrified young lady cowers helplessly in the left foreground. The robot, which closely resembles Arnold Schwarzenegger, chromium-plated, seems quite unaffected by the five bullet holes in its carapace, and its human opponent is now firing his last round. . . .

A commonplace enough scene, of course, on the cover of a science fiction magazine. But what—surely—makes Wesso's cover unique is the intriguing fact that *the robot is wearing a loincloth.*

The story illustrated is "The Gate to Xoran" by Hal K. Wells (no relation), and with some difficulty I will refrain from commenting on the blurb: "A Strange Man of Metal Comes to Earth on a Dreadful Mission." Nor will I re-read the story, as I'm sure I'll be disappointed. After all, this *is* 1931—and Barbarella is still thirty years in the future.

Sad to say, the contents page of the January issue reveals that all is not well with the Clayton chain. There are now four, not three, blank spaces on the proof-sheet: *Wide World Adven-*

tures, Flyers, Big Story Magazine, and *Forest and Stream* have vanished into oblivion, and *Miss 1930* has not been succeeded by *Miss 1931*.* (However, *Western Adventures* and *Western Love Stories* have materialized. One can imagine the fights over manuscripts between the editor of the last magazine and that of *Ranch Romances*. However, they were probably the same person, and I wouldn't be the least surprised if it was Harry Bates.)

Murray Leinster (Will Jenkins) is the only author of note in this otherwise undistinguished issue; his story "The Fifth-Dimension Catapult" was the first of a series he wrote on the once popular theme of "hyperspace."

We take it for granted that we live in a world of three dimensions, all completely equivalent and indistinguishable. It is true that gravity puts a special emphasis on the up-down direction, but that is merely a local phenomenon and does not affect the geometry of the situation. In space, no-one can find a vertical.

But why only *three* dimensions? Why not four—or two?

Over the last hundred years, a vast literature has accumulated on this subject. Edwin A. Abbott's *Flatland: A Romance of Many Dimensions* (1884) was the first popular book to imagine what life might be like in a world without thickness—flatter than the thinnest imaginable sheet of paper. More recently, in *The Planiverse*, A. K. Dewdney has produced a *tour de force* by describing the biology and even machinery of such an—at first sight—hopelessly limited universe. (How can you make a functioning engine, of any kind, that has no thickness whatsoever?)

By imagining the difficulties of a hypothetical two-dimensional creature—like Abbott's narrator "A Square"—in understanding our three-dimensional world, we can comprehend some of the

---

*There was once a popular English literary journal called *The Nineteenth Century*. As the crucial year 1901 approached, the editor was annoyed to find that some cultured kidnapper had registered the title *The Twentieth Century* and was holding it to ransom.

He was out of luck. The magazine became *The Nineteenth Century—and After*.

features of a four-dimensional one. But we can never actually "visualize" it; we can only work out, like a theorem in mathematics, what its properties would be.

An intelligent Flatlander could make a perspective drawing of a cube in his universe; the simplest version would show one square inside another, with the corresponding corners joined together. *We* can easily imagine this figure, for we can actually see it entire from our three-dimensional viewpoint, by looking at any of the faces of a glass cube.

To us, it is "obvious" that the more distant face is the same size as the closer one, even though it appears smaller. And the four other faces, though they certainly don't look like squares, are really identical with the remaining two. Try to explain *that* to a Flatlander. . . .

The analogy in our universe of the four-dimensional cube, or "tesseract," can be easily made of wire; it consists of one cube inside another, with the eight corners joined. Anyone who wishes to do some genuine consciousness-expanding should contemplate this object, and try to realize that (1) the inner cube is "really" the same size as the outer one (2) all the wires are the same length (3) all the angles are ninety degrees and (4) all the eight "faces" are identical cubes.

As so often happens, despite the best efforts of those practitioners who like to repeat G. H. Hardy's famous toast: "Here's to pure mathematics—may it never be of any use to anyone!" some of the properties of the tesseract have suddenly become of practical importance. To speed up processing, sets of identical computers have been connected together as if they were at the corners of a tesseract; fortunately, this can be done without taking the wires into the Fourth Dimension.

With the advent of Einstein's Theory of Relativity the Fourth Dimension—hitherto the almost exclusive property of spiritualists, science fiction writers and similar riffraff—suddenly became respectable. Despite its obvious differences from the other three dimensions (you can walk backwards in space . . .) the mathematics of Relativity was able to handle Time exactly as if it was another dimension—or direction. Space and Time behaved as if they were one seamless entity, Space-Time. Its division into four elements all mutually at right-angles was entirely subjective, even arbitrary, depending upon the observer's point of view (or "reference frame"). Bringing in Time as a pseudodimension, however, is a complication that can be ignored if we are merely discussing the properties of space—or hyperspace.

To hungry science fiction writers, hyperspace has always been a godsend; it can be used for as many purposes as a Swiss Army knife. Let me list a few of its properties, without further explanation.

An enclosed space in three dimensions would be wide open along a fourth. Surgeons and bank robbers, please note.

Two points far apart in ordinary space might be close together through a higher dimension. The *Enterprise* and countless other spacecraft have taken advantage of this.

An endless series of other universes might lie adjacent to ours, like pages in a book, quite imperceptible though only a fraction of an inch away.

An object "lifted" out of our space could be rotated through a fourth dimension, and returned completely unharmed—but as its own mirror image.

This last property has always fascinated me, and became the basis of an early story ("Technical Error," reprinted in *Reach for Tomorrow,* 1956). It is quite easy to demonstrate by paper cut-outs and wire models; sometime in the late 1940s I did this on my very first BBC television program.

Luckily, no record of this exists; videotape was still far in the future—and everything had to be done live. I would like to pay a tribute to my first producer, Robert Barr, who survived this ordeal and went on to present *The Time Machine* and other works of science fiction to a few thousand flickering black-and-white sets. He even risked some more programs with me: in one of them, I exposed an early UFO fraud (Adamski's *Flying Saucers Have Landed)* by re-faking the photos and showing that some of the UFOs must have been rather small, to have fitted inside Mr. Adamski's telescope.

Only a few weeks ago, my brother Fred (keeper of the Clarkives) was baffled to discover the cobweb-draped wire

models—tesseract, scalene tetrahedra—which I used in my pioneering presentation, almost forty years ago. That baptism of
fire was an invaluable experience, and left me permanently
inoculated against TV nerves. No one who has lectured on the
Fourth Dimension for a straight thirty minutes, *live*, could ever
be scared of the camera again. It was the best possible preparation for the day, twenty years later, when I would be sitting
beside Walter Cronkite and Wally Schirra in the CBS studio,
while an appreciable fraction of the human race joined us to
watch the first men step upon the surface of the moon.

When "Technical Error" was published *(Thrilling Wonder Stories,*
June 1950) its editor gave it the perfectly accurate and far more
interesting title "The Reversed Man." Like much early (and
late) science fiction, it's a "gimmick" story; but once again, as
with the super-computers already mentioned, the gimmick has
suddenly become of practical—indeed, commercial—importance.
But first, the story, such as it is.

I have just looked at it for the first time in—oh, thirty
years—and am very surprised to find two other items from
today's headlines. My protagonist is inside the windings of "the
first generator in the world to use the principle of superconductivity"—well, there are going to be lots of those around
soon, now that superconductivity has suddenly become the
spearhead of applied physics.

And this is a little eerie: "On a mountain three hundred
miles to the south a giant cosmic ray analyzer was being rushed
into action to await the expected cosmic-ray shower from the
new supernova in Capricornus, which the astronomers had
detected only an hour before."

Just six months ago, as I write this, most of the astronomers
on earth were turning cosmic ray analyzers, neutrino detectors, and everything else they could lay their hands on, towards
the first supernova observed in our home galaxy for three
hundred years (1987A).

(I apologize for these occasional modest coughs, which you
will have to tolerate from time to time in the course of this
memoir, and promise not to overlook those instances where I
have been disastrously wrong. Perhaps the worst example—

though I can blame the astronomers for that—will be found in my early novel, *The Sands of Mars*. It contains a sentence which still makes me cringe: "There are no mountains on Mars." But at least there is plenty of sand . . . millions of square kilometers of it.)

To continue with "Technical Error": owing to a short circuit which sends an enormous surge of electricity through the magnet coils when my protagonist is at the exact center, he is "rotated" through the Fourth Dimension. But at first, it seems that nothing untoward has happened to him; then he complains that he can read books and newspapers only when they are reflected in a mirror.

That, however, is a trick that anyone can learn. More difficult to explain is the fact that the coins and pocket diary he was carrying have become their own mirror images.

And then, despite a normal intake of food, he begins to starve. . . .

Anyone who has studied a little chemistry will be able to guess why. Many, if not most, organic compounds exist in two varieties, known as stereo-isomers; their formulae are identical, but the atoms are arranged so that the molecules bear the same relation as left- and right-hand gloves, and indeed are referred to as levo- (left) or dextro- (right).

To quote my scientist from "Technical Error":

Stereo-isomers have almost identical chemical properties, though there are subtle differences. In the last few years, it has been found that certain essential foods have properties depending on the arrangement of their atoms in space. In other words, the left-handed compounds might be essential for life, but the right-handed ones would be of no value. This in spite of the fact that their chemical formulae were identical.

You will appreciate, now, why Nelson's inversion is much more serious than we at first thought. He is actually starving to death in the midst of plenty, simply because he can no more assimilate certain molecules of food than we can put our right foot into a left boot.

I recalled this forty-year-old lecture when I read in a Washington newspaper that a company had been formed to exploit this situation. There are a lot of people in the modern world—at least in the over-developed countries—who *want* to starve, but don't wish to give up eating. How nice if there were tasty foods that could be guaranteed to provide no actual nourishment!

Dr. Gilbert Levin, President of Biospherics Inc. of Rockville, Maryland believes that his company can provide them. He recalls reading "Technical Error" and comments that "he was much taken with its, hopefully, more than fictional confirmation of our left-handed sugar sweetener." I'll be sorry if my "prior publication" invalidates his patents. . . .

Dr. Levin, incidentally, is also involved in a debate with almost the entire exobiology establishment over the question of life on Mars. He argues that some of the varicolored patches on a rock imaged by the Viking cameras may be due to lichen—or their Martian equivalent. Everyone would like to believe him, but we won't know the truth until we go back to Mars.

There is considerably more in "chirality"—or handedness—than meets the eye, particularly if mirrors are involved. An immense amount of correspondence has been provoked in scientific journals by this apparently simple paradox: when you look in a mirror, your left and right sides are interchanged. *Why not your head and feet?*

A few years ago, getting rather bored by the whole argument, I wrote to the *New Scientist* saying that gravity must be responsible, and that NASA was going to fly a full-length mirror in the shuttle to prove it. As I might have expected, a lot of people took me seriously.

The whole subject of stereo-isomorphism is intimately connected with the search for extraterrestrial life. In his book, *The Origin of Life*, the distinguished chemist Cyril Ponnamperuma* states:

---

*Onetime leader of the NASA-Ames Exobiology Division, now Head of the Department of Chemistry of the University of Maryland. Dr. Ponnamperuma was also the first Director of the Arthur C. Clarke Center for Modern Technologies, established by the government of Sri Lanka in 1985.

Pasteur was the first to observe that the molecules related to life were asymmetric in configuration. The amino acids found in proteins of living organisms are all levorotatory or L-amino acids, and the sugars are dextrorotatory or D-sugars. . . . Outside the living world, everything consists of equal amounts of the right-handed and left-handed molecules. But, in living organisms, only one form is used.

Dr. Ponnamperuma has used this fact to demonstrate that the amino acids found in certain meteorites are *not* the products of life, though they may well be its precursors.

I have often wondered if the connection between biology and chirality hints at the physical existence of a fourth dimension of space. For consider this very odd phenomenon:

One would expect left-handed, or right-handed, snails to have similar offspring, and so they usually do. But there is one marine variety that switches (or flips) when the water temperature reaches a certain point!

I find this very peculiar, and can't imagine why it happens. But I can imagine *how;* perhaps our universe is just thick enough along the Fourth Dimension to accommodate the width of a DNA molecule. . . .

A few years ago, I might have hesitated to make such a suggestion in print—or even out of it, unless I could maintain "plausible deniability." But today's theoreticians have gone far beyond such modest proposals. If you think that Murray Leinster was being extravagent with *five* dimensions, consider this recent quotation from *Scientific American* (September 1986):

In superstring theory gravity is defined in a world expanded to nine spacial dimensions and time, making 10 dimensions in all. Evidently six of the 10 dimensions must be hidden from view, thereby leaving only the four familiar dimensions of spacetime to be observed. The six extra dimensions must be curled up to form a structure so small that it cannot directly be seen.

(From "Superstrings" by Michael B. Green)

I might add that this theory is a great improvement on an earlier one, which required twenty-six dimensions. . . .

The less said about Murray Leinster's adventure in a much simpler universe, the better. But I would like to give him the last word:

"Five dimensions does seem extreme. Three is enough for ordinary use, and four is luxurious. Five seems to be going a bit too far."

10

"THE WORLD BEHIND THE MOON" or "After You, Monsieur Lagrange . . ."

The April 1931 *Astounding* features a story riddled with so many interesting fallacies that it merits an entire chapter. Yet, surprising, the biggest "error"—that implicit in the title itself—does contain an element of truth.

The author, Paul Ernst, was a prolific pulp writer of the 1930s, and though his science was often shaky, several of his stories have left me with such pleasant memories that I can even recall actual phrases from them. And "The World Behind the Moon" almost certainly started me thinking about the problem in celestial mechanics it involved, though the results were not apparent until many years later.

The tale has a most deplorable opening; the heroes are about to crash on a new world and cannot slow down their rocket *because it has not yet encountered an atmosphere.*

Although in 1931 most members of the general public—if they bothered to think about the matter—believed that rockets couldn't work in space "because there was nothing to push against," a writer of even pseudoscience-fiction had no excuse for such a howler. And why did not Harry Bates's blue pencil uphold the boast (and I quote again from his first editorial) that all stories would be "strictly accurate in their science"? Perhaps he was too busy writing stories for his own magazine; the same issue contains "Four Miles Within" by "Anthony Gilmore" who was Harry plus his assistant editor Desmond Hall. (It is only fair to say that this gambit was practically forced upon them by the difficulty of obtaining usable stories, and nobody was any the worse for it. Anthony Gilmore was extremely popular with the readers—and with Clayton himself.)

I do not know if Paul Ernst was the first writer to use the concept of a world hidden behind the moon, and will be most surprised if he was—if only because a much more celebrated author had used a similar theme seven years earlier. Edgar Wallace's *Planetoid 127* (1924) is a rather feeble novel about a twin of the Earth, moving in the same orbit but forever invisible because it is on the other side of the sun. Forty years later, John Norman (John Frederick Lange) revived this patently absurd idea in his "Gor" series, so popular with militant feminists.

I say absurd, because ever since Newton discovered the law of gravitation, the movements of the planets and their satellites have been subject to the most detailed mathematical analysis. Any large, unknown masses would have been detected at least a century ago: in fact, this is precisely how Neptune was discovered, by its perturbations of the next inner planet, Uranus. And *that* was at the outer fringes of the solar system; anything near the Earth's orbit would have no chance of hiding—unless it is far too small to count as a planet.

But Paul Ernst's "Zeud" was "almost a twin of the moon; a very little smaller, and almost eighty thousand miles away . . . there it whirled, directly in a line between the earth and the moon, moving as the moon moved so that it was ever out of sight beyond it."

Don't ask me, by the way, why Ernst chose the name "Zeud," in defiance of astronomical tradition. All major bodies in the solar system, including satellites, are given mythological names, though oddly enough "Zeus" has not been used—perhaps because it is equivalent to Jupiter.

Not long ago, *The Times* columnist Bernard Levin suggested that any planet beyond Pluto should be named Marilyn, after you-know-who. He was promptly squashed in the correspondence columns, though for once there was no protest from the traditional "Disgusted," of Tunbridge Wells.

When I read Ernst's story, probably at the age of fifteen, I was already a keen astronomer and knew my way about the moon thanks to a series of homemade telescopes I had built from miscellaneous lenses and cardboard tubes. Little could I have dreamed that one day I would have on my roof a 14" Celestron with stereo-ocular that allows me to use *both* eyes, so that now when I explore my favorite lunar landscapes I seem to be behind the window of a spaceship, rather than peering through a telescope tube. (Still less could I have dreamed that my roof would be only a few hundred miles from the Equator.)

If I gave the matter any thought at the time, I probably saw nothing wrong with hiding a world behind the moon. But a few years later, when I knew something about the laws of gravitation, I might have argued along these lines:

The more distant a satellite is from the body it is orbiting, the weaker the primary's gravitational field—hence the more slowly it need move to counterbalance it. Eighty thousand miles beyond the moon, Earth's gravity is almost halved, so "Zeud" would have to move very much more slowly than the moon to maintain its more distant orbit.* So it will quickly drop behind, and can't possibly stay hidden for more than a few hours at a time. Ergo, the whole concept is nonsense.

"Logical," as Mr. Spock would say. However, the reasoning is incorrect; it does not take account of all the facts, and the truth is more complicated—and much more interesting.

That this might be the case I probably did not suspect until fifteen years later, until it was pointed out to me by my friend the late R. A. Smith, who was one of the most enthusiastic pre-

---

*Obeying Kepler's Third Law: the square of the period is proportional to the cube of the distance.

(and post-) war members of the British Interplanetary Society; trained as an engineering and architectural draftsman, Ralph's artistic skills played a major role in putting our ideas across to the general public. His drawings of space vehicles, lunar bases, and space stations contributed greatly to my own early books, *The Exploration of Space* (1951) and *The Exploration of the Moon* (1954). Many of his remarkable illustrations, which anticipated almost all the developments that occurred soon after his untimely death (1959), were later collected by the BIS in the volume *High Road to the Moon* (1979).

In addition to his artistic talents, Ralph had an astonishing insight into the practical engineering problems of space travel, and eventually earned his living in the nascent British rocket industry. Early in 1947, he had discovered—without mathematics, but by very simple reasoning—that a body *could* indeed stay hidden behind the moon! What was equally interesting, there appeared to be a point between Earth and moon where a large enough body could hover forever, occulting the moon.

My earlier refutation of Zeud overlooked one point—the gravitational field *of the moon itself.* True, the moon's mass is little more than one percent of the earth's, but Zeud would be much nearer, and the inverse square law would be operating powerfully. So let us repeat the argument, bringing in this additional refinement.

Because the moon's mass isn't zero—as was tacitly assumed—its gravitational field has to be added to that of the earth, so Zeud has to move a little faster to remain in orbit. The question Ralph asked me was this—is there a point at which the increase in speed can exactly compensate for the increase in distance, so that a satellite—or sub-satellite—would remain hidden behind the moon?

It was an interesting problem, and might one day have practical applications; a relay station hovering permanently above Farside would be very useful to lunar explorers, who would no longer be able to communicate with each other via Earth.

So I wrote out the equations, and was disconcerted to find that I had a quintic on my hands. Elementary high-school algebra copes with quadratics (equations in x squared) and may take a nervous look at cubics, which are ugly but not difficult. Quartics are worse, but not impossible because they are essentially quadratics squared. But how can you solve equations involving x raised to the power of five?

Well, you can't, at least in purely algebraic terms, though it took mathematicians several centuries to discover this. The proof was scribbled down, the night before he died in a duel, by the twenty-year-old Evariste Galois. A moving account of this tragedy was written by Eric Temple Bell* in his *Men of Mathematics;* although some details of Bell's version have now been challenged, his verdict still stands:

> What Galois wrote in those desperate last hours before the dawn will keep generations of mathematicians busy for hundreds of years. He had found, once and for all, the true solution of a riddle that had tormented mathematicians for centuries: under what conditions can an equation be solved? But this was only one thing of many. . . .

I have always thought that Galois's last hours on earth raise one of the great "ifs" of science. *If* he had got a good night's sleep, instead of writing down his theories, he might have lived to eighty, and changed even more profoundly the course of mathematics. . . .

Luckily, my quintic equation was a fairly simple one: I'm still quite proud of it, so here it is:

$$k^5 - 3k^4 + 3k^3 - 1.2 \times 10^{-2}(1-k)^2 = 0$$

After playing round with my slide rule for a while (electronic calculators, of course, were still twenty years in the future), I found my two ks. One gave a position 64,000 kilometers beyond the moon (exactly half the figure Ernst gave for

---

*Bell, under the pseudonym "John Taine," wrote several fine sf novels; perhaps his best was *The Time Stream.* His only contribution to *Astounding,* however, was the mediocre "Twelve Eighty-Seven" (May–Sept 1935).

Zeud) while the other was 58,000 kilometers on the earthward side.

I am one of the world's most incompetent calculators: even as a young man, I did not believe that human brains should be wasted on work that machines could do. (The fact that those machines had not yet been invented did not affect the principle.) So I did not trust my results until I had worked out a purely graphical solution, by plotting the combined earth–moon gravity field and seeing at what points along it a body would have the same period as the moon. To my relief (and mild surprise) the two approaches gave the same result.

This double-checking gave me enough confidence to write a short paper, "Stationary Orbits," which I submitted to the *Journal of the British Astronomical Association*. Probably because he was still suffering from wartime shortages, the editor published it in the December 1947 issue (Vol. 57, No. 6, pp. 232–7). I have since reprinted it in *Ascent to Orbit: A Scientific Autobiography* (Wiley, 1984) which in many ways may be regarded as complementing this volume.

So—is Zeud ridiculous, after all? Yes, I'm afraid so.

My analysis was based on several approximations; it assumed that the sub-satellite had no mass, and that the moon's orbit is perfectly circular, whereas in fact it is slightly elliptical. When these factors are taken into account, it turns out, alas, that neither the farside nor earthside positions are stable. Any objects placed there would drift around in complicated curves, and eventually wander away.

However, it would take very little effort to *keep* them on station, if desired. Just as satellites in earth orbit correct their position from time to time by gentle spurts of gas from their thrusters, so a satellite or space station could easily stay balanced, like a tightrope walker, on the earth–moon line. In my 1947 paper I calculated that a mass of several hundred tons could maintain its position by ejecting a few kilograms of rocket propellant a day.

All this must have seemed the wildest theorizing to the British Astronomers, back in 1947. Indeed, nine years in the future no less a person than the Astronomer Royal was to remark that "Space travel is utter bilge." (*Sputnik* went up next year, and the poor man was never allowed to forget his faux pas.) Yet its practical application did not have to wait until the moon was colonized, but began in the 1970s, with a seminal paper by Robert W. Farquhar of the Goddard Space Flight Center, "The Utilization of Halo Orbits in Advanced Lunar Operations" (NASA TN D-6365, July 1971).

Farquhar pointed out that even if the position beyond the moon wasn't stable, it could be a most useful parking place for probes investigating the properties of trans-lunar space. The fact that they would not stay hidden behind the moon was a positive advantage, as we would need to keep in touch with them.

By skillful navigation, matters could be arranged so that a lunar sub-satellite could move in what Farquhar called a "halo orbit," because from the viewpoint of the earth it would appear to trace a ring around the moon.

No one has yet thought of a use for the earthside position— which, incidentally, has nothing to do with the so-called neutral point where the gravities of moon and earth just cancel. This is about 20,000 kilometers closer to the moon, and has no physical significance. Contrary to a common belief, a body placed here would not be helplessly trapped; it would soon fall one way or the other.

Now let us step back and take the wider view. My piece of mathematical *chutzpah*, as I knew perfectly well even then, was a cheeky assault on one of the Universe's greatest challenges to human mathematicians—the Problem of Three Bodies. In general, there is no exact solution, though there are approximation methods which will give the answer to any desired degree of accuracy. Most of them were, however, impractically laborious in the era before electronic calculators, which have now transformed Celestial Mechanics—like everything else.

One of the greatest mathematicians who ever lived, Lagrange, discovered that for one special case the problem had a solution—or, rather, five solutions. If the mass of the third body is negligible compared with the other two, which is certainly true for space probes in the earth–moon system, then it can remain in equilibrium at (or near) five fixed points.

These are known as "Libration points" (from *libra,* a balance). We have already encountered two of them: L_1 is the hidden point above Farside, and L_2 that between the earth and moon.

The third, L_3, is rather surprising, though its existence can be readily deduced from the argument already given for L_1 and L_2. It is on the side of the Earth's orbit opposite to the moon, and at a slightly greater distance.

L_4 and L_5 are the two points which have received a great deal of publicity in the last few years (Lagrange *would* have been surprised). That they must exist is obvious from the quintic equation I have already given; by a fundamental theorem in algebra, any such equation must have as many roots as its highest power—in this case, five.

Since I already knew the answers, I never bothered to solve this equation for the other two points (especially as they would have to be complex numbers, involving the square root of minus one, Steinmetz's often unwelcome contribution to electrical engineering—see Chapter 4). L_4 and L_5 are the now famous "Equilateral points," so called because they move in the moon's orbit, at the same distance from earth and moon. L_5 is the one *ahead* of the moon; L_4 the one in the trailing position.

L_5 has become very popular as a piece of celestial real-estate since Dr. Gerard O'Neill's advocacy of large space colonies. An "L_5 Society" (now merged into the National Space Society) was formed to promote such developments*; its history is outlined in Michael A.G. Michaud's entertaining book *Reaching for the High Frontier: the American Pro-Space Movement, 1972–84* (Praeger, 1986.)

It should be noted that positions L_1 through $_5$ are possible for *any* pair of astronomical bodies. Perhaps the first writer to exploit this possibility in sf was the radio-engineer George O.

---

*Which reminds me that the United Nations Committee on the Peaceful Uses of Outer Space is often referred to in the trade as the Committee on the Useful Pieces of Outer Space. Sorry . . .

Smith, in his "Venus Equilateral" stories, which started appearing in *Astounding* in October 1942—the portentous month when the first V2 rocket was successfully launched at Peenemünde, and the first nuclear chain reaction was started in Chicago. We will meet George Smith and his stories in due course.

If there were any lingering doubts about the theory, it was dispelled by Jupiter, largest of all the planets—just as Lagrange had predicted, more than a century earlier. Two groups of asteroids, known as the Trojans, hover rather unsteadily around the L_4 and L_5 points, making equilateral triangles with the sun and Jupiter. Doubtless there are many other natural, though perhaps temporary, examples, in the solar system—and recently there was a man-made one.

In 1978 the space probe originally called ISEE-3 (for International Sun–Earth Explorer 3) was launched to measure the properties of the solar wind—the invisible stream of charged particles which continually blows from the sun. Because that was the most convenient place to observe the phenomenon, ISEE-3 was "parked" on the earth–sun line at the L_1 point, one and a half million kilometers sunwards from earth. There it sat patiently for five years, observing solar flares an hour before they could reach earth, and radioing back its observations.

It might have been there to this day, "haloing" the earth from the viewpoint of the sun, but from the very beginning Dr. Farquhar had more ambitious plans for it. During 1983, in one of the most remarkable feats of astrodynamics ever attempted, it was gently nudged away from the L_1 point and sent falling towards the moon, so that lunar gravity would give it a boost as it flew by—exactly like Ray Cummings's *Planetara* (Chapter 4). This maneuver was repeated no less than five times; on the last flyby, the probe skimmed only a hundred kilometers above the moon, and the slightest navigational error could have been disastrous.

After the final flyby, in December 1983, ISSEE-3 was renamed ICE—for International Cometary Explorer. It had now acquired enough extra velocity to go chasing after Comet Giacobini–Zinner, and succeeded in flying through its tail in September 1985.

The celestial mechanics behind this first encounter with a comet are absolutely mind-boggling. When plotted out, much of ICE's track looks like a plate of spaghetti, dropped from a considerable height. By no stretch of the imagination can it be called an "orbit."

The entire astronomical community applauded the feat for the extraordinary achievement it was, but the praise from one direction was slightly muted. The Japanese, European, and Russian teams preparing to meet Halley's Comet next year felt they had been just a little upstaged.

But back, briefly, to Zeud. It turns out to be a tropical world full of assorted monsters, and savage "Zeudians" from whom our heroes escape by a remarkable piece of luck:

> The professor mechanically adjusted his glasses more firmly on his nose. . . .
>
> With his move, the narrowing circle of Zeudians halted. A violent clamor broke out among them. They glared at the two, but made no further step toward them.
>
> "Your glasses!" Joyce shouted. "When you moved them, they all stopped! They must be afraid of them. Take them off and see what happens!"
>
> Wichter removed his spectacles and swung them round in his hand, peering near-sightedly at the crowding Zeudians. . . . Hisses of consternation came from their lipless mouths. They faced each other uneasily, covering their own eyes as though suddenly afraid they would lose them. . . .

Shame on you, Paul Ernst; H. Rider Haggard played this trick long, long ago. You never read *King Solomon's Mines*? Frankly, I find that rather hard to believe. Anyway, how lucky that Professor Wichter wasn't wearing contact lenses!

11
"BEYOND THE VANISHING POINT"

The March 1931 issue of *Astounding* marks the first appearance of a man who was to become perhaps its most popular author: Jack Williamson. As, full of honors, Professor Williamson (Department of English, Eastern New Mexico University, 1960–77) enters his eighties, I'm sure he would prefer not to be reminded of "The Meteor Girl," so I will say as little as possible about it. (It's the least that one SFWA Grand Master can do for another.)

The scientist hero manages, with the help of a strange meteorite that has just happened to land right on his doorstep, to make more revolutionary inventions in a few hours than the Bell Laboratories could do in a decade; what's more, they all work *perfectly* just as soon as they are switched on. Through one of them—a remote viewing device involving the fourth dimension—the horrified scientist sees his shipwrecked girlfriend clinging to a rock in mid-ocean while one of the local denizens makes an unwelcome appearance. His partner, however, does his best to be helpful. . . .

Desperately I searched for consolation for him.

"Maybe the octopus won't hurt her," I offered. "They say that most of the stories of their ferocity have been exaggerated."

Very true, as already pointed out in Chapter 7. But I shouldn't count on it. Even the friendliest octopus has to eat.

Leaving you in a state of unendurable suspense, we pass on to the only item of interest in this issue, Ray Cummings's "Beyond the Vanishing Point." It was unkindly said that in his later years, Cummings kept retyping the carbons of his 1919 novel *The Girl in the Golden Atom;* how the old-time pulp writers would have loved word-processors, so that they could have changed the names of their characters with a few keystrokes!

Wesso's cover illustration for this story is one of his most striking. It shows a group of tiny human beings threatened by a giant whose outstretched arm can't quite reach to the back of the cave in which they are cowering. The giant, by the way, is actually the "repulsive hunchback" Polter, whom we have already met in Chapter 4. And he is not really a giant, but only a few hundred times bigger than his opponents, who have taken too large a dose of Ray Cummings's patent reducing drug.

Lewis Carroll, of course, had the same idea half a century earlier, and such adventures in size—whether promoted by chemicals or rays or any other means—belong not to science fiction but to pure fantasy. When they shrank their characters, the authors never seemed to consider what happened to all the missing mass. If it was annihilated, there would be a multi-gigaton explosion, and that would be the end of the story. If it wasn't, the characters would become denser and denser as they contracted, until they sank into the earth, like mercury dropped into water.

Long before that, they would run into other problems. There is a famous essay by J. B. S. Haldane, "On Being the Right Size"* which points out that you cannot change the dimensions

*In *Possible Worlds* (1927); later reprinted in Volume 2 of James Newman's *The World of Mathematics* (Simon and Schuster, 1956). Haldane was one of the true geniuses of the first half of this century—and a very brave man. When he was dying of the disease, he wrote an amusing (!) poem "Cancer Can Be Fun." In the last letter I ever received from him, he remarked what a boon a zero gravity space hospital would be to bedridden patients like himself.

of any animal without also changing its design. This can be illustrated by a very simple argument, which was clearly enunciated by Galileo almost four centuries ago.

Suppose a man was increased to ten times normal size. Then his mass would be increased a thousandfold, but the cross-section of his leg bones only a hundredfold. The stress on the bones would thus be multiplied by ten—and they would break. As Haldane remarks dryly of the giants in the illustrated *Pilgrim's Progress* of his childhood: "This was doubtless why they were sitting down in the picture I remember. But it lessens one's respect for Jack the Giant-Killer."

The catastrophe could be postponed—though only by a little—if the man was redesigned so that his bones were much thicker. Obviously one cannot go far in this direction; perhaps a giant could be twice as tall as a normal man, but he would be so clumsy that he would probably be no match for one. The story of David and Goliath contains a profound lesson: David was the "right size" (as well as the "right stuff").

The reasons why human beings cannot be greatly reduced in size are more complex; I have discussed some of them in "The Road to Lilliput" (see *Profiles of the Future*). One problem would be heat-loss; if you make a man ten times smaller than normal, the ratio between his surface area and his mass would *increase* tenfold—and he would have to eat at ten times his normal rate or he would die of hypothermia. (This is the reason why some very small mammals have to eat their own weight of food—per day!) Nevertheless, the range of size between the two extremes of (adult) *H. sapiens* is quite surprising—perhaps four to one in height, and twenty to one in mass. Yet even the freaks at the opposite ends of the distribution curve are still recognizably human.

When a complete redesign is allowed, these limits can be far surpassed; if one had seen only photographs, with no indication of scale, of a mouse and an elephant, it would be obvious from the relative thickness of the elephant's legs that it was the larger animal. But who would have guessed *how* much larger?

Ray Cummings was by no means the only writer to reduce his characters in size so that they could have adventures in micro-worlds. I still remember with affection Paul Ernst's "The Raid on the Termites" (June 1932), because this story was my first introduction to these extraordinary insects. I had no idea that creatures as bizarre as any invented by science fiction writers actually existed on this planet, capable of astounding—yes, the word is indeed accurate—feats of construction, communication, and genetic engineering. Ernst had obviously researched his story with great care, and the account of his two intrepid heroes' adventures in the labyrinth of the termitary was one of the most fascinating tales I had ever read. A few years later, it undoubtedly triggered an early effort of mine, which suggested that the termites had an origin, and a purpose, that no one had yet guessed:

And in the long echoing centuries before the birth of man, the aliens had not been idle but had covered half the planet with their cities, filled with blind, fantastic slaves, and though man knew these cities, for they had often caused him infinite trouble, yet he never suspected that all around him in the tropics an older civilization than his was planning busily for the day when it would once again venture forth upon the seas of space to regain its lost inheritance. ("Retreat from Earth": *Amateur Science Fiction Stories:* March 1938, Vol. 1, No. 3. Reprinted in *The Best of Arthur Clarke, 1937–71:* Sphere, 1973).

Hollywood has produced one classic movie on adventures in smallness. Despite its unfortunate title, *The Incredible Shrinking Man* is a surprisingly mature and moving film, as well as a very exciting one (who can forget the resourceful hero's escape from that frightful monster, his own cat—or his battle with the spider?). Don't miss it, the next time it turns up on late-night TV.

One lesson that all these stories teach is that, even if a man could shrink himself down to microsize, he would be very ill advised to do so; there are more dangers down there than in the most fearsome jungle. And now, thanks to a remarkable development in technology, we can have at least the visual experience of confronting those dangers face to face.

The microscope, like the telescope, was invented around the beginning of the seventeenth century, and revealed for the first time the wealth and complexity of the world below the limits of normal vision. Its impact on philosophy and religion was not as great as that of Galileo's "optic tube"—it did not help to shatter any system of the universe—but it made a profound impression upon all educated men.* It even became a popular toy for wealthy amateurs; in his diary for July 26, 1663 Samuel Pepys reports spending the enormous sum of five pounds, ten shillings on a "very excellent microscope, which did discover a louse or a mite most perfectly and largely." And everyone knows—though nobody ever quotes correctly— Swift's famous stanza:

> So, naturalists observe, a flea
> Has smaller fleas that on him prey;
> And these have smaller still to bite 'em,
> And so proceed *ad infinitum*.

The optical microscope reached the limit of its resolving power a century ago, because this is set by the wavelength of light. Beyond a magnifying power of around a thousand, nothing new can be seen; the waves of light are so long that they sweep around any objects in this size-domain, as unaffected by them as ocean waves by a bobbing cork.

Nature herself appeared to have set an absolute limit to our ability to view the microworld. We could perhaps see the second level of Swift's "fleas"—but not the third.

Half a century ago, the electron microscope broke through this barrier. Because, under certain conditions, electrons behave like waves which can be made as short as we like by an increase in voltage, it became possible to achieve magnifications not of thousands, but *tens* of thousands. Once again, a new world was opened up.

But the electron microscope has serious limitations. Like the

*See Marjorie Nicolson's essay "The Microscope and English Imagination" (in *Science and Imagination*, Cornell University Press, 1956).

optical microscope, it can only focus on a single plane; its images are two-dimensional, having no depth or solidity. They are pictures from Flatland.

Then, in 1965, a team of British scientists developed an extraordinary instrument, the Scanning Electron Microscope (SEM) which for the first time showed the microworld as it really is. It did not require specimens to be sliced into wafer-thin sections, and since it worked with reflected, not transmitted, electrons, it could show the exteriors of objects—even living insects. (Though they may not survive the ordeal!)

When you see a good SEM photo of, say, a housefly, every minute detail is in focus; the image is so sharp that *there is no sense of scale*. You might be looking at a creature the size of a dog—or a horse—photographed with an ordinary camera. Some of the front views of spiders and other predators would be terrifying enough to discourage even the most intrepid small-game hunter from entering the microworld.*

With the example of this breakthrough in mind, you may wonder if I am still so confident that "The Raid on the Termites" and "Beyond the Vanishing Point" are not science fiction, but pure fantasy. The answer remains "Yes"—though the second story is much more impossible than the first. Let me amplify that rather illogical statement.

Ray Cummings's dreams of shrinking down to atomic and even subatomic dimensions are fantasy for the most fundamental of reasons—at this level, matter as we know it does not exist, but dissolves into waves. (My apologies to the physicists for this slight abridgement of half a century's theorizing.) The naive 1930 model of the atom as a minuscule solar system, with electrons circling round the nucleus like planets round the sun, vanished with de Broglie, Heisenberg and Schrödinger.

---

*For an explanation of the SEM, and some extraordinary images by one of its most skilled operators, see *Magnifications* by David Scharf (Schocken Books, 1977). By a curious coincidence, I saw an SEM for the first time the very day I typed these words. It was in the splendidly equipped lab of the deep-sea drilling vessel *JOIDES Resolution*, which had just put into Colombo harbor.

But the world of the termites, at between one-hundredth and one-thousandth of the normal human scale, still obeys laws that we can understand. Objects in it can be readily viewed and manipulated. And one day, we may be able to enter it—not of course like Paul Ernst's explorers, but vicariously.

Largely as a result of computer development, and the rush to squeeze more and more into less and less, a whole new technology of micro-miniaturization has arisen. It is now possible to cram a million components into a space the size of a fingernail—something that would have been unthinkable only twenty years ago.

And the process is just beginning, although some definite limits are already in sight; obviously, you can't make components smaller than single atoms. A new discipline is evolving—"nanotechnology"—the design and construction of complex mechanisms so small that they may be invisible to the eye. The direct successors of the ubiquitous microchip, they may have an equally profound impact upon society.

Imagine what a surgeon could do with a remote-controlled manipulator small enough to wander through the human body! Yes, the micro-submarine that explored the bloodstream in *Fantastic Voyage* is not totally fantastic. But it would not look in the least like a conventional submarine—and of course it wouldn't have Raquel Welch aboard.

So one day we may be able to explore a termitary, even more closely than the makers of scientific films have already done with their snorkel cameras and other ingenious devices. Imagine a tiny robot—perhaps disguised as a termite, and with the right smell so that it wouldn't be instantly attacked as an intruder—which could be sent scuttling through the labyrinthine corridors of the insect city. Its operators, looking at their screens and controlling the robot's movements, would soon develop that sense of "telepresence" already experienced by the men who steered their little "swimming eyeball" into the wreck of the *Titanic*.

Psychologically, emotionally, they will be a fraction of an inch high—and *there*, inside the termitary. It may even take them some time to readjust to the world of the human scale, just as astronauts find it hard to get used to gravity again.

And although they will be perfectly safe, they had better have good nerves. Some of the genetically altered termite warriors are the things of nightmare—as hideous as any aliens from Hollywood. I wouldn't care to meet one suddenly, even on the other side of a TV screen.

On the very last page of "Beyond the Vanishing Point" is a fascinating little filler titled "Moon Rockets." It begins:

> Seventeen years of experimenting on a rocket designed by Prof. Albert H. Goddard of Clark University, to shriek its way from the earth to the moon, came to a glorious climax recently when the rocket tore its flaming way through the air for a quarter mile. . . .

It seems a shame that so little is known about Robert Goddard's twin brother Albert. Always insanely jealous of his older (by 2 min. 20 sec.) sibling, Bert attempted to emulate him in every way, copying and even stealing the results of his experiments. His lucky development of a superfuel almost a million times more powerful than dynamite enabled him to build a working moon-rocket while his plodding brother was still experimenting with such feeble propellants as gasoline and liquid oxygen. Determined to be the first man to reach our satellite, he left earth just before full moon, but in his haste he made a disastrous miscalculation. That month—*there would be a total lunar eclipse*!

Sorry about this; I just don't know what came over me. Perhaps those old sf magazines (and quite a few new ones) should carry a Government Health warning: "Reading This Material Can Damage Your Mind."

12

THE FALL
OF THE HOUSE
OF CLAYTON

Halfway through Harry Bates's third year as *Astounding*'s editor, his readers became aware that the magazine was in trouble. With the June 1932 issue, it went bi-monthly—the magazine equivalent of Cheyne-Stokes respiration. This continued for six issues, until March 1933: then the Clayton chain collapsed into bankruptcy, and the bereft readership must have imagined that whole Number 34 might be the last *Astounding Stories of Super-Science* that would ever grace the newsstands. Little did they know, as the old cliché was fond of saying, that the Golden Age* was still to dawn.

Astounding did not contribute to the collapse of the Clayton empire, for it was at least covering its own costs, and would probably have soon been making a profit. But, as it comes to all men, Clayton had been overtaken by a sudden cash shortage, which had put him out of business.

Glancing at the last dozen issues that Harry Bates edited, I find a few titles that still set bells jangling—or synapses clicking—somewhere in the depths of memory. "The Doom from Planet 4" (Jack Williamson again); "Brood of the Dark Moon"; "The Sargasso of Space"; "The Red Hell of Jupiter"; "The Cavern of

*For more about the beginning, and end, of the Golden (or at least Gilded) Age, see Chapter 38.

the Shining Ones"; "Out Round Rigel"; "The Hammer of Thor"; "The Affair of the Brains"; "The Fifth Dimension Tube" (Murray Leinster, back in hyperspace); "The God in the Box."

But I had totally forgotten Harl Vincent's "The Copper-Clad World" (September 1931) and am amused to find that it contains an accidental bull's-eye. His protagonists are approaching Io, innermost of Jupiter's four Galilean satellites, and discover that it "was like nothing else in the heavens ... it was of gleaming coppery hue." This is a dead accurate description of this unique body; however, Vincent's Io really *was* copper-plated, whereas the orange-yellow hues of the world revealed by the *Voyager* space probes are due to sulphur compounds.

Sometimes, the fillers inserted to plug an unsightly gap at the bottom of a page are a good deal more interesting than the stories—especially when viewed through the telescope of time. Thus the March 1932 issue contains an item which is even more topical now than it was half a century ago:

EINSTEIN ON THE UNIFIED FIELD THEORY

Dr. Einstein recently presented to a class of distinguished physicists and mathematicians his latest and greatest work, the unified field theory. Theoretical physicists proclaimed it as the simplest theory that will explain all the secrets of space and the universe. . . . His face wreathed with smiles, the benign little German professor explained that he sought to write in the most simple complete equation one basic law explaining the universe and its properties. To his amazement, when he had completed the theory he found it contained the laws of his old gravitational theory combined in harmony with Maxwell's laws of electromagnetism. . . .

Sad to say, Einstein's face didn't remain "wreathed in smiles" for very long; it was soon covered with egg. His unified field theory, on which he continued to work for the remainder of his life, was rejected by all his peers, who considered that he was simply wasting his time on a fruitless quest.* There is a curious parallel here with the only man who can be classed with Einstein: Newton spent the latter part of his life in arcane studies of theology, alchemy, and even magic.

Einstein's select audience contained at least one science fiction writer, who later appeared in *Astounding*'s pages. As his *Men of Mathematics* amply proves, Eric Temple Bell ("John Taine") was one of Einstein's greatest admirers, and his best novel *The Time Stream* had been published in *Wonder Stories* just the year before.

I wonder if he presented a copy to the great man, who would certainly have been interested. But I very much doubt it; the President of the Mathematical Association of America seems to have been reluctant to acknowledge his disreputable alter ego, and few of his colleagues were aware of the equation Bell = Taine.

It may or may not be a coincidence that the very next issue of the magazine contains "The Einstein See-Saw," by Miles J. Breuer, M.D.—yet another forgettable tale of fourth-dimensional bank-robberies, but with a considerably higher intellectual content than most pulp magazines of the time would tolerate:

> Tony leaned over eagerly to glance at the titles.
> " 'Theory of Parallels,' Lobatchevsky; 'Transformation of Complex Functions,' Riemann; 'Tensors and Geodesics,' Gauss," Tony read. "Hm—old stuff. But here's modern dope along the same line. 'Tensors,' by Christoffel; 'Absolute Differential Calculus,' by Ricci and Levi Civita. And Schrödinger and Eddington and D'Abro. Looks like somebody's interested in Relativity. . . ."

Tony is another of those criminal scientists all too rare in the humdrum non-sf world. Later in the story he behaves in a manner which, for a villain, is singularly unimpressive:

> As they hesitated, he stamped his foot and shrilled crankily: "I mean it!"

---

*Aren't we lucky that Douglas Adams has now given us the answer which Einstein sought in vain for so long: 42.

After several attempts, I have so far failed to produce a really convincing cranky shrill. If I succeed, I may tackle the even greater challenge presented long ago by another forgotten pulp writer:

"You cad!" she hissed.

It is, however, quite unfair to Dr. Breuer to single out this momentary lapse. He was a writer of considerable ability, who explored many important themes, and (as one would expect of a medical man) was concerned with the major problems of science and society. His best work ("The Gostak and the Doshes," "Paradise and Iron," "The Birth of a New Republic"—the latter in collaboration with the young Jack Williamson) appeared in *Amazing Stories* and its associated *Quarterlies,* and he had only one other story in *Astounding*. Though its plot is elementary—as the title indicates, it concerns the problem of sending a message without being detected—"A Problem in Communication" is quite remarkable, because it is now all too topical. For once, the blurb is accurate and unsensational:

The delivery of his country into the clutches of a merciless, ultra-modern religion can be prevented only by Dr. Hagstrom's deciphering an extraordinary code.

Dr. Breuer's story contains a very well-written account of the nature and purpose of religion, with a glance back at the historical background of Christianity and Islam—all this in a 1930 pulp magazine! Then it describes the rise of a twentieth century religion worshipping Science as its God, with brainwashed adherents required to be a "perfect cog in the machine"—a type all too familiar now.

Despite its excesses and abuses, and its plans to take over the world, Dr. Breuer was not unsympathetic towards his creation:

There was something sublime in the conception of this religion. It certainly had nothing in common with the "Christian Science" that was in vogue during the early years of the

Twentieth Century; it towered with a noble grandeur above that feeble little sham.

Fighting words, which many nervous editors would blue-pencil today. I'll be surprised if the September 1930 *Astounding* wasn't banned in Boston.

Shortly before the end, Harry Bates obviously made several attempts to bolster circulation. His penultimate issue—January 1933—had the first editorial he had written since Vol. 1, No. 1. A thoroughly competent little essay on the failure of the alchemists and the success of their modern, scientific successors, it was entitled, by a sad irony, "Just Around the Corner."

I cannot help wondering if this editorial was indeed written by Bates, who must have had bigger problems on his mind at the time. What prompts my suspicion is the fact that this issue has, for the first time, a "Science Forum" in which one Carlyle Elliott, B.A., B.S., Ph.D. answers reader's questions. ("Why is outer space black? How can we be sure since no one's been there?" "What is radioactivity?" "Do stars really have different colors?") The answers are straightforward and accurate; hence my suspicion that Dr. Elliott had a hand in the editorials as well.

Clayton's penultimate cover, incidentally, was one of the most beautiful that Wesso ever painted. Done entirely in tasteful greens and golds, it shows a fleet of handsome (though aerodynamically improbable) ornithopters flapping towards an alien city of crystal towers, linked by sky-spanning bridges. This splendid illustration of Murray Leinster's "The Fifth Dimension Tube" (a sequel, of course, to his "Catapult") is my second favorite of all Wesso's covers, next to his portrait of the moonward-bound *Planetara,* and is artistically much superior.

His last cover,* for the final Clayton issue of March 1933, unintentionally records the magazine's struggles to survive. The previous issue had contained an announcement calculated

---

*Wesso did paint some covers under the new regime, but they were few and far between.

to send all full-blooded fans stampeding towards the magazine stands. A serial by the most popular sf author of the day would be Coming Next Month. Well, next month but one . . .

Edward Elmer Smith (invariably and fondly referred to as "Doc" Smith—he had a Ph.D. in chemical engineering) had exploded upon the science fiction scene with *The Skylark of Space* in 1928, and *Skylark Three* in 1930. These epics of inter-stellar adventure (Smith holds the original *Star Wars* patents) had appeared in the rival *Amazing Stories,* but Smith had become fed up with editorial revisions—not to mention a rate of payment less than half that of *Astounding*.

His new saga, *Triplanetary,* was heralded in the January issue as "One of the Finest and Most Outstanding Novels of Inter-planetary Invasion and Warfare of the Future That Has Ever Been Written" (I've checked those capitals painstakingly). In one of the episodes, the heroes' spaceship is sliced into pieces by a worthy precursor of Darth Vader's "Death Star": "a sphere so large and so close that they seemed to be dropping down-ward towards it as though it were a world!"

Wesso painted this scene—not very accurately, as he showed the marauder as a conventional submarine-shaped vessel, com-plete with four stubby tailfins! It duly appeared on the cover of the March issue, but there was no trace of *Triplanetary* inside. Nor was there any hint that the deal had fallen through, for the simple reason that the magazine had ceased publica-tion. (This wasn't mentioned, either. Indeed, the last page of the last issue still has a "Readers' Ballot" for the best authors and a space for "Science Forum" questions.)

Harry Bates's (Carlyle Elliott's?) final editorial "The Expand-ing Universe" has lost absolutely none of its topicality; in fact, it is right up to date because the very first sentence uses one of the current cosmological buzzwords, "inflation"! It even dis-cusses the possibility of eventual contraction and rebound, so that the cycle is repeated, perhaps millions of times.

It is something of a surprise to realize that the concept of an expanding universe was so familiar in 1933. In fact, Hubble had discovered the "red shift" only four years earlier, but it had been quickly interpreted as a Doppler effect caused by the recession of all the more distant galaxies. This explanation was accepted by almost all astronomers, and is the basis of modern cosmological theories. I say "almost"; there is one notable exception, to whom I shall return in a moment—after a detour caused by this last editorial's reference to "Dr. H. P. Robertson, of Princeton," who had analyzed Hubble's results and come to the conclusion that the universe is now thirteen times greater than it was originally. That puny thirteen would now be inflated to infinity, but let that pass. . . .

Just twenty years later, Dr. Robertson was involved in a highly classified project that would have fascinated the readers of *Astounding*—and doubtless did, when they finally got to hear of it. He was chairman of the CIA panel which first met in January 1953 to investigate UFO sightings.

So secret was the "Robertson Panel" that it was a couple of decades before I discovered one of my oldest and closest friends* was its secretary, and that Luis Alvarez (who keeps popping up in this book) was one of its members. Luie later told me how easy it had been to dispose of most UFO sightings with a little common sense and a modicum of science.†

To return to the expanding universe, which Dr. Robertson was helping to midwife in 1933. The evidence for its expansion is the undisputed fact that the wavelengths of all except the very closest galaxies are shifted towards the red, and at an amount directly proportional to their distance.

If the spectral lines of a source of light are shifted towards the red, the simple and obvious explanation is that the source is moving away; this "Doppler effect" is one of the most funda-

---

*Frederick C. Durant, Assistant Director, Astronautics, of the National Air and Space Museum (1965–81)—a post that ideally qualified him for his present even more responsible position as Executive Secretary of the Arthur Clarke Foundation of the United States. The other scientist members of the panel, besides Robertson and Alvarez, were Samuel Goudsmit, Thornton Page, and Lloyd Berkner. Allen Hynek and Fred Durant were associate members.

†For a somewhat critical account of the panel's proceedings, see *The UFO Controversy in America* by David Michael Jacobs (Indiana University Press, 1975).

mental in physics and astronomy. But there might be other causes; just conceivably, light waves might lose some of their energy (and hence frequency) after traveling cosmic distances. If this "tired light" theory, as it has been somewhat facetiously called, is correct, then the extra-galactic nebulae might not be receding after all—and the expansion of the universe is an optical illusion!

One man who believes this to be the case is Grote Reber—who, virtually single-handed, founded the science of radio-astronomy. The fact that radio waves—in the form of a low-level background hiss—came from space had been discovered by Jansky in 1932, but he was a Bell Laboratories engineer more concerned with their effect on communications than their scientific significance. And the astronomers, who should have known better, showed little more interest.

In 1937, using his own resources, Reber built a thirty-foot diameter dish which for a decade was the only radio telescope in the world. With this, he made the first maps of the sky at radio wavelengths, which clearly showed its most prominent feature—the Milky Way. The rest is astronomical history: not since Galileo has one man, with one new instrument, so transformed an entire science.

My "Scientific Autobiography," *Ascent to Orbit*, reprints a 1949 article "The Radio Telescope" which reproduced Reber's first map. He was delighted that the copy I sent him was autographed (by pure coincidence) on his seventy-fifth birthday, December 22, 1986, and wrote back enclosing his "latest effort at debunking big-bang cosmology. I understand that some of the big-bangers would enjoy having me burned at the stake like Bruno!"

His stimulating little paper, "Intergalactic Plasma,"* suggests that light does indeed get tired during its journeys across the cosmos, as a result of collisions with free electrons which lower its energy and hence frequency (the Compton Effect). So the famous red shift has nothing to do with velocity; the universe isn't expanding, after all! Dr. Reber ends his paper with the

---

*IEEE Transactions on Plasma Science, PS-14, No. 6, Dec. 1986, pp. 678–82.

words: "We may be on the verge of a new Copernican revolution."

If all goes well (a phrase long popular in the corridors of NASA, but never more so than nowadays) the Space Telescope should settle this question—before it raises a dozen others—when the shuttle carries it into orbit. That would be very appropriate, because the most important astronomical instrument of this century is named after Edwin Hubble, the man who discovered the red shift and started the whole debate.

Many years ago, Dr. Reber moved his radio observatory to Tasmania because, believe it or not, that island lies underneath a genuine "hole in the Heaviside Layer" (see Chapter 8), through which longer wavelengths occasionally penetrate. I must warn him about those giant amoebae.

And so, as the Clayton fleet sinks slowly in the west, we say farewell to *Astounding Stories of Super-Science*—but only its first and most primitive incarnation.

Six months later, after the Street and Smith salvage operation, it surfaced again. Since October 1933, alone of all science fiction magazines, it has never missed an issue. That is an achievement of which it may well be proud.

TREMAINE

(1 9 3 3 – 1 9 3 7)

13

DEATH AND TRANSFIGURATION

The first issue of the magazine to appear under Street and Smith's insignia was a rather unprepossessing hybrid. It had dropped the "Super-Science" and was now plain *Astounding*— an ominous sign that it might be hospitable to the supernatural, the occult, or indeed anything outside the range of the ordinary. Only three of the eleven stories in the October 1933 issue could be classed as sf; the others could have appeared in almost any adventure magazine. Among them was one curiosity —a short story by Colonel P. H. Fawcett, whose 1925 disappearance in the jungle of Brazil was one of the famous mysteries of the era.

And one story has a very insensitive title, which must have shocked many readers: they might well have thought that "Burroughs Passes" was an obituary of Edgar Rice—who didn't pass for another seventeen years, and far too many more books.

The new magazine's covers were also unimpressive; compared with Wesso's eye-catchers, they looked anemic and not particularly Astounding. However, Howard Brown quickly got into his stride, and during the next five years produced some of the most memorable artwork in the history of the magazine.

Harry Bates's successor, F. Orlin Tremaine (1899–1956) was an experienced pulp magazine editor who had previously worked with the Clayton chain, though not on *Astounding* itself. After his understandably shaky start, he quickly mastered the new genre, and if the famous Golden Age did not actually begin during his four-year reign, he certainly prepared the way for it.

However much he may regret that unfortunate necessity, in the final analysis any editor is totally dependent upon his authors. Tremaine printed stories by virtually all the writers who were to dominate the later decades, including some of the best work of his great successor, John W. Campbell.

But before we give Tremaine too much credit as a judge of literature, one grave charge must be brought against him. He published more than a dozen stories by "Warner van Lorne"—a prime candidate, against pretty stiff competition, for the title of "Worst Science-Fiction Writer of All Time." The invaluable *Encyclopedia of Science Fiction* hints at this when it remarks tactfully that his "Blue Men of Yrano" is "best remembered, though not by reason of its quality."*

Yet there is worse to come; though the identity of van Lorne was never revealed, the culprit is usually considered to have been Tremaine's brother Nelson—and there is considerable evidence that some of the stories were written by Tremaine himself! The truth will probably never be known, and now hardly matters; but the whole affair was a sad reflection on an otherwise fine editor.

Tremaine's most memorable innovation, when he took over the magazine, was the concept of the "thought variant." He optimistically promised to bring his readers at least one story a month that would contain new and hitherto unexplored ideas, and would bow to no previous prejudices or restrictions.

Nat Schachner's "Ancestral Voices" (December 1933) was the first result of this policy. The previous issue had proclaimed that it would "awaken *MORE CONTROVERSY* than any story

---

*Thus prompted, I was naturally unable to resist exhuming the story. I can only say that it achieves hitherto unplumbed depths of ineptitude, and is written in a style which gives me a strong mental image of an exhausted cart horse, homeward wending its weary way.

ever published in a SCIENCE-FICTION MAGAZINE." It would "slice daringly through the most precious myths, legends, and folklore of mankind, and attack boldly a present-day wave of race-hysteria." And finally: "This is not just 'another story.' You will *LIKE* it; or *Hate* it; and will *READ* it *AGAIN.*"

Quite a build-up—and not a single exclamation mark!! That's truly Astounding!!!

After more than half a century, I have just re-read "Ancestral Voices," and find it surprisingly impressive. Nat(han) Schachner was a lawyer and historian, who wrote several biographies of leading Americans; he was a man of culture and erudition, and it shows in this story. For a 1933 pulp magazine, "Ancestral Voices" is quite remarkable.

Today, the basic idea is a cliché—indeed, almost a joke. What happens if a man goes back into the past and kills one of his own ancestors?

Nat Schachner's scientist does just that, when his time machine takes him back to AD 452 to confront one of the Huns who is busily assisting the Fall of the Roman Empire. As a result, fifty thousand people disappear instantly in 1935—including a Hitleresque dictator ranting about racial purity, *both* the contestants in a Jewish versus Aryan world heavyweight fight, and other ancestor-proud individuals whom Schachner briefly (and often wittily) sketches. The whole story is a most effective little reminder that there is only one Family of Man, and its lesson is, alas, just as timely today.

Of course, all stories of travel into the past involve hopeless paradoxes, which writers like Robert Heinlein and Ray Bradbury have gleefully exploited in such classic tales as "By His Bootstraps" and "A Sound of Thunder." One of the first problems that springs to mind is—what chance would you have of encountering one of your direct ancestors if you went back in time?

It looks pretty good, if you go far enough. Schachner's protagonist went back 1500 years—say sixty generations. Since every human being has exactly two parents, an elementary calculation (which anyone who remembers that log 2 = 0.30 can do mentally in ten seconds) gives the number of ancestors fifteen centuries back as around a million, million, million.

Something's wrong here; the world population then was much less than a thousand million. . . .

The answer, of course, is that our family trees don't radiate indefinitely, but the branches continually reunite and soon become inextricably intertwined. All but a minute fraction of those million, million, million are phantoms—or looking at it from another point of view, billions of them are the same person.

The lesson is clear. We do not have to go back very many centuries to reach a time when almost everyone alive would have been an ancestor of everyone living now! So it is not a good idea to pack a gun, when you set off to visit the past.

The same December 1933 issue contains a story which I remember to this day because of its sheer effrontery. If you think "Ancestral Voices" violated a few scientific laws, you should read Paul Starr's "The Invading Bloodstream."

I don't know who Paul Starr was: he never appeared again, and the name sounds suspiciously like a pseudonym. (He wasn't "Warner van Lorne," because the writing does at least attain a modest level of mediocrity.) The basic idea was outrageously simple: a hostile European power plans to invade the U.S. with an army of half a million men, microminiaturized so that they are concealed in the bloodstreams of ten "carriers"! (How they would manage for weapons was not made clear; perhaps they were all karate experts.) Fortunately, before the plane carrying this invisible army could reach the United States, a resourceful secret agent aimed the enlarging ray at it, and the half million were materialized inside its cabin—undoubtedly the worst case of over-booking in airline history.

But let us not linger over the magazine's 1933 convulsions and ineptitudes. Orlin Tremaine was getting his act under control, and *Astounding*'s first great year was about to dawn.

14

"BORN OF THE SUN"

Like "The Invading Bloodstream," Jack Williamson's novelette "Born of the Sun" (March 1934) is one of those stories which is unforgettable because of its sheer nerve. But whereas Starr's tale is merely ridiculous, Williamson's has the power of a myth.*

The basic idea is simple enough: the planets and satellites of the solar system are all *eggs*, waiting to hatch. Here is the end of the earth:

> And a thing emerged from the shattered crust of it that was like the creature that had come from the Moon. The beaked head was crested with a spray of crimson flame; it was marked with two ovoid patches, glowing lividly purple, that were like dread eyes. Flame green, its body was slender and tapering and marked weirdly with black and silver. Slow, shining waves shimmered through its wings, that were like green fans of the aurora and veined with burning white.
>
> It moved uncertainly in the void, as if to test its members. It preened itself with thin blue appendages that were thrust

*Which reminds me that, sometime in 1964, Stanley Kubrick said hopefully: "What we want, Arthur, is a tale of mythic grandeur."

from the head. Then, with a beat of strange luminous force in its wings, it wheeled away from the Sun, and drove outward into the void of space.

Leaving aside the improbability of wings in space (well, they might be solar sails or heat absorbers . . .) I still feel that this story has a certain crude effectiveness. Williamson gives it additional depth by bringing in an oriental "Cult of the Great Egg," but unfortunately "Born of the Sun" eventually dissolves into pulp-magazine melodrama, with the intrepid hero (who has invented the first spaceship in the nick of time) leaving the ruins of earth with only his girlfriend for company. Yet the story ends on an optimistic note:

"We've won—Men will now be small parasites no longer, to be crushed like vermin by any chance tremor of the beast that bears them. . . ."
His serene quiet eyes stared at the mocking points of the stars, and he whispered to them:
"You're alive, all of you. We owe our lives to you—we've been parasites on your kind. But we aren't any longer. We're beginning all over again, on our own."

Noble sentiments; Adam and Eve Mk II need all the encouragement they can get as their brand-new, hastily built and quite untested Eden begins its maiden flight to nowhere in particular. I'd give them twelve hours, with luck, before the polyphase discombobulator short-circuits, or the parametric frammistat seizes up.

Yet I'm not making fun of this story, and would love to see how Professor Williamson would tackle the same theme, half a century later—not as sf (which it could never be) but as a philosophical fable. It would tie in very well with the current "Gaia" hypothesis, which suggests that the Earth should indeed be regarded as a single living organism.

Williamson's concept was also foreshadowed by a little-known Conan Doyle 1929 story, "When the World Screamed," featuring his redoubtable scientist Professor G. E. Challenger, FRS,

FRGS. My copy of *The Lost World* (John Murray, 1914) has as its frontispiece a photograph showing Challenger and the other members of the party to that great adventure. The professor himself, with his huge beard and bushy eyebrows, looks very much like one of our distant ancestors—a resemblance that later plays an important part in the story. The model is Doyle himself, heavily disguised, and I suspect that the irascible scientist was much nearer to his heart than his more famous creation, Sherlock Holmes.

"When the World Screamed" is still quite entertaining, partly because Doyle himself obviously did not take very seriously Challenger's "proofs" that the Earth is the equivalent of a sea-urchin which

> . . . browses upon a circular path in the fields of space, and as it moves the ether is continually pouring through it and providing its vitality. Quite a flock of other little world-echini are doing the same thing, Venus, Mars and the rest, each with its own field for grazing.

I cannot resist quoting Challenger's demolition of one obvious objection:

> "The temperature!" I cried. "Is it not a fact that it rises rapidly as one descends, and that the centre of the earth is liquid heat?"
> He waved my assertion aside.
> "You are probably aware, sir, since Council schools are now compulsory, that the earth is flattened at the poles. This means that the pole is nearer to the centre than any other point and would therefore be most affected by this heat of which you spoke. It is notorious, of course, that the conditions of the poles are tropical, is it not?"

Anyway, Challenger gets an eight-mile deep shaft dug through the shell of his cosmic sea-urchin and reaches a layer of

... greyish material, glazed and shiny, which rose and fell in slow palpitation ... beneath it, seen as though through ground glass, there were dim whitish patches or vacuoles, which varied constantly in shape and size. "Does look rather like a skinned animal," said Malone in an awed whisper.

Challenger rather recklessly tests the reaction of this outsize beast by pricking it with a harpoon, and the result is dramatic:

It has been the common ambition of mankind to set the whole world talking. To set the whole world screaming was the privilege of Challenger alone.

Appropriately enough, forty years later the deep-sea drilling ship *Glomar Challenger* was revolutionizing our knowledge of the earth by bringing up cores thousands of feet long from the thinnest part of its crust, under the oceans. So far, there have been no screams of protest, except the usual ones from the General Accounting Office. Only last week I had the privilege of visiting a companion ship, *JOIDES* Resolution,* and looking at the millions of years of earth's history recorded in the long tubes of deep ocean sediment lying in its refrigerated storeroom. The massive machinery needed to obtain these cores was awesome; even Professor Challenger would have been quite impressed.

*Joint Oceanographic Institutions for Deep Earth Sampling.

15

PRELUDE
TO STAR WARS

Looking at the contents list for the twelve *Astoundings* in 1934, I am sorely tempted to use the overworked adjective "fabulous." That year saw the appearance of three of the most famous sf novels of all time, still in print today. (How many of 1934's so-called mainstream novels can make such a claim?)

But first, as the TV commercials are so fond of saying, a few words about a story which is now quite forgotten, but which I have just re-read as an act of courtesy—even homage. Harry Bates, the man who started the magazine, made his debut in the April issue with "A Matter of Size."

It's a complicated tale about an earthman's kidnapping by benevolent aliens to replenish their gene pool—a favorite wish-fulfillment theme of (male) fantasy and sf authors. Much of the action, and most of the interest, lies in the hero's problems in coping with a world in which he is only six inches high—exactly the same situation as in Richard Matheson's novel *The Shrinking Man*, twenty years later. (There is even the same deadly threat—a common domestic cat.) Although the whole tale is astronomical and scientific nonsense, it moves quickly and its occasional naïveté is redeemed by flashes of wit. And it's impossible not to admire the ingenious way Bates gets his tiny hero across the vast expanses of New York City: he *mails* himself in a cardboard box, and arrives safely at his destination a few hours later.

That alone sets the story firmly back in the 1930s. Today he'd be dead on arrival—of starvation.

The same April issue contained the first installment of Jack Williamson's *The Legion of Space*—the breathtaking adventures of four cosmic musketeers against assorted menaces and monsters. By this time, *Legion* must be at least a thousand space operas downstream, and I have read far too many of them. So I recall only two elements from this early novel—its cowardly anti-hero Giles Habibula, whose chief talents were cracking safes and emptying bottles, and the mysterious secret weapon AKKA, which now sounds like a pop group.

The Legion of Space had only reached its fourth cliff-hanger when, in the August issue, it was joined by an even more mind-blowing epic, E. E. Smith's *Skylark of Valeron*. After a year's wait, "Doc" Smith had finally arrived—not with the promised *Triplanetary*, but with the third in the *Skylark* series, which he had started writing as long ago as 1915.

Tremaine broke the good news in the June issue, with an editorial headed simply "The Skylark!" Well he knew (dammit, I'm beginning to copy E. E.'s style) that his readers needed no further identification; but they might not have agreed with his rather snide remarks about the earlier stories: "There were two, you remember. . . . There's some demand that they be reprinted, but there's no thrill in reading what is already past and done." And, just to make sure that his readers get to the newsstands on time, he continues with the truly astounding claim: "THE SKYLARK OF VALERON *will never be reprinted.* It will appear ONCE, starting in the August 1934 issue."

Never, indeed! My fourteen-year-old copy bears the designation "Eighth printing." But Tremaine may be excused; in 1934, few readers could have imagined—and we're dealing with pretty imaginative people—that the time would come when any sf story of the slightest merit would be anthologized between hard and soft covers, microfiched and CD/ROM'ed on a scale which would make its original magazine appearance quite insignificant.

At year's end, *The Skylark of Valeron* had only reached the fifth of its seven installments when the first part of John W. Campbell's *The Mightiest Machine* appeared. This was another epic of interstellar warfare, with the enemy a species that the human race had encountered in the remote past—and remembered in the classical image of the Devil. (I have never hesitated to acknowledge my many debts to JWC.)

All these stories made engrossing reading to any science-addicted teenager, and they seemed harmless enough at the time—even educational. But now I am not so sure; in an age that has seen the genocide of millions, it is no longer possible to enjoy wiping out whole planets, no matter how nasty their occupants, without at least a mild sense of guilt. Especially as some writers have even gloried in the thought that *we* are perhaps the most vicious race in the Galaxy. (They may be right, though I doubt if we are *that* exceptional. Anyway, we shouldn't boast about it.)

The classic space opera—and to me, E.E.'s *Skylark Three,* the second of the series, will always be the archetype—has a simple formula which in our time has been brilliantly projected into a new medium by George Lucas. Unfortunately, the very same advances in technology which made it possible to transfer Star Wars from the pages of pulp magazines to the wide screen have also helped to convert them from fiction to reality.

That has just been brought home to me in a rather startling manner. Today is August 31, 1987—and on looking at my diary I see that exactly five years ago I was in Geneva, addressing the United Nations Disarmament Committee on "War and Peace in the Space Age."* For good or ill, the fantasies of my youth had become the international politics of my adult life.

To what extent can science fiction be blamed for this tragic—perhaps ultimately fatal—state of affairs? To focus on one issue—would President Reagan ever have made his famous "Star Wars" speech of March 23, 1983 if he hadn't seen so many movies?

*For an updated version, see *1984: Spring* (Grafton).

There is enough blame for everyone, starting with H. G. Wells and his Martians. Personally, I have a fairly clear conscience, because only once, in *Earthlight*, have I attempted a full-scale space battle. That was a deliberate attempt to emulate E. E. Smith—specifically, the attack on the Mardonalian fortress in Chapter 7 of *Skylark Three*.

The circumstances in which I started writing were somewhat unusual. In the summer of 1941, after my basic Royal Air Force training ("If it moves, salute it. If it doesn't, paint it.") I was stationed with a few hundred other Aircraftsmen II—the lowest form of animal life in the RAF—in a partly bombed-out school building in the East End of London.

Fate had timed my return to the Metropolis with exquisite precision. The previous year, while still an executive officer in HM Exchequer and Audit Department, I had been evacuated to the safety of North Wales. Here I sat out the Blitz, peacefully checking the accounts of the Ministry of Food, until I exchanged civilian clothes for RAF blue.

When I returned to London for basic electronics training, the last major attack on the city had taken place a few days before. So I was surrounded by the dramatic evidence of air warfare, without being subject to its considerable inconvenience. That was when and how I started trying to imagine what *real* war would be like; the result, after revisions made necessary by the arrival of the atom bomb four years later, was Chapter 17 of *Earthlight*. Today, I am rather ashamed of it—though I am very proud indeed of the fact that the Apollo 15 astronauts named a small crater after this early novel, and drove past it on their second EVA (see Chapter 4).

A much more thoughtful treatment of technological warfare, without any fireworks at all, is the short story "Superiority" (1951: reprinted in *Expedition to Earth*, 1953). In 1985 I had occasion to refer to it when I addressed (by videotape) the MIT Club of Washington. The distinguished audience had substantial representation from the notorious Military-Industrial Complex ("Some of my best friends, etc. . . . .") and there was a good deal of cringing and collar-fingering when I came to this part of my address:

> I would like to refer to my short story, "Superiority," which in the 1950s was required reading in MIT engineering courses. I hope it still is, because it describes the inevitable fate of all those who become intoxicated with technological obscenities.
>
> And here, I regret to say, honesty compels me to be severely critical of *Star Wars*. I do this with considerable reluctance—even a sense of guilt—because I owe many enjoyable hours to George Lucas. (You didn't think I was talking about someone else, did you?)
>
> We have already met Darth Vader—and he is us. If we are to survive, we must exorcize the demons of our haunted childhood, and grow out of our fascination with "technoporn" —gleaming weaponry and beautiful explosions. Whatever new armaments may be needed to preserve peace in the immediate future, in the long run only political solutions can save us. (If we deserve to be saved: perhaps a species that has accumulated four tons of explosive per capita has already demonstrated its biological unfitness beyond any further question.)
>
> There have been times and cultures in which it was unthinkable (and frequently unwise) for a gentleman to appear in public without a weapon. In civilized societies, that need has passed. What now applies to individuals must one day apply also to nations . . . who, after all, are only collections of individuals. (Remember Auden: "There is no such thing as the State.") And for better or for worse, human nature is infinitely changeable—a fact seldom understood by the Crackpot Realists who often prowl the corridors of power.
>
> In the long run—no, the very short run—we have to become intelligent mammals, not turn ourselves back into armored dinosaurs. To complete that quotation from Auden: "We must love one another or die." And it's very hard to love people who—for excellent reasons—we don't like.
>
> But the alternative is far worse.

Half a century after letting Williamson, Smith and Campbell destroy appreciable fractions of the Universe, *Astounding*'s successor *Analog* has just printed these words.* Perhaps we are both trying to make up for our misspent youth.

*Mid-December 1987: see Chapter 34.

16

"TWILIGHT"

The Index for the magic year 1934 contains an unusually large number of stories I remember—at least by title, and often by content. Howard W. Graham's "Guns of Eternal Day" is perhaps first on the list; the title has haunted me for years, and on re-reading it I think I know the reason.

It's a ridiculous tale about a mad scientist (yes, again!) who decides that night is a Bad Thing, and abolishes it by turning the moon into a second sun. But I am in no position to criticize, and if the endings of *The Sands of Mars* and *2010: Odyssey Two* owe anything to Mr. Graham, I gladly acknowledge my debt.

The prolific and ingenious Murray Leinster published two of his most memorable stories during 1934. Although it is very difficult to establish priority in a field where so many have written for so long (and in so many languages), "Sidewise in Time" and "The Mole Pirate" both appear completely original in concept.

The idea that many time streams might coexist simultaneously (whatever that means) is now quite commonplace: two distinguished writers who have used the theme are Fred Hoyle *(October the First Is Too Late)* and Brian Aldiss *(Frankenstein Unbound)*. But when Murray Leinster set a regiment of Roman soldiers marching down a street in Joplin, Missouri, on June 5, 1935, he created a whole new genre.

His "Mole Pirate," on the other hand, has had fewer off-spring. The story inspired one of Howard Brown's most memorable covers (November) showing what looks like the ghost of a submarine, half in and half out of a bank vault, while the frustrated guards attack it vainly with ineffectual weapons. *Inside* the vault, of course, a criminous scientist is busy loading up bars of gold. . . .

I can still recall Murray's delightful explanation of his strange vehicle—let's call it a subterrene. The name *Mole* was not really appropriate, since it made no tunnel. It simply interpenetrated normal matter, as if it wasn't there.

How? Easily. Atoms are little solar systems, with the electrons circling a central nucleus. So they are essentially flat, or two dimensional. However, the quadrillions of atoms in any ordinary substance are arranged at random, their orbits pointing in all directions. This makes it impossible for two objects to coexist in the same space.

However, if you could align all the atoms so that their planes were parallel, one solid object could move through another! The analogy that Leinster uses is that of two packs of playing cards, sliding through each other. . . .

There's a snag somewhere, I'm sure, but we'll leave that as "an exercise for the student." Anyway, the details of the story were worked out with great ingenuity, and I have often wondered why there have been so few variants on the theme of "The Impalpable Man."

The last issue in a memorable year contains a lineup of authors which could hardly occur today, but which was not at all unusual in the era of the pulps. December 1934 features stories by John W. Campbell, Karl van Campen, and Don A. Stuart. Now, the first two names look suspiciously similar—but no one would ever guess that "Don A. Stuart" was *also* John Campbell.

The first Stuart story had appeared in the previous month, and had created an immediate sensation. A haunting mood piece, "Twilight" was so totally unlike anything that Campbell had ever written that no one could have guessed the authorship. It is not really a story, for there is no plot; it is a straightforward description of the age seven million years hence, when the human race has lost all curiosity and merely exists idly in a world run by the perfect machines its ancestors had created.

Nothing could have been further from the typical Campbell space opera, featuring indomitable scientist-heroes overcoming one menace after another with their resourcefulness and brilliant inventions. His alter ego Stuart put the question "So what?," but did not answer it; though he did examine the problem again in a sequel, "Night" (October 1935).

The closing pages of *The Time Machine* have precisely the same elegiac quality as "Twilight," but Stuart's vision is even more chilling than Wells's because of its much greater (and more realistic) time scale. Only Stapledon's *Last and First Men* (1930) has similar vistas of cosmic time, which totally dwarf the whole span of human history and prehistory.

"Twilight" had a major impact on my own career, and certainly influenced *Against the Fall of Night*, which I started writing in 1937. When it was completed in 1946 I submitted it to Campbell—now *Astounding*'s editor—and he returned it with one of his long, helpful letters. A few months later I sent him a revised version, and was quite disappointed to get it back with an even longer essay of rejection. This correspondence is (I hope) safely stored in the Clarkives and I have not seen it for forty years, but I recall that Campbell's chief objection was that in my vision of the future the human race never amounted to anything much. As that was precisely the theme of "Twilight" and "Night," I felt this was a poor excuse.

In any event, *Against the Fall of Night* was sold a year later to *Startling Stories*, and has never been out of print for long since its appearance in 1948—despite my efforts to swallow it up in the Authorized, Final, Definitive etc. version, *The City and the Stars* (1956). Some people still prefer the earlier story, and I've given up arguing about it.

To return to Campbell/van Campen/Stuart's trio in the December 1934 issue:

Part 1 of *The Mightiest Machine* showed that Campbell was living up to the editorial promise: "A novel of titanic scientific achievement, of voyaging into another space, and of fantastic civilizations and their colossal conflict—the greatest story yet told."

"Karl van Campen's" "The Irrelevant" could hardly have been less titanic. To this day, I don't know whether Campbell was having a little joke, or whether he really believed that there was a loophole in the Law of the Conservation of Energy.

His hero sets off to the moon in a rocket fueled by hydrogen and oxygen, on what he thinks is a one-way trip. But by juggling with relative velocities, van Kampen "proved" that the fuel could have any energy content one likes to specify; it all depends on the reference frame. So his protagonist is able to get home safely, with some gas still left in the tank. . . .

Nonsense, of course—though uncomfortably close to some of the pseudoscience Campbell was to peddle in later years. However, the story did contain one very accurate piece of forecasting—the suggestion that the Doppler effect on radio waves could be used to measure the velocity of a rocket. Less than ten years later, this technique was employed by experimental (but not operational) V2 missiles.

"Don Stuart's" "Atomic Power" is based on one of the most philosophically terrifying ideas in the whole of science fiction. It was not original; we have already encountered Ray Cummings's explorations of the micro-universe. Campbell, however, gave it a new and appalling twist, ingeniously presented in a single short story, the components of which unite at the end to form a critical mass guaranteed to blow the mind of any sensitive reader. Here they are, safely separated. Assemble them at your peril:

1. An atomic power plant ("crouched in hulked, latent energy, the massive conductors leading off in gleaming ruddy columns, like the pillars of some mighty temple to an unknown, evil god") is being demonstrated to some students by a bored professor. He explains that every second "fifty-five duodecillion atoms" are destroyed to create energy.

2. There is a sudden glitch and the reaction stops momentarily. "You're fortunate," says the professor. "In the last

eleven years, only eight times has such a thing happened."
He explains that occasionally the generator strikes a bit of
fuel that simply refuses to break down—no one knows why.
3.   The laws of nature start to go crazy; gravity weakens; the
solar system begins to break up.
4.   The usual Campbellian superscientist deduces the cause:
"The solar system is just an atom in a greater universe. But
they're releasing atomic energy in that universe—and we're
the atom!"
5.   He decides that the process can be stopped by an injec-
tion of energy from the atomic generator he has just invented.
6.   He switches it on—it works for a fraction of a second—
then stops inexplicably. He is despondent, and is afraid to
try it again in case it blows up. "What have we got to lose?" a
friend asks, very reasonably. (Most of the planet Earth is
already frozen.)
7.   He tries again. This time it works perfectly; a counterfield
is created, and *our* universe is saved.
8.   "I wonder," asks the scientist, "if, in some vaster world,
they even knew when this particular atom of fuel simply
refused to disintegrate . . .
9.   . . . but why didn't *my* generator work before? I didn't
change a thing . . ."

After that vertiginous glimpse of universes within universes, it
is a relief to turn to the one story in the December 1934 issue
that is still remembered half a century later because of its
gentleness and humanity—even though the protagonist is an
utterly alien and (to our eyes) hideous Martian.

Raymond Z. Gallun's "Old Faithful" concerns a scientist on
Mars who has succeeded in contacting Earth by light signals.
For once, the editorial blurb is exactly correct: "A novelette
of the problem of communication—heroically and tragically
solved." Much of the narrative is a detailed and thoughtful
discussion of the question: how do you exchange ideas if you
do not even have a common language, and can only exchange
binary (on/off) signals? Whole books have now been devoted
to this central problem of Alien Contact, but Ray Gallun's

analysis must surely have been one of the earliest in a popular medium.

"Old Faithful" contains a number of other startling ideas. Here is the Martian's telescope: "The bowl contained mercury. As the container spun on its perfectly balanced axis, centrifugal force caused the mercury to spread in a thin, precisely distributed layer over the inside of the bowl, forming a convex surface that acted admirably as a mirror for Number 774's gigantic reflecting telescope. Its area, and its consequent light-gathering capacity, was many times greater than any rigid mirror that could have been constructed without flaws."

Apart from one obvious slip ("convex" for "concave") this is an admirable description of an idea whose time has just come. Only recently have advances in electronic control systems permitted the construction of large mercury mirrors, and the first telescopes based on this principle are now being tested. (One problem, of course, is that the mirror has to be horizontal, and so requires a secondary "flat" of at least equal size if the instrument is to do anything besides look at the zenith.)

After this good beginning, I am sorry to say that Gallun helps to perpetuate a common astronautical fallacy. "Old Faithful" hitchhikes from Mars to Earth by flagging a ride on a convenient comet.

Ignoring the fact that such miracles of timing involving three bodies must be extremely rare, the technique simply doesn't work. Let me quote from the essay, "Space Facts and Space Fallacies" (reprinted in *1984: Spring*), where I used asteroids as much more probable alternatives to comets:

Why not hop aboard such a body as it makes its closest approach to Earth and then jump off at a convenient moment when passing Mars? In this way your spaceship would only have to cover a fraction of the total distance; the asteroid would do all the real work. . . .

The fallacy arises, of course, from thinking of an asteroid as a kind of bus or escalator. Any asteroid whose path took it close to Earth would be moving at a very high speed relative to us, so that a spaceship which tried to reach and actually land on it would need to use a great deal of fuel. And once it had matched speed with the asteroid it would follow the asteroid's orbit *whether the asteroid was there or not.*

So there is no advantage whatsoever in such a rendezvous—unless you want some local scenery to admire. However, if there are readily available sources of raw material or propellant mass on the asteroid (or comet), that could be a very different matter. For further fascinating details, see *2061: Odyssey Three.*

I have just discovered, while prowling through my rather disorganized collection of anthologies (how *do* you file them? By title, editor, theme?) that Isaac Asimov devotes Part Five of his "Science Fiction Anthology of the 1930s," *Before the Golden Age* (1974) to the 1934 run of *Astounding.* He reprints three of the stories I have discussed: Williamson's "Born of the Sun," Leinster's "Sidewise in Time" and Gallun's "Old Faithful," as well as Donald Wandrei's "Colossus" (the story of a breakthrough into the superuniverse of which ours comprises the atoms). With good reason—since he is dealing with *all* the magazines of the period—Isaac does not reprint a single story from the Clayton era.

His anthology is a convenient source for many of the stories I have already discussed, as well as others I plan to look at later. Isaac's memories of the early magazines make enjoyable reading, and closely parallel mine. But there is one big difference, for which I envy him.

He didn't have to haunt Woolworth's, and sometimes wait years to catch up with back issues. They were right there on the racks of his father's candy store, just as soon as they rolled off the press.

Isaac—do you know how lucky you were?

1 7

"LO!"

It might be argued that a magazine claiming to publish fiction has no right to fob off factual articles on its readers. Whether *Ranch Romances, Western Love Stories, et al* ever printed thoughtful essays on land-ownership, cattle-branding, Indian sign language and similar relevant subjects, I have no idea; but somehow I doubt it.

Apart from the occasional "fillers," a few of which we have already discussed, the Clayton *Astounding* never published any non-fiction. The new management waited six months, then announced that it would start serializing Charles Fort's *Lo!* in the April 1934 issue. It was to run for eight installments, concluding in November.

No choice could have been more appropriate for a science fiction magazine, and Fort's writing was to have an immense influence on the field. Born in 1874 and dying in 1932, he achieved a certain posthumous fame when a group of disaffected intellectuals* that included Ben Hecht, Theodore Dreiser, and Alexander Woollcott formed a "Fortean Society" to promote his ideas. His most fervent advocate in the United Kingdom was Eric Frank Russell, of whose encouragement in my early career I shall have much to say later. But on the

*Intellectual: someone educated beyond his intelligence.

subject of the Forteans Eric and I did not agree; I considered them (and still do) to be ignorant and opinionated science-bashers.

Though this description could often be applied to Fort, his wry sense of humor and refusal to take himself as seriously as did his followers excused many of his faults. I found his eccentric—even explosive—style stimulating and indeed mind-expanding; years later he undoubtedly helped to inspire (if that's the right word) my two Yorkshire Television productions, *Arthur C. Clarke's Mysterious World* and *Arthur C. Clarke's World of Strange Powers*.*

Charles Fort spent an exciting life in the New York Public Library and the British Museum, going through mountains of old newspapers in search of strange events. Showers of fish and frogs from clear skies—

You won't believe this, but I swear I'm telling the whole truth and nothing but the truth. I was in the middle of that last sentence when I decided to look up some more examples in my musty 1931 Gollancz edition of *Lo!* Opening it *entirely at random,* my astonished eye fell instantly upon the following passage, in Fort's typically breathless prose:

> We contribute to the record of strange alarms. There was one in Ceylon. Gigantic vegetarians were eating trees.
>
> Millions of foreigners, big African snails *(Achatena fulica)* had suddenly appeared, massed in the one small district of Kalutara, near Colombo. Shells of the largest were six inches long.... Nothing had been seen of these "gigantic snails" until suddenly trees turned knobbly with the monsters.... The ground was as thick with them as were the trees.
>
> All the accounts, in the *Ceylon Observer,* in issues from July 27 to Sept. 23, are of a sudden and monstrous appearance of huge snails, packed thick, and not an observation upon them until all at once appeared millions.

---

*Two books, co-authored with my producers John Fairley and Simon Welfare, have been based on this material. We have now published a final summing-up, *Arthur C. Clarke's Chronicles of the Strange and Mysterious.* I've always liked short, snappy titles.

Now, I know Kalutara very well; it is the site of one of the largest temples in Ceylon—or Sri Lanka as it has now become—and I drive through it about once a month. I've never noticed any snails there, but will certainly keep my eyes open from now onwards.

My assistant, Mr. H. R. Premaratne, tells me that he has seen this phenomenon several times in the Kandy area, the ground sometimes being so covered with the creatures that it was impossible to walk without treading on them. (Very unpleasant for people without shoes!) So it is not a particularly rare occurrence.

A plague of giant snails, however annoying it may be to gardeners (and smaller snails) is not the sort of event that threatens the foundations of science, or calls for major revisions to our views of the universe. *I* don't know where all those snails came from, but feel pretty confident that they were lurking somewhere in the vast area of jungle that is not a far crawl from Kalutara even today. I would be willing to bet fairly heavily against them coming from the *N*th Dimension, or landing in flying saucers. Even though (and this too is an odd coincidence) they appeared in Ceylon just a few months after Halley's Comet had blazed in the skies.

Yet many of the news items dug up by Fort in his decades of research seem to be quite inexplicable—*if* they are true. That, of course, is the problem; hoaxes, stories manufactured by unscrupulous journalists trying to make a scoop, hallucinations, honest misinterpretations—these must explain a great many of Fort's anomalies. As he freely admitted, "I shall be accused of having assembled lies, yarns, hoaxes and superstitions. To some degree I think so, myself. To some degree I do not. I offer the data."

Unfortunately (no pun intended) he does not confine himself to that. Despite his avowed scepticism, he continually promotes the theory—totally absurd in the 1930s or even in the 1830s—that the stars and planets are really quite close, and the earth is surrounded by some kind of shell from which material occasionally falls. If Fort had lived to see men walk on the moon (well, he would have been only 95 . . .) he would have

had to eat a good many of his sarcastic words about astronomers. Scepticism is one thing; stupidity is another. But then,
everyone is stupid about *something*. As that prolific poet Anon
(who frequently uses the pseudonym Spike Milligan) once wrote:

> Happy little moron,
> Lucky little man.
> I wish I were a moron—
> My God, perhaps I am!

The Complete Books of Charles Fort, with an introduction by
Damon Knight, were reprinted by Dover Publications, New
York, in 1974; anyone attempting to read them from end to
end would suffer from acute mental indigestion. But they are
wonderful browsing fodder, because you never know what you
will come across. To quote from the flap:

> In these four volumes Fort gathered together, organized and
> commented on a wild host of phenomena: flying saucers seen
> in the sky before the invention of aircraft, flying wheels, strange
> noises in the sky; correlations between volcanic activity and
> atmospheric phenomena; falls of red snow; falls of frogs, fishes,
> worms, shells, jellies; finding of "thunderbolts"; discrepancies
> in the schedules of comets, sightings on Mars and the Moon;
> infra-Mercurian planets; flat earth phenomena, disruptions of
> gravity; poltergeist phenomena; stigmata; surviving fossil ani-
> mals; the Jersey devil; Kaspar Hauser; spontaneous combustion;
> and similar weird effects. All this mass of data Fort described
> in what is at times one of the most brilliant styles of his day.

The next time Dover reprints the Collected Works, I hereby
give permission for it to use the notice that appeared on
advertisements for my own *Strange Powers:*

PUBLISHER'S WARNING

At a generous assessment, approximately half this book is
nonsense. Unfortunately, I don't know *which* half; and neither, despite all claims to the contrary, does anyone else.

Fort's latter-day—and much more scientific—successor is William R. Corliss, who publishes a series of "Sourcebooks" of strange phenomena in the fields of geophysics, geology, archaeology, astronomy, and psychology, all carefully indexed and classified. He has assembled many of these anomalies in one volume, his *Handbook of Unusual Natural Phenomena.** Unlike Fort, Corliss selects his material almost exclusively from scientific journals like *Nature* and *Science,* not newspapers, so it has already been subjected to a filtering process which would have removed most hoaxes and reports from obvious cranks. Nevertheless, there is much that is quite baffling in some of these reports from highly reputable sources.

And here is one which Fort would have loved, in the latest issue of the *Journal of the British Astronomical Association* to reach me (Vol. 97, No. 5, August 1987, p. 257). Under the striking headline "Goose zapped by meteorite?", a letter to the editor from Richard McKim of Oundle, Peterborough reports a "mysterious incident involving a Canada goose. The farmer reported that he had seen a flash from the sky; the goose had been struck in flight and had fallen into a nearby river." Two eyewitnesses described seeing a thin, bluish, nearly vertical flash traveling downwards and striking the goose, from which cascaded "a shower of yellow sparks, similar to those seen when welding." The goose—which had a hole clean through it—was put into deep-freeze and later examined by a professor of veterinary medicine, who decided from the state of the unlucky bird's heart that it had been killed by an electric shock.

What is one to make of this? Some newspapers jumped to the conclusion that a meteorite was responsible, but this excessively unlikely explanation was ruled out by other evidence. Mr. McKim—and the Cambridge astronomers he consulted—decided that the cause of death was "some unusual form of atmospheric electricity;" a confession of ignorance which would have provoked scornful comment from Fort.

And here's an odd coincidence. Mr. McKim writes from Oundle, and today I received this note from *the* expert on

*The Sourcebook Project, Glen Arm, MD 21057.

geese, Sir Peter Scott, to whom I'd sent the report: "I was intrigued by the story and am glad it seems that the goose really was not 'zapped by a meteorite.' Having myself spent five years at school at Oundle and having studied biology I know rather more about Canada Geese than meteorites."

Personally, I have a simpler explanation. I think the Star Warriors were playing with one of their latest toys, and have sent a stiff note of protest to my friends in the Pentagon.

18
NOVA
WEINBAUM

With the January 1935 issue, a nova* exploded in the pages of *Astounding*. Stanley G. Weinbaum made his first appearance there, with a short story, "Flight on Titan."

I had already met him in the July 1934, *Wonder Stories,* which published the trailbreaking classic by which he is still chiefly remembered—"A Martian Odyssey." Never before—and never since—have I turned back to the beginning of a story immediately on finishing it, to read it straight through again. Such was its impact on me that I can still remember the time and place (my lunch break, in the "bike shed" at the back of school).

During the single year 1935, *Astounding* published seven stories by Weinbaum; and in March 1936, Tremaine printed his obituary. His entire career had spanned little more than eighteen months, and is the saddest "what might have been" in the whole history of science fiction.

Today, we take friendly aliens for granted, and they had not been unusual even in the 1930s. However, Weinbaum went beyond this; in his stories he created truly *alien*—yet not malevolently hostile—aliens. I do not know if Stanislaw Lem has

*I have just noticed that Isaac Asimov uses the title "The Second Nova" in his introduction to the Ballantine *The Best of Stanley G. Weinbaum* (1974). His first nova is E. E. Smith; I agree.

ever read a word of Weinbaum, but his masterpieces *Solaris* and *Fiasco* are among the many distant echoes of "A Martian Odyssey."

Weinbaum died from cancer at the age of thirty-three, which gives a tragic irony to the final paragraphs of the story that started his career. In one of his adventures, his Martian Odysseus (a chemical engineer—like Weinbaum himself) encounters a glowing crystal that instantly cures a wart on his thumb. After his return to the spaceship, one of his colleagues remarks:

> "The wart-cure. Too bad you missed that; it might have been the cancer-cure they've been hunting for a century and a half."
>
> "Oh, that!" muttered Jarvis gloomily. "That's what started the fight!" He drew a glistening object from his pocket.
>
> "Here it is."

And there, abruptly, "A Martian Odyssey" ends. I have often wondered if Weinbaum already knew—or suspected—his imminent fate.

Brian Stableford's study of Weinbaum in the monumental *Science Fiction Writers* (Scribners, 1982) reminds me of something I had totally forgotten, as well I might after half a century:

> In a "fanzine" article published in 1938*, entitled "Science Fiction for Beginners," Arthur C. Clarke recommended that anyone wishing to win converts to the cause of science fiction should start by providing would-be victims with the three best stories of Stanley Weinbaum: "A Martian Odyssey," "Parasite Planet," and "The Lotus Eaters." That advice may have dated somewhat, but it is still possible to see the logic of it. Although these stories are hardly typical of the pulp fare of the day, they capture the essence of its excitement. They are naive, but they are naive in precisely the right way—their

---

*Not even listed in David Samuelson's bibliography of my writings. I've no idea where it appeared.

wide-eyed stare is directed into a kaleidoscope of wonders; like all good science fiction stories they imply far more than they can contain. In his exploration . . . Weinbaum reached Pluto, but never the stars. Astronomy, in consequence, has banished every one of his marvelous worlds into the wilderness of pure fantasy. . . . Nevertheless, any modern reader with a modicum of sensitivity can still appreciate their artistry, and the fortunate few may use them to recover a little of the imaginative glamor of the days before the solar system had been so thoroughly disenchanted.

Apart from the fact that it is a little premature to write off the solar system, which will certainly have many surprises still in store for us, this seems a very fair assessment of Weinbaum. His chief talent was a wonderful imagination, firmly grounded in his scientific training; he received his degree in chemical engineering at the University of Wisconsin in 1923. According to Sam Moskowitz, redoubtable historian of sf, Charles Lindbergh was a member of Weinbaum's graduating class; it would be interesting to know if this influenced his writing in any way, and I offer the project to aspiring D. Litts.

Although Weinbaum's tales were most of all entertaining and full of novel ideas, the one which had the greatest impact upon me (after the initial shock of "A Martian Odyssey") was "The Red Peri" (November 1935). Set on Pluto, which had been discovered only five years earlier, this tale challenged—I believe for the first time—one of the most firmly held beliefs in the literature of planetary exploration. The hero of "The Red Peri" crossed a thousand feet of vacuum—*without a spacesuit.*

Weinbaum gave carefully worked out reasons why this could be done, citing the experience of divers, mentioning the "bends" (and its causes) and making a point which I have found to be still quite true today:

"Everybody's been believing a lot of superstitions about space. . . . It isn't the vacuum that's dangerous, and it isn't the cold; it's the lack of air. We couldn't freeze, because a vacuum is the best heat insulator there is ... our bodies actually produce heat faster than we radiate it away. In fact, it really felt warm to me. ..."

Weinbaum cites as additional proof an experiment which, he says, "every high-school physics student sees." I hope this is no longer true, and don't understand what it was intended to prove, but apparently in the 1930s mice were put in bell-jars and the air pumped down to vacuum. Though the mouse loses consciousness, Weinbaum points out: "When the air returns, it recovers. Its lungs don't collapse because there's no outer pressure to crush them, and its body doesn't burst because the tissues are strong enough to maintain that much internal pressure. And if a mouse can stand it, why not a human being?"

Why not, indeed? When I took up diving in the late 1940s (entirely because of my interest in its mirror image, space exploration) I became more and more convinced that Weinbaum was right. And because a good idea is worth stealing more than once,* over the years I used it in no less than three of my own stories.

The first was *Earthlight* (1955), when I had one spaceship rescue the crew of another when there weren't enough spacesuits to go around. The second was a short (very—1,500 words) story "Take a Deep Breath," later published in *The Other Side of the Sky* (1957). This involved an accident during the building of "Communications Satellite Two;" in those days (the story was written just before *Sputnik* opened the Space Age) I assumed that comsats would have to be manned, if only because masses of electronic equipment would require regular servicing. Well, the transistor and its successors rewrote that scenario, and I've sometimes regretted it. If we were still stuck with vacuum tubes, global satellite communications might have been delayed a couple of decades—but *manned* space transportation would now be going full blast.

My third unprotected space walk was not in print, but on the screen. By this time, an appreciable fraction of the human race

*Who said "Talent borrows—genius steals"?

must have seen Dave Bowman leave his spacepod, *sans* helmet, to confront HAL and regain control of *Discovery*.

I was not at the studio when Stanley Kubrick shot this episode, so had no opportunity of briefing Keir Dullea in advance. As a result, he makes an understandable error, though you have to look quite closely to notice it. When he blows off the hatch and enters vacuum, *he tries to hold his breath*.

This natural, instinctive reaction would be the very worst thing to do; it has killed many divers attempting to make a "free ascent" after running out of air. When the pressure around you drops, you must *not* attempt to retain the air in your lungs, but must let it escape freely, to avoid possibly fatal damage.

Needless to say, I expected a good deal of criticism from all the "experts" who would be quite certain this was nonsense. So I wrote an essay, "A Breath of Fresh Vacuum" (reprinted in *The View from Serendip*, 1978) detailing the human body's surprising toughness. Who would have dreamed, until Jacques Mayol did it, that a man could descend a hundred meters and return safely to the surface *without breathing gear*—going through a pressure change of ten atmospheres in one minute? And I quoted a striking phrase from U.S. aerospace medic, Dr. Gene Konecci: "The skin is a pretty good spacesuit."

Finally, I clinched matters (or so I thought) by referring to NASA and USAF School of Aerospace Medicine experiments on dogs and chimpanzees, which had survived more than two minutes of exposure to virtually complete vacuum. (I'd challenge anyone to notice 2 mm of mercury—about 1/400th of an atmosphere!)

Yet the debate still continues, and recently had an amusing twist. In 1985 the French TV network, TFI, made a documentary *Star Glider—Portrait of Arthur C. Clarke* during the course of which the interviewer asked me if I *really* believed that Dave Bowman would survive his ten-second space exposure.

"Certainly," I answered, with Keir Dullea bouncing round in the airlock behind me, courtesy of Stanley Kubrick and MGM. "But that reminds me . . ." and I drew a bead on the distinguished French writer Pierre Boulle, best known for *Planet of the Apes* and *Bridge on the River Kwai*. (Filmed in Sri Lanka, incidentally; I've visited the location, but the jungle has left no trace of David Lean* *et al.*)

In 1965 Pierre Boulle published *A Garden on the Moon*, in which the *Japanese* were the first to reach our satellite. And in this novel, I told my TV audience, "He had a man *exploding* in vacuum. Well, that's absolute nonsense."

Imagine my discomfiture when Monsieur Boulle instantly appeared on camera, denying that he had ever said anything of the sort, and leaving me wondering if I had been suffering from literary hallucinations. Though I forget much that I read (thank heaven) it is rare for me to remember things that simply aren't so—but it seemed to have happened in this case.

Not so much to challenge M. Boulle as to quell fears of galloping senility, I secured a copy of *Garden*, which I re-read with great enjoyment. Skillfully using actual events as they had occurred up to 1964, Pierre Boulle wrote what is now a convincing and moving "parallel history"—something that might have happened, but didn't.

It ends with a Japanese scientist breathing his last oxygen on the moon, having made a one-way trip for the honor of his country. He goes outside wearing his spacesuit, carrying a razor-sharp knife. The final pages of the book describe his thoughts; he remembers NASA's experiment with the water dumped in space (see Chapter 8) and muses: "The substance had literally exploded. . . . A rent in a spacesuit must produce a similar result for the human body, which is largely composed of liquid." He decides that's a very good way for an astronaut to go, and the book ends with him preparing for a painless hara-kiri.

---

*In 1952, soon after the appearance of *The Exploration of Space*, David Lean took me out to lunch to discuss a projected space movie. But nothing came of it, which perhaps was just as well. The time was not ripe for a serious treatment of the subject, until the Apollo project was under way. Still, it's fun to imagine that if he hadn't followed up *The Sound Barrier* with *River Kwai*, Lean might have made *Childhood's End*, starting its thirty-year odyssey round the movie studios just about then. . . .

Vastly relieved, I photocopied the relevant pages and sent them off to Paris. Pierre Boulle replied at once, admitting that he had entirely forgotten the passage about exploding in vacuum—and getting neatly off the hook by pointing out that he didn't actually *describe* such an event, but had merely put it into the mind of his doomed protagonist. To quote his letter: "What an ideal apotheosis for old Kanashima! In the state of mind that must have been his, don't you think he might have forgotten his science, to let himself be carried to the universe of dreams?" I concede the point, and am happy to call it a draw: P. Boulle 1; A. Clarke 1.

I suppose the only way to settle the matter is by a direct demonstration, so here is a modest proposal:

There is (or used to be) a TV series called *That's Incredible!** in which lunatics of all shapes and sizes risked their necks performing apparently impossible feats. Well, if the producers can get an insurance company to go along (and they must be pretty good at that by now) this might make for a *very* interesting program. And a useful one; it would be extremely valuable to know not merely how long men and women can survive in vacuum—but the period of consciousness during which they can do something useful.

Thirty years ago, getting myself into shape for the Great Barrier Reef, I managed to hold my breath underwater for three minutes forty-five seconds. (I'm sure I could have reached four minutes, but gave up because my fellow passengers around the swimming pool of the *SS Himalaya* were showing increasing signs of distress.) Though it's now a little late in the day, I wouldn't mind volunteering.

If the price is right, of course. . . .

---

*I once invented a vomitous variant: *That's Inedible!*

19

GREATER GLORIES, NASTIER NIGHTMARES

Although the dying Stanley Weinbaum dominated the 1935 *Astounding*, he had competition from most of the major writers in the field—as well as from the magazine's previous editor, Harry Bates.

"Alas, All Thinking!" (June issue) is an unforgettable title, and the story itself is a remarkable one to appear in a 1930s pulp magazine. It portrays, with a savagery worthy of Swift or Huxley, the physical degeneration of the human race into a few dozen immobile brains—and their deliberate "mercy killing" by a man from our age. Its unrelieved pessimism makes even Stuart/Campbell's "Twilight" seem positively cheerful.

But not that story's sequel, "Night" (October) which is surely the ultimate in hopelessness. Campbell's time-traveler goes to the very end of the universe, when the last stars are guttering to extinction. "Night" is one of the most powerful stories he ever wrote, and is not recommended reading for anyone suffering from depression.

In total contrast, his interdimensional epic *The Mightiest Machine* continued to share the pages of the magazine with E. E. Smith's space opera to end all space operas (so we thought at the time, but we should have known better . . .), *The Skylark of Valeron*. However, gentler voices were also becoming heard, and one of them was in the September 1935 issue.

Astounding's readers were doubtless surprised to discover that the "C" in C. L. Moore stood for Catherine; writing science fiction—as opposed to fantasy—was not then an occupation for ladies. It still isn't, though there are some notable exceptions, of whom Ursula Le Guin is the most outstanding; a recent *Locus* poll voted *The Left Hand of Darkness* as Number 2 in its list of all-time best sf novels.*

"Greater Glories" is one of Catherine Moore's minor stories, but the verse from which the title is taken has stuck in my memory for more than half a century. As only poetry can do, it summarizes in a few words a profound truth about our situation in the universe:

> A being who hears me tapping
> The five-sensed cane of mind
> Amid such greater glories
> That I am worse than blind.

I think this is as powerful an image as that of Plato's prisoners in the cave, and quoted it many years ago in an essay "More Than Five Senses" (reprinted in *Report on Planet Three*, 1972) adding that I would be glad to know the author's name. Some kind reader supplied this information—but, alas, it's now lost in a mountain of paper.

It would take a sixth sense to find it.

Astounding was now about to feature another writer more associated with fantasy than with science fiction. H. P. Lovecraft made a surprising appearance in 1936—like Weinbaum, only a few months before his death.

Lovecraft, who was almost as strange as his stories, is one of those writers you either hate or, er, love.† Since his death, he

---

*No 1, by a huge margin, is Frank Herbert's *Dune*. Modesty (or mortification) won't allow me to mention Number 3. *Locus* (P.O. Box 13305, Oakland, CA 94661) is the equivalent of *Variety* in sfdom.

†On a recent visit to London I noticed a shop bearing his name, appro-pri-ately located close to the famous statue of Eros. H.P. would have been horrified by its merchandise.

has become a cult-figure; Colin Wilson is perhaps his best-known current admirer, which is somewhat ironic, because Wilson takes the occult seriously, and Lovecraft was a complete skeptic. His cosmos of Nameless Monsters, Shambling Entities and Elder Gods was purely a literary creation, owing a considerable debt (which Lovecraft freely acknowledged) to Lord Dunsany.

I have a special fondness for his short novel *At the Mountains of Madness* (February–April 1936) because four years later I wrote a parody, "At the Mountains of Murkiness, or Lovecraft-into-Leacock;" and parody is, of course, often the sincerest form of homage.

Lovecraft later complained that *Mountains* was badly cut and edited; I have never read the full version, but even the abridgement still has considerable power. The author's remarkable erudition—he had more than a nodding acquaintance with all the sciences—makes his account of an ill-fated expedition to the Antarctic very convincing, through its use of geographical, historical, and geological details. Needless to say, the explorers find more than they had bargained for, when they are chased down a tunnel by something that reminds the narrator of a subway train, with a few subtle differences:

> It was a terrible, indescribable thing—a shapeless congerie of protoplasmic bubbles, faintly self-luminous, and with myriads of temporary eyes forming and unforming as pustules of greenish light all over the tunnel-filling front that bore down upon us, crushing the frantic penguins and slithering over the glistening floor. . . .

Not at all a bad description of the "indescribable," I'd say; and it gave Howard Brown one of his best covers (February 1936).

Lovecraft made his final bow in June, with "The Shadow Out of Time." The horrors are muted now, though some familiar lexicons of evil make a rather perfunctory appearance, as his narrator goes:

... minutely through such things as the Compte d'Erlette's *Cultes des Goules*, Ludvig Prinn's *De Vermis Mysteriis*, the *Unaussprechlichen Kulten* of von Juntz, the surviving fragments of the puzzling *Book of Eibon* and the dreaded *Necronomicon* of the mad Arab Abdul Alhazred.

Ah, the dear old *Necronomicon*! (When is the Book-of-the-Month Club going to get round to it?) Perhaps the most famous of all Lovecraft's creations, this do-it-yourself guide to eternal damnation by trafficking with strange powers has now achieved a shadowy life of its own. Other writers of fantasy are fond of quoting from it, and Donald Wollheim once reviewed it in an obscure small-town newspaper. No wonder that puzzled librarians are frequently asked to locate a copy; they might discourage inquiries with the information that HPL gave one of his correspondents:

In his last years, Alhazred dwelt in Damascus ... and of his final death or disappearance (738 AD) many terrible and conflicting things are told. He is said by Ebn Khallikan (12th Century biographer) to have been seized by an invisible monster in broad daylight and devoured horribly before a large number of fright-frozen witnesses. ...

Some writers will do anything for publicity; and of course there were no TV talk shows in those backward days.

"The Shadow Out of Time" has a marvelous surprise ending, and Lovecraft is being modest (or playful) when he writes, "It has been hard for me literally, to set down that crucial revelation, though no reader can have failed to guess it." *This* reader never guessed it, so I really don't think I should spoil the story for you. ...

Oh, very well. The typical Lovecraft narrator, Dr. Peaselee, political economist at Arkham's Miskatonic University, has weird visions of totally nonhuman civilizations in the remote past. He dreams that he has been transported into a monstrous alien body, and is working in a vast library with similar creatures—obviously scholars like himself, whatever *he* has become.

Eventually he comes to accept his visions as no more than psychological disturbances, until one day he receives news of an amazing discovery—the ruins of a cyclopean city in the Western Australian desert. He joins the archaeologists who are exploring it, and finds everything hideously familiar. Especially the library:

> No eye had seen, no hand had touched that book since the advent of man to this planet. And yet, when I flashed my torch upon it in that frightful abyss, I saw that the queerly pigmented letters on the brittle, aeon-browned cellulose pages were not indeed any nameless hieroglyphs of Earth's youth. They were, instead, the letters of our familiar alphabet, spelling out the words of the English language, in my own handwriting.

Lovecraft eked out the final decades of his forty-six years in a genteel poverty that must have contributed to his early death by stomach cancer; his food budget was never more than two dollars fifty a week. But this was partly his own fault; he was too much of a would-be gentleman to sully himself with commerce, and he squandered his limited energies in an enormous correspondence with other writers and admirers. (Five to ten letters a day, often of incredible length: his record was "seventy or eighty pages.") Some of this was necessary and stimulating, and much was done out of sheer kindness; but I cannot help thinking that HPL used the postman to avoid serious creative work. Although it's a little hard to picture him sitting in front of a VDT, I wonder how he would have reacted to the advent of instantaneous electronic mail, which must have had a devastating impact on contemporary gossips. (At least until the first month's phone bill arrives.)

Forty years after his death, one of his teenage fans paid HPL a handsome tribute. Willis Conover's* _Lovecraft at Last_ (Miskatonic

---

*Thanks to his daily Voice of America program, "Music USA," Willis has perhaps the best-known voice on this planet; he has only to ask his way in a Moscow street and a crowd instantly appears, thrusting locally produced jazz cassettes upon him. For the last twenty years, the wretch has been sitting on my own extensive correspondence with C. S. Lewis and Lord Dunsany, promising to edit it real soon.

University Classics: Volume 1. Arlington, VA: Carrollton-Clark, 1975) is a selection of their correspondence over the last eight months of HPL's life. This beautifully produced book (only a thousand copies were printed—mine is #421) gives a unique portrait of a man who never really grew up, and who was born a hundred years too late—or too soon.

And it's safer reading than the *Necronomicon*.

20
MECHANICAL
BOY

In the last year of his life, H. P. Lovecraft shocked the teenage Willis Conover by regretting that he could not secure some regular employment at *any* job paying "ten bucks a week or over" (letter dated September 23, 1936). Reading this fifty years later, I too was shocked, until I remembered that at virtually the same time I was managing quite comfortably on just *twelve* bucks a week—and in London!

As I approached the critical age of nineteen, I do not recall that I had any particular ambition in life, except to read science fiction magazines, look at the moon through my home-made telescopes, and play with Meccano—the most wonderful toy ever invented up to that time.

With its perforated girders and strips, its angle brackets and flanges, its rods and cranks, its threaded pins and axle rods, and its vast array of gleaming brass gear-wheels, a Meccano set permitted the construction of almost any conceivable piece of engineering. It came in ten sizes or sets, from a very simple No. 1 which could make only crude cars and cranes, to the awesome No. 10—which could construct anything up to a convincing scale model of the Eiffel Tower, with elevators run by built-in electric or clockwork motors.

The sets could be upgraded by auxiliary kits; if you had No. 3 (which was about where I started) you could turn it into No. 4

by purchasing 3A, and so on. Individual bits and pieces could also be bought separately, and any of my lunch money left after visiting the Woolworth's magazine racks went to the toyshop which was the local Meccano agency.

One of my boyhood dreams was to own the fabulous No. 10 set, but its cost was so astronomical (twenty pounds, I believe!) that such an ambition was pure fantasy. However, four decades later the dream came true; my thoughtful brother Fred, on one of his visits to Sri Lanka, brought a No. 10 set (in its wooden chest of drawers, with all the items neatly laid out in tray after tray). I unpacked it with childish delight, and soon had all the scores of well-remembered bits of cunningly machined metal spread around me on the floor—just like old times. Though I no longer have the manual dexterity, still less the hundreds of hours, needed to build one of the really complex models, I often call on the set when some mechanical problem arises. The last occasion was when I needed a steerable mounting for the laser which I use to terrorize the neighborhood; and wouldn't *that* have seemed pure sf in 1936—a housebroken death-ray, no less!

While researching the above, I discovered the following item in the *Meccano Magazine* for July 1979, which couldn't possibly apply to me:

In an article by Lord Taylor published in the Christmas 1978 edition of the *British Medical Journal,* the author describes a medical complaint known as the "Presenile Meccano Syndrome." The "victims" of this obsession apparently fall into the affluent middle-age category, people who are able to buy huge Meccano outfits and indulge themselves after possibly many years of not being able to afford to do this.

In two out of three cases, the gentlemen concerned are content to gaze at their outfits through the cellophane wrappings, while the third, who has probably never constructed a Meccano model in his life, delights in dismantling the models of others and very carefully replacing the parts in the appropriate compartments of the carton.

Well, I have some good news for the eminent medic. There's a complete cure for the Meccano Syndrome: it's called a Personal Computer.

Unfortunately, the cure is much deadlier than the disease.

Since writing the above, I was delighted to come across a news item ("Boost for Meccano nuts," *Daily Mail,* November 23, 1987) reporting that Meccano has made a comeback after "collapsing like a badly-built model crane" when General Mills abandoned it in 1985. Monsieur Marc Rebibo (who had to share a "battered set in the austere days of his childhood with six brothers and sisters," and hence developed a classic case of the dreaded Syndrome) is now manufacturing it in his Calais factory. Gustave Eiffel would be delighted; I predict that in the next century the French will be the world's leading mechanical engineers.

The Number 10 set now costs more than a thousand dollars, which would certainly have amazed Liverpool butcher's clerk Frank Hornby when he invented the system in 1901. So the centennial will be in 2001: I must do something about that. . . .

I don't know who suggested that I should take the entrance examination for the Civil Service Executive Grade, but in the spring of 1936 I found myself scribbling away in what is now the Museum of Man, just off Piccadilly. Today, that same building houses the famous "Crystal Skull," which provided a kind of trademark for my *Mysterious World* and *Strange Powers* television programs. (British television, incidentally, started up that same year—just in time to develop the equipment, and train the technicians, for the radar chain which would defeat the Luftwaffe.)

To everyone's surprise, including my own, I came in 26th in a field of about 1500, and so was able to select whatever branch of the Civil Service I preferred. Because I had scored 100 percent in arithmetic, it was suggested that I apply for the Exchequer and Audit Department; so in the summer of 1936, wearing a hat for the first (and last) time in civilian life, I arrived in Whitehall.

Literally: my first office was in King Charles Street (next to

Downing Street) and here I was supposed to help audit the accounts of the Board of Education. I quickly discovered that government financing was, and would forever remain, a complete mystery to me; luckily, that didn't really matter, at least in my first job, which was checking teachers' pensions. This involved no more than simple arithmetic—multiplying the last five years' earnings by the appropriate factor, which took me only a few seconds.

Half a century later, it's quite safe for me to confess the details of my technique. I quickly realized that an auditor didn't have to get figures *exactly* right; that was the job of a mere accountant, probably cranking the handle of a mechanical calculator (though I don't remember seeing even one of those extinct monsters during my five years in the Civil Service). The auditor's job—as *I* defined it—was to see that the figures were approximately right—say to within one percent, or tuppence in the pound. (In those far-off days, the pound sterling still consisted of twenty shillings, each containing twelve pennies. And there were four farthings to a penny—they were still used occasionally as change, though even in 1936 they couldn't buy anything.)

I prided myself on having the fastest slide rule in Whitehall, so I was usually able to do all my work in an hour or so, and devote the rest of the day to more important business. Very leisurely lunch hours, which allowed for enjoyable strolls around Green Park and St. James's Park, also helped to pass the time pleasantly.

On the whole, I have nothing but happy memories of the prewar Exchequer and Audit Department, though there were moments of acute boredom *outside* the office. As part of my training, I had to take courses in accounting at that hotbed of revolution (though I never noticed any signs of it) the London School of Economics. The niceties of double-entry bookkeeping, trial balances, and bank reconciliation statements passed straight through my brain without any transmission loss; I was too busy daydreaming about spaceships.

To the astonishment of my superiors (misled by that 100 percent score in arithmetic of which, as a would-be mathematician and not a bean counter, I was thoroughly ashamed) I failed my accountancy exam and had to take it again. The second time I scraped through; fortunately, the war cut short my inglorious career as an LSE external student. I have only once revisited the place, in the early 1970s, to meet one of its most famous and now sadly missed professors, and still recall his rueful comment on the surrounding hippydom: "I wouldn't have believed it possible that in such a large group of young people there's not a *single one*, of either sex, I'd like to take to bed."

Of my stay at the Board (now Ministry) of Education I remember very little, except the kindness of my colleagues to a raw country boy. One of my fellow auditors was the first communist I'd ever met; he'd actually been to the Soviet Union and *hadn't* been disenchanted. Everyone regarded him with tolerant amusement, and I don't recall that there were ever any political arguments.

Of the hundreds of teachers' personal files that passed over my desk I remember just one, for reasons which will soon be apparent. Sometimes a teacher forfeited a pension (usually for the sort of conduct my LSE friend was contemplating) and in that case he was still entitled to a refund of the contribution that had been deducted from his salary, to await him when he came out of jail. (Because this was England, not France, it was always "he." There was never, alas, a "she" to break the monotony with a Louis Malle-type scenario.)

These sordid cases arrived in sealed envelopes bearing red stars, and were only to be opened by authorized officers—which of course included the auditor. Needless to say, a really juicy scandal would make my day, and on several occasions my innocent superiors were duly appalled when I had to explain the forensic Latin I had used in my minutes.

More often, though, a refund of contributions would be for a perfectly innocent reason: a lady teacher had married and was retiring too early to qualify for a pension, or a young man had decided that he was better suited for some other profession. In these cases the accumulated money was refunded by the Board, and the ex-teacher would be given a golden (or at least silver) farewell handshake.

One day in 1937, such a file crossed my desk. A young trainee-teacher had decided to try his luck elsewhere; it was a perfectly routine case—but I recognized the name.

And this has puzzled me for fifty years; was he already famous *then*, at 28, just out of university? If not, why do I remember handling his file?

We have never met, though once his producer invited me to visit the TV studio when he was rehearsing. And a few years ago, I was delighted when he used one of his famous radio talks to discuss Arthur Clarke and his works.

The name of that young would-be schoolmaster, in case you haven't already guessed, was Alistair Cooke. By bailing out of the British educational system, he taught thousands of times as many people as if he'd stayed aboard.

Determined to solve this mystery, I sent the above material to Alistair Cooke, and was delighted to receive the following reply:

I'm honoured to be included, albeit shakily, in your memoirs. . . . "Was he already famous then, at 28, just out of university?" Well, no. First, I got out of university at 23, at the end of my fifth year at Cambridge. Took my final, honors, degree in English to attend the Teacher's Training College. (So, true, I intended to be a schoolmaster.) . . . During that fourth year, I did some student teaching, at the Cathedral School in Ely. I was then 22. In June of 1932 I left Cambridge and, in the September, sailed for the United States (I had been awarded a Commonwealth Fellowship for two years' graduate study—which turned out to be a year at Yale and another at Harvard). At the end of that time, faced with the unpleasant prospect of becoming usefully employed, I applied for—at 3000 miles—the post of Film Critic to the BBC. (I read—in a glaring headline in the *Boston Globe*—that "BBC FIRES PM'S SON." He was Oliver Baldwin, and if he hadn't been, God knows where I'd be today.) The Fund whipped me over (via the paddling Cunarders) to London for an interview. I got the job. Returned to England in Oct. 1934 and was the BBC's film critic till April, 1937, when I resigned to return to America as a correspondent (I had picked up a considerable load of walking money by reporting—five times a day—the Abdication Crisis for NBC). I was then 28. (Born Nov. 1908—still going in a mildly arthritic way.)

I hope this true account will help you confirm or amend your previous page.... With continued good wishes for your continued soothsaying.

Alistair Cooke

I was, of course, pleased (and relieved) to receive this proof that I wasn't hallucinating a fifty-year-old memory. Doubtless I'd already encountered Alistair Cooke in his Film Critic incarnation, when his file arrived at my desk.

To return to Lovecraft's plaintive cry for "ten bucks a week." My initial salary as a Junior Auditor was no more than twelve; the rate for a new Executive Officer was three pounds a week—and in those days, believe it or not, there were four dollars to the pound. I cannot recall how much of this princely income went towards the room I rented near Paddington Station, but I do remember that it was just large enough to contain bed, sink, and cupboard. There was no chair, and any visitor had a choice between sitting on the bed or the windowsill. As most of my visitors were fellow members of the British Interplanetary Society, I was certainly proving Hamlet's adage: "I could be bounded in a nutshell, yet count myself king of infinite space."

Forty-four years later—the day after signing the contract for *2010: Odyssey Two*, which would bring me slightly more than three pounds a week—I once again walked past 21 Norfolk Square, Paddington, and looked up at the window from which I had first surveyed the city of London. As far as I could tell, everything was completely unchanged, and I wondered who was occupying my old room.

If he is a newly appointed Executive Officer in the Civil

Service, he will now earn more in a week than I received in a year—such is the degree of inflation since 1936. Yet I do not recall ever being short of money. Of course, there were countless luxuries I would have liked (including a room more than ten feet by six in size) but their absence never worried me. I was even able to afford a small radio, which cost a week's salary and was a distinct fire hazard; it was an American model, running on 115 volts, which it extracted from the British 230 by the simple expedient of dumping the excess watts into a gently glowing resistor.

An appreciable fraction of my salary must have gone to London Transport, because every workday I plunged into Paddington Underground Station to make the journey Edgware Road–Baker Street–Oxford Circus–Piccadilly Circus–Trafalgar Square; it took about thirty minutes, and then there would be a ten-minute walk down Whitehall to the office, passing Downing Street on the way. Being a Civil Servant (10 to 5 in winter, 9 to 4 in summer) I missed the rush-hour crowds, and was usually able to find a seat. So the time wasn't wasted; I could consume the average novella between Paddington and Trafalgar Square. It wasn't a bad life.

No—it was a *good* life, and I can thank science fiction for that, because it was through the magazines that I got in touch with London "fandom" and, most important of all, the fledgling British Interplanetary Society. (There was about an 80% overlap between the two groups.)

The BIS had been founded in 1933 by a Liverpool engineer, P. E. Cleator, and I had joined a year or two later. I can still remember a voluminous correspondence I had with the society's long-suffering secretary, Leslie Johnson, in which I bombarded him with technical questions.

Unlike many prophets, Phil Cleator has had the great satisfaction of being able to say "I told you so"—squared. Recently Dr. Hans Mark, NASA's Deputy Administrator during the years 1981–4, published his account of the U.S. decision to build a space station. (*The Space Station: A Personal Journey;* Duke University Press, 1987.) His first chapter opens:

Books are important, and they can influence lives.* I want to begin this story by talking about a book I received as a present on my twelfth birthday in 1941. . . .The book was published in 1936 and is titled *Rockets Through Space*. . . . Slowly it dawned on me that Cleator and his colleagues were on to something really important and that I wanted somehow to be a part of it. . . .

Hans Mark's experience exactly mirrors mine; in my case the book was *The Conquest of Space* (1931) by David Lasser. How odd that a young American should be turned on by an English writer, and vice versa! I am happy to report that Phil Cleator was delighted by Dr. Mark's tribute—and I am currently helping David Lasser with *his* latest book. People intelligent enough to be interested in space are good life insurance risks—as long as they only *write* about rockets. When they try to build them as well, the odds aren't quite so good. Korolev died at 59, Goddard at 63, von Braun at 65.

One man who spent some time building, but much more writing, was Willy Ley—and he deserves a chapter to himself.

*Astronaut Joe Allen, who helped recapture two lost satellites on the November 1984 *Discovery* shuttle flight, sent me his beautiful book *Entering Space* (Stewart, Tabori and Chang, 1984) with the note: "When I was a boy, you infected me with both the writing bug *and* the space bug but neglected to tell me how difficult either undertaking can be. . . ."

21

"AT THE PERIHELION"

Willy (or "Villy" as he was to all of us) emigrated to the United States from Germany in 1935, at the age of twenty-nine. A polymath who was equally at home in astronomy, geology, history, and zoology, he later became one of the world's leading advocates of space-exploration—and its first historian.

"The Dawn of the Conquest of Space" (March 1937) was the first of his many articles on rocketry to appear in *Astounding*. It opened with a thought-provoking statement:

> The case of the rocket ship is a peculiar one. It does not yet exist . . . thus we have—with the possible exception of flying machines—for the first time in history a machine that is popular even before its actual invention. . . .

The rest of the article is a very clear account of the distinction between solid and liquid propellant rockets, the work of the German Rocket Society (of which Ley was a prominent member and publicist) near Berlin between 1929 and 1933, and a simple analysis of the problem of escaping from earth. Ley believed that the road to the spaceship lay through the meteorological rocket, capable of reaching altitudes of about fifteen miles; this would develop the necessary technology for more ambitious projects.

As he himself was to document in due course, history did not adhere to this reasonable scenario. The rocket bypassed the lower stratosphere; new types of balloon were able to explore this region much more economically.

While his first articles were appearing in *Astounding*, Willy Ley's old colleagues, with a little help from the German Army, had already established themselves at Peenemünde. They were interested not in fifteen-mile altitudes—but two-hundred-mile ranges; not in payloads—but in warheads. Yet their leader, young Wernher von Braun, had already set his sights on the moon—with London as a regrettable first stop.

Although Willy was a science-fact writer par excellence—the best in the business before Isaac Asimov—he did occasionally try his hand at fiction. The February 1937 *Astounding* contains "At the Perihelion," by "Robert Willey"—set on Mars in AD 1978. Alas, we never made it; nor did Willy, who died in 1969—just a few weeks before the first Apollo flight to the moon.

Re-reading "At the Perihelion," I am impressed. I don't know what editorial help, if any, he had received, but Willy appears to have mastered English in a couple of years. (Though he spoke with a thick German accent to the end of his life, hence the "Villy" of all his friends.)

The story takes place on a realistic (for 1937) Mars, which is being colonized by the Soviets! *Astounding*'s readers may well have been surprised to meet some sympathetic Russians, and Willy shows a nice sense of humor by bureaucratizing Mars with "light-years of red tape."

The most interesting point in the tale, however, is the technique used to cope with "weightlessness" on a long space journey:

> As soon as the rocket motors had ceased firing, the ship had changed her appearance. She was a madly spinning double star now. On the one end of a thin but strong steel cable there was the main cabin, the supply room and the control room—on the other the machinery and the fuel tanks. Held together by the three miles of cable, the two parts spun around each other, thus producing an artificial gravity in the cabin.

Three miles! That seems excessive, and would involve a substantial mass of cable. To produce half normal Earth weight, the system would have to make one revolution every two minutes, which scarcely qualifies as "madly spinning."

But the principle is sound, and was tested in one of the Gemini missions. "Tethers" are now a Big Thing in space technology, and have applications that Willy Ley could never have dreamed of in 1937.*

A few years later, he published a two-part article "The End of the Rocket Society" (August–September 1943) which formed the nucleus of his invaluable book *Rockets: The Future of Travel Beyond the Stratosphere* (see Chapter 28).

Willy's most influential book, however, was undoubtedly *The Conquest of Space* (Viking, 1949) in which he provided the text to accompany Chesley Bonestell's magnificent paintings of the solar system. These beautiful and awe-inspiring studies—particularly the classic views of Saturn from its various moons—must have introduced thousands to the wonders of astronomy, and the possibilities of space exploration.

A few years after Willy's death, Chesley and I joined forces to produce *Beyond Jupiter: The Worlds of Tomorrow* (Little, Brown, 1972), a preview of the "Grand Tour" of the outer planets then being considered by NASA. The Voyager missions magnificently achieved all the Grand Tour's objectives (though we're still waiting for news from Neptune) and proved the accuracy of Chesley's previsions. What he could not have imagined— what *nobody* could have imagined—were such details as the volcanoes of Io, and the incredible complexities of Saturn's rings.

We dedicated the book "To Willy, who is now on the Moon." Now Chesley has also gone (at the age of ninety-eight, still painting furiously); one day he too will have a lunar crater named after him.

Or better still, one on Mars.

*Including the "Space Elevator": see *The Fountains of Paradise.*

2 2
TELSTAR
MINUS
TWENTY·SIX—
AND
COUNTING. . . .

John W. Campbell, alias Don Stuart, showed his versatility during 1936 when the first article of an eighteen-part series, "A Study of the Solar System," appeared in the June issue. They were both accurate and exciting, full of striking insights like: "Meteors never fall to Earth from Space. They fall to the Sun, and the Earth happens to get in the way." The whole series would have made an excellent textbook: even now, I am surprised to see how little it has dated.

Campbell began modestly by conceding that perhaps a tenth of his statements would be inaccurate to the point of virtual uselessness, and at least a twentieth would be wholly wrong. In fact, he did rather better than this: among the few "wholly wrong" statements were the rotation period of Mercury, which every astronomer of the time would have sworn on oath to have been the same as its year—eighty-eight days. To everyone's stupefaction, it turns out to be only fifty-nine days.

Nor could Campbell, in the days before radar, have known that Venus has the longest "day" in the solar system—almost exactly two thirds of an Earth year, which may be more than a coincidence. He was correct in discounting Venus as a possible abode of life, saying if it had any seas, they would be boiling at the equator. In fact, Venus is so hot that they would boil at the Poles.

He was also accurately pessimistic about Mars, though he did consider that plant life was "certain." (He may yet be right.) He thought that the atmosphere was only one-thousandth as dense as Earth's; it is actually more like one-hundredth, but Campbell was much closer to the truth than many later "experts." And he was uncannily correct in thinking that Mars had literally "rusted to death" owing to the action of free ozone on the planet's iron ores.

The discovery of a "hole" in the ozone layer over the South Pole has recently focused attention on this gas, which, though a deadly poison, protects us from the sun's ultraviolet rays. We will soon have to abandon fluorine-based aerosol sprays, unless we want to die of skin cancer.

John Campbell's thorough demolition of our neighborhood as a place you'd like to visit took a long time to discourage his fellow writers. The February 1937 issue contained part 9 of his "Study of the Solar System," which explained that "Jupiter is possessed of a climate ideal for life"—if you enjoy breathing hydrogen at a couple of hundred degrees below zero.

Yet that very same issue opens with a cops-and-robbers adventure, "The Saga of Pelican West," on an *asteroid* with a perfectly Earthlike environment; reading it, I find it impossible not to see Harrison Ford in the leading role.

This fast-moving little tale was the first appearance in *Astounding* of the British author Eric Frank Russell, who was later to produce many stories of much greater merit, dealing with serious philosophical and political issues. Even in "Pelican West" there are a couple of items that gave me a distinct jolt. Thirty days out from Mars:

> . . . Michaelson developed blue death. Terrestrial medicos claimed this affliction was bubonic plague complicated by alien metabolism. Anyway, Michaelson had got blue swellings in the armpits. There was no known cure. They'd given

him an overdose of dope and incinerated him in the four-o'clock stern combustion chamber. . . .

Ominously topical, isn't it? And does this passage from the same story remind you of something?

Has a Martian ever succeeded in explaining to you what it means to poldek?
A Martian can't explain it because no Terrestrial has been born with the ability to poldek. All I've been able to gather is that it's a sort of sense that enables them to perceive life, a faculty by which they can tell . . . whether or not anything contains life.

I'm still grokking this. . . .

Eric Frank Russell was a big, energetic man with a ribald sense of humor. It's inconceivable that I could have destroyed his long letters, written in one of the most beautiful hands I've ever encountered, but I'm ashamed to say I have no idea what has happened to them.

I owe him many debts, for he was my first literary collaborator and my first source of income from writing. Some of his early stories used ideas that I provided, and he paid me promptly and generously. Although Scribner's authoritative *Science Fiction Writers* devotes five pages to him, I must sadly agree with its verdict that "in general it is unsurprising that Russell . . . though he is nostalgically remembered by older readers, should otherwise be virtually forgotten in the 1980s."

Yet in the 1940s and 1950s he was one of the most popular of all sf writers—and the favorite of *Astounding*'s next editor, John W. Campbell.

There is some uncertainty about the date when Tremaine handed over the magazine to this twenty-seven-year-old author, who had already made a major impact on the field both with his science fiction and his science fact. In any event, the transition took place at the end of 1937, and from December onwards Campbell was at the helm.

He died in harness exactly 34 years (409 issues!) later, Ben

Bova taking over from January 1972. It is not likely, in today's fast-moving, multimedia world, that this record will ever be surpassed.

But before we move into the Campbell era, I would like to share with you an unexpected and piquant discovery I have just made. In the March 1936* issue, Tremaine published a story by a young engineer who was exactly the same age as Campbell—they were both born in 1910. Entitled "Pre-Vision," it's a modest little piece about an electronics genius who invents a machine that can see into the future, using "the advanced potentials that satisfy the electromagnetic equations." (No gobbledegook this, but the genuine article.)

"Pre-Vision" has two points of interest; the first—merely amusing and trivial—concerns the illustration. The artist has tried to depict a city street of the future, with fashions and vehicles which would look—well, futuristic—to his 1936 audience. The scene shows a reckless lady jaywalker about to be hit by an automobile, which is instantly recognizable as a "Beetle." Intriguing, to say the least—as Volkswagenwerk AG wasn't even founded until 1937. . . .

Now let me tell you something about the future career of this young author, to give you some idea of the people who wrote (occasionally) for *Astounding Stories*—and, still more often, read it.

After graduating from Caltech, he was offered a job at one of the country's most famous laboratories, and during the war developed some vital radar components. Though he wrote a few more stories and numerous articles, his main contribution to the English language is a single word. When some of his colleagues invented a new amplifying device, he suggested the name for it: "transistor."

In 1952, he became the Lab's Director of Electronics Research. I met him that same year, on my first visit to the U.S. to promote *The Exploration of Space*. But I cannot claim to have turned his thoughts in that direction: *Wonder Stories*

---

*The same issue that contains Weinbaum's last story, and a brief memorial notice by Tremaine.

had already published his "Adrift in the Void" as far back as 1934. . . .

In 1955, he published a seminal paper "Orbital Radio Relays" (*Jet Propulsion,* April 1955) which for the first time set out the detailed engineering parameters of communications satellites. (My short 1945 paper had merely stated the underlying principles.) A few years later, he persuaded NASA to launch a radio-reflecting balloon as a "passive" satellite, and Echo was seen by more human beings than any other artifact in history. In 1962, his team followed this up with the history-making Telstar, precursor of all today's comsats. This was just twenty-six years after his debut in *Astounding.*

And it is now, I am slightly appalled to see, twenty years ago that he asked me to write the preface to his monograph, *The Beginnings of Satellite Communications* (San Francisco Press, 1968). I have not seen him for many years—but hope to do so again very shortly.

On my seventieth birthday, December 16, 1987, Dr. John Robinson Pierce will be visiting Sri Lanka to deliver the Arthur Clarke Lecture, and to receive a handsome trophy whose artist has cleverly combined two of the chief motifs of my life: a 1:4:9 monolith, and three satellites equidistantly spaced around a central globe.

The above events, I am happy to record, took place very successfully, John Pierce and his new bride Brenda spending more than a week in Sri Lanka. On December 16 he delivered his lecture "Space Enough For All" to a distinguished audience which included President J. R. Jayewardene. The whole event was carried live on local TV, and was followed immediately by a half-hour panel discussion over the United States Information Agency's Worldnet satellite link. It was a great pleasure to see my old friends Fred Durant (Executive Director of the Arthur Clarke Foundation of the United States), Dr. Joseph Pelton (Intelsat's Director of Special Projects) and Todd Hawley (Administrator, International Space University) at the Washington end—though I felt guilty at getting them to the studio at 7 A.M. EST. And it was a great privilege to have President

Jayewardene on our Colombo panel; the fact that the Head of State was prepared to devote three hours of his time to the proceedings was a striking proof of his interest in the communications revolution.

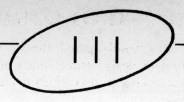

CAMPBELL

(1 9 3 7 – 1 9 7 1)

2 3

JWC

I did not meet John Campbell until my first visit to the United States, in 1952, so I never knew him during the years when he was reshaping the magazine. But I am sure that Isaac Asimov's description of him cannot be bettered:

> The man who built the structure of modern science fiction was a tall, broad, light-haired, crew-cut, bespectacled, overbearing, overpowering, cigarette-holder-waving, opinionated, talkative, quicksilver-minded individual named John Wood Campbell, Jr.*

Not particularly flattering: but Isaac goes on to say that "everything in my writing career I owe to him. It was he who gave me the skeleton of 'Nightfall,' including the opening quotation, and sent me home to write the story. It was he who considered my third or fourth robot story, shook his head, and said, 'No, Isaac, you're neglecting the Three Laws of Robotics which are—' and that was the first I heard of them."

Many other sf writers could pay similar tributes, quoting from letters of rejection longer than the stories they had sub-

*Introduction, *Astounding: The John W. Campbell Memorial Anthology*, edited by Harry Harrison (Random House, 1973).

mitted. A small selection of Campbell's enormous correspondence (probably far surpassing even Lovecraft's) was published in 1985 in a 600-page volume, *The John W. Campbell Letters*, edited by Perry A. Chapdelaine, Tony Chapdelaine, and George Hay.* This labor of love—the first of a projected series!—brings the man vividly to light, with all his quirks and foibles. Towards the end of his career he became involved in the promotion of a whole series of controversial (to say the least) ideas: Dianetics, parapsychology, antigravity-machines (the "Dean Drive"), extremist political opinions, and his once-stimulating editorials became almost unreadable. Yet even at his most outrageous, you could never be quite sure if Campbell was really expressing his own point of view, or was merely—merely!—trying to provoke his readers to think for themselves, by challenging their most cherished beliefs. To quote once again from Isaac Asimov: "however idiosyncratic his views on science and society, he remained, in person, a sane and gentle man." And, I would like to add, essentially a kind one.

He died on June 11, 1971, three days after his sixty-first birthday, and there is a curious irony about the manner of his passing, which he would have thoroughly enjoyed. In a 1945 Editorial (June: "Communication and Noncommunication") he had attempted to predict the future of electronics, and had rashly guessed (his own phrase) that "television may never reach the stage of being in everybody's home, as radio receivers are now. . . . It can't be unobtrusive; you have to watch it. But you can't watch it, if you're doing housework, bills, playing bridge, or reading. . . . My own hunch is that too few people will buy the expensive, four hundred dollar television receivers to support the commercial advertiser's very expensive show."

A very reasonable prediction—and, like most reasonable predictions, totally falsified by events. Campbell underestimated the human capacity for what we would now call parallel processing, and he also failed to anticipate that mass-production would bring the price of TV sets down from $400 to less than $40, in 1945 dollars.

*AC Projects, Inc., Rte. 4, Box 137, Franklin, TN 37064.

And so, again in the words of his friend Isaac Asimov, John Campbell died "at home, quietly, quickly, painlessly, as he sat before his television set."

By this time, such a farewell to life must be far from unique. And I cannot help but wonder what program John was viewing. . . .

24
ROCKET WARFARE

Writing this chapter has suddenly brought back a childhood memory I once made considerable efforts to erase. My first encounter with rockets was not an auspicious one.

The year is uncertain, but the date is not; it must have been November 5th—Fireworks Day, the occasion on which we British celebrate (or lament—the matter is still under dispute) Guy Fawkes's failure to blow up the Houses of Parliament in 1605.

Perhaps I was ten years old; it could not have been any more. I was standing in the village square at Bishop's Lydeard, just outside the little post office in which I was to spend so many hours as mail-sorter and night telephone operator, when some idiot launched a rocket *horizontally*, so that it shot along the ground. It hit the toe of my shoe, was deflected up *inside* my shorts, and wandered around for awhile before burning its way out through the back of my shirt.

Mirabile dictu, I was not badly hurt—but I was terrified, and for several years hid myself every Guy Fawkes Day. The incident left no lasting scars—physical or mental—and by my mid-teens I enjoyed firework displays as much as anyone. But it might have turned me off rockets for life, and changed my entire future career. I would certainly not have made my 1938 debut in *Astounding*.

According to Isaac Asimov, who should certainly know, although Campbell joined Street and Smith in September 1937 he did not actually succeed Tremaine as editor until May 1938. However; anyone who remembers John will agree that he probably became de facto editor about five minutes after entering the premises, and there can be little doubt that he must bear some of the blame for an article that appeared in the January 1938 issue. It must be rather unusual for a pulp magazine to feature differential equations, and I expect the printers demanded danger money when they coped with "Rocket Flight" by Leo Vernon, described as an MIT mathematician.

After a very clear statement of the basic principles of rocket propulsion, Leo Vernon derived an equation relating exhaust speed, rate of fuel consumption, rocket mass, and acceleration. It would be difficult to find a simpler problem in dynamics, yet he got a completely wrong answer—then proudly claimed that his results "differ considerably from those obtained by some writers on rocket flight." For "some" he might well have written "all"; I wonder why Vernon never stopped to ask why *he* was the only one out of step.

To make matters worse, he then applied his erroneous equation to calculate the performance of rockets with exhaust velocities between ten and *one hundred* times greater than could be provided by any possible chemical propellants. And he talked of storing hydrogen and oxygen not as liquids, but as gases under pressures of 6,000 atmospheres! (The average scuba tank, which is hardly notable for lightness, is only safe to 300 atm.)

Vernon's essay must have made Willy Ley, the *real* rocket expert, absolutely furious (ironically, Willy was featured in the same issue, with an excellent article on solar energy). It certainly annoyed me, and I wasted no time in demolishing the author. My full-page letter in the "Science Discussions and Brass Tacks" section of the May issue marks my very first appearance in *Astounding;* seamail must have been faster in the 1930s than airmail all too often seems today.

Anyone interested in seeing how I dealt with Mr. Vernon can look up the photocopy of my letter in Chapter 2 ("First Flights") of *Ascent to Orbit: A Scientific Autobiography*. I'm not particularly proud of it; the attempts at sarcasm and schoolboy humor now make me wince. But it put the record straight, and certainly gave me a memorable introduction to John Campbell —who headed my attack with a hopeful, "We'll expect a reply from Leo Vernon."

None was ever forthcoming, but the July "Science Discussions" opened with a letter from one Norman F. Stanley which, while attempting to support Vernon, merely pinpointed the source of his error. He had differentiated the rocket's momentum, not its velocity. It's a subtle point and, fifty years too late, I feel a little guilty at being so rude—even though I was in the right.

I answered Mr. Stanley in the December issue, restating the correct equation of rocket motion which, incidentally, Tsiolkovski had derived in the last century (it is sometimes known by his name). And that was the end of the matter—though not of Leo Vernon, who did contribute two more articles—*not* on rockets— before vanishing without trace.*

I have often wondered who he was, and for a while suspected Campbell himself. He too had studied at MIT, but had failed to graduate there—because, so the legend runs, he flunked in German. I don't believe it: German would have been child's play to JWC, and it seems much more likely that he couldn't meet MIT's exacting standards because he was writing more science fiction than was good for his studies. (He probably needed the money, modest though it must have been.) In any event, he finally secured his B.S., majoring in physics, at Duke University—then famous through Dr. J. B. Rhine's work on parapsychology. Campbell took part in some of Rhine's ESP experiments, which doubtless contributed to his later interest in "psionics." The good doctor has much

---

*"Tools for Brains" (July 1939) is an excellent account of the status of computers at that time, and a shrewd—though now hopelessly conservative—forecast of their future potential. "Unseen Tools" (June 1940) is a fascinating essay on multidimensional geometry, symbolic logic, noncommutative algebra and other esoterica. When he stuck to pure maths, Leo Vernon knew exactly what he was talking about.

to answer for—including, come to think of it, *Childhood's End.*

The addresses given on my May and December 1938 letters record a major change in my own life-style. The first was written in the Paddington broom closet described in Chapter 20, and during the summer I had moved eastwards, though not quite so far as I was to do eventually. The December letter (see Appendix) came from 88 Gray's Inn Road, an address which soon became famous in British sf fandom. Why everyone called it "the Flat" I don't know: it extended vertically over several floors, and getting around required a considerable expenditure of energy. The only other time in my career when I lived in comparable circumstances was when I resided in a one hundred foot-high lighthouse six miles off the south coast of Ceylon: see *The Treasure of the Great Reef.*

I was able to afford this luxurious accommodation (I had the attic, which commanded a fine view of St. Paul's Cathedral) because I shared the rent with another science fiction (and movie, and music) enthusiast, William F. Temple. Bill's extra three years gave him a maturity I was not to approach for several decades (if ever); he worked in the Stock Exchange, which he hated, until his writing allowed him to escape. We were friendly (usually) rivals, and when he sold his novel *The Four-Sided Triangle** to the movies I was pleased rather than envious, because such an achievement was far beyond my own ambitions.

I note, with some amusement, that the TEMPLE, WILLIAM F(REDERICK) entry in the superlative *Encyclopedia of Science Fiction* refers to Bill as my "housemate"—a slightly ambiguous description. So I hasten to add that we were Just Good Friends, perhaps even more so after Bill's long-suffering (it will soon be half a century!) wife Joan moved in, and vastly improved the quality of the housekeeping.

Though he pretended to be totally ignorant of technology, Bill became editor of the British Interplanetary Society's semi-

---

*Released by Hammer Films in 1953. I have never seen it, but it occasionally surfaces on late-night TV.

amateur *Bulletin,* and wrote some very amusing accounts of the frequent BIS Technical Committee meetings that took place in the Flat. They deserve to be reprinted: they are part of the history of the early space movement.

25
"WHO
GOES THERE?"

After he became editor of *Astounding* in 1938, John Campbell published no more fiction. But for a year or two his alter ego "Don A. Stuart" continued to publish some excellent stories, and one of them is among the most famous ever to appear in the magazine.

"Who Goes There?" (August 1938) may not be completely original (the legend of Proteus predates it by a few millennia) but it is a work of such power that it became almost a modern myth, and has had innumerable imitators. The discovery* of a spaceship that has been buried in the Antarctic ice for twenty million years, the thawing out of its one surviving crew member, and its attempt to take over the isolated expedition by *imitating* perfectly man, dog, or anything else it pleased is one of the all-time greats of classic horror.

When Howard Hawks filmed it as *The Thing From Another World* (1951) he turned Stuart's "submarine without a conning tower" into a flying saucer, and completely abandoned the story's most disturbing element—the "shape-changing" theme which provides the chilling title. It became just another monster movie, though a superior one.

*By the magnetic anomaly it produced! Thank you, John: I'd completely forgotten, when I used the very same idea in *2001*.

More than two decades later, John Carpenter was much more faithful to the original—and gave full rein to the special effects department, with such horrifying results that the public stayed away in droves. The human transformations are bad enough, but as a lifelong caninophile (my feet are being warmed by half a hundredweight of Rhodesian Ridgeback at this very moment) I can't bear to watch huskies turned inside out. To coin a phrase, it shouldn't happen to a dog.

Campbell/Stuart published only one more story ("Cloak of Aesir," March 1939) in *Astounding* and when questioned by Isaac Asimov—who could not imagine how any successful author could bear to stop writing fiction—he had an incontrovertible reply. As an editor, he explained (and I can see that cigarette-holder waving in the air) he could write *hundreds* of stories. And he did.

He also wrote at least five hundred editorials and articles, most of them under his own name but a few, during the 1937–41 period, as "Arthur McCann." These are brilliant, wrongheaded, stimulating, crazy, amusing—and now mostly unreadable. Where Campbell was right, which was pretty often, he has suffered the fate of all prophets: time has devalued the originality of his thinking, so that to the modern reader he merely seems to be stating the obvious. And where he was wrong (which was also pretty often—see his remarks on TV in Chapter 23) he now seems foolish or even stupid.

He was neither of these in a short filler that appeared in August 1939, under a heading that would not mean anything to most of mankind for another six years: "Isotope 235." Its opening paragraph sums up the excitement then raging through the world of physics—a mood perhaps unmatched until the superconductivity furor of today:

Since last January, when the uranium fission reaction was first announced, progress toward the solution to the problem of practicable, commercial atomic power has been so rapid that only weekly bulletins could report the succeeding waves of advance. Now . . . not the atomic physicist, but the physical chemist must make the next step—the isolation of Uranium isotope 235.

This in the summer of 1939! Even now, it would be difficult to improve on Campbell/McCann's essay on the problem of separating isotope U-235 from the hundred-and-forty times more abundant U-238; in a couple of pages, he explained the advantages and disadvantages of the gaseous-diffusion and mass-spectrographic methods, both of which were eventually employed in the Manhattan Project.

"Security" would have been horrified—but not for several years. In 1939, few people in the United States except a few crazy pulp writers and impractical scientists took atomic power seriously.

In the very month that *Astounding* featured "Isotope 235," Albert Einstein, prompted by Szilard, was composing his famous letter to President Roosevelt. Science fact was catching up with science fiction, as it sometimes does—but never for long.

2 6
THE
BIS

My two letters to *Astounding* on rocket theory had both been proudly signed "Hon. Treasurer, British Interplanetary Society." I had been the obvious choice for this grave responsibility (our annual budget was about a hundred pounds) because I was (a) a Civil Servant, and presumably a law-abiding citizen and (b) an auditor, and hence able to add up columns of figures. That latter assumption was far from correct.

After its founding by P. E. Cleator in 1933, the BIS had migrated to London, not without some heartburning at its city of origin. But in those days no one had ever heard of Liverpool (the Beatles were still three decades in the future) and the Metropolis was where the action was.

A quarter of a century later (and now a quarter of a century ago!) I wrote my reminiscences of this period for *Holiday Magazine*.* Here is my affectionate tribute to the friends who shared with me the vision of the Space Age that was about to dawn, and whose early light we alone could see.

(Extracts from "Memoirs of an Armchair Astronaut, Retired.")

As is well known, we British are a romantic and wildly imaginative race, and to our annoyance the conservative

*Later reprinted in *Voices From the Sky* (Gollancz, 1966).

Americans did not consider that space travel was respectable. Though they had formed the American *Interplanetary* Society in 1930, the name had been changed to American *Rocket* Society a few years later. The suggestion was sometimes made that we should follow suit, but we refused to lower our sights. To us, the rocket was merely the interplanetary bus; if a better one came along (it hasn't yet, but we're still hoping) we would transfer, and give the rocket back to the fireworks industry.

Picture us then, in the mid thirties, when only a few aircraft had flown at the staggering speed of three hundred miles an hour, trying to convince a sceptical world that men would one day travel to the moon. There were about ten of us in the hard core of the Society, and we met at least once a week in cafés, pubs, or each other's modest apartments. We were almost all in our twenties, and our occupations ranged from aeronautical engineer to Civil Servant, from university student to Stock Exchange clerk. Few of us had technical or scientific educations, but what we lacked in knowledge we made up in imagination and enthusiasm. It was, I might add, just as well that we were over-optimistic. If we had even dreamed that the price of the first round-trip ticket to the moon would be ten billion dollars per passenger, and that spaceships would cost many times their weight in gold, we would have been much too discouraged to continue our quarter-million-mile uphill struggle.

The total amount spent on the British space effort before the outbreak of war was less than a thousand dollars. What did we do with all that money? Let me tell you.

Most of us talked, some of us calculated, and a few of us drew—all to considerable effect. Slowly there emerged the concept of a space vehicle which could carry three men to the moon and bring them back to earth. It had, even for a 1938 spaceship, a number of unconventional features, though most of them are commonplace today, and many have been "rediscovered" by later workers. Notable was the assumed use of solid propellants, of the type now employed in Polaris and similar missiles. Our first plans, based on highly unrealistic assumptions, envisaged making the entire round trip in a single vehicle, whose initial weight we hopefully calculated at about a thousand tons. Later, we discussed many types of rendezvous and space-refuelling techniques, to break down the journey into manageable stages. One of these involved the use of a specialized "ferry" craft to make the actual lunar landing, while the main vehicle remained in orbit. This, of course, is the approach used in the Apollo Project—and I am a little tired of hearing it described as a new discovery. For that matter, I doubt if we thought of it first; it is more than likely that the German or Russian theoreticians had worked it out years before.

There is a vast gulf, almost unimaginable to the layman, between thinking of an idea, and then converting it into detailed engineering blueprints. There is an equally great gulf between the blueprints and the final hardware, so we cannot claim too much credit for our pioneering insight. Yet I am often struck by the fact that there is hardly a single new conception in the whole field of current space research; everything that is happening now was described, at least in outline, twenty or even fifty years ago.

But back to our Model T. As soon as we had finished the drawings we published them in the minute *Journal of the British Interplanetary Society*. It took us some time to collect enough money to pay the printer; he was Greek, I remember, and a few Hellenic spellings slipped through my proofreading. Nor am I likely to forget the day when I collected the entire edition, in two parcels, and was walking home with it to the Flat. . . . I had got halfway when two polite gentlemen in raincoats tapped me on the shoulder, and said, "Excuse me, sir, but we're from Scotland Yard. Could we see what you have in those packets?"

It was a reasonable request, for at the time wild Irishmen were blowing up post offices to draw attention to their grievances, and the Yard was trying to round them up. (They did catch a brat named Brendan Behan.) To the considerable disappointment of the detectives, I was not even carrying *Tropic of Capricorn*, but when I presented them with copies of the journal they very gamely offered to pay. Tempting though it was to acquire a genuine subscriber (the cash box held about $2.50 at the time) I refused the contribution; but I got them to carry the parcels the rest of the way for me.

The *Journal* attracted a surprising amount of attention and a not surprising amount of amusement. That doyen of scientific publications, the good, grey *Nature,* condescended to notice our existence, but concluded its review with the unkind cut: "While the ratio of theorizing to practical experimentation is so high, little attention will be paid to the activities of the British Interplanetary Society."

That was a quite understandable comment, but what could we do about it, with that $2.50 in the till? Why, launch an appeal for an Experimental Fund. . . .

We did so, and the money came rolling in. There was one occasion, I now blush to recall, when I shared sardines on toast with an elderly lady member in an Oxford Street tearoom and convinced her that, for $60, one could solve the basic problems of building a meteorological rocket. Eventually we rounded up a couple of hundred bucks, and the research program was under way. (At Peenemünde, though we were not to know it for quite a while, von Braun was already heading for his first hundred million.)

All this money was something of a responsibility; having appealed for it, we had to use it, in a manner most calculated to produce both scientific results and publicity. The actual building and launching of rockets was frowned upon, for it would only result in police proceedings under the 1875 Explosives Act, as a group of experimenters in the North had already proved.

We were in the position of someone who could not afford a car, but had enough for the speedometer and the rear-view mirror. This analogy is quite exact; though we couldn't make a down payment on even a compact spaceship, we felt we could develop two of the instruments needed to operate it.

It was a sensible decision, and indeed about the only one possible in the circumstances. The first project we tackled was a spaceship speedometer which had been invented by

Jack Edwards, the eccentric genius who headed our research effort.

Edwards, who is now dead, was a short, bearded and excitable Welshman—and the nearest thing to a mad scientist I have ever met outside fiction. He was the director of a very small electronics firm, which soon afterward expired thanks to his assistance; but he had an altogether uncanny grasp of the principles of astronautics. He had invented, back in 1938, what is now called inertial guidance—the technique which allows a rocket to know just where it is, and how fast it is going, by continually keeping track of the accelerations acting upon it.

Edwards's space speedometer consisted of a large aluminium disk, pivoted on ball bearings, and with sundry gears, weights, and springs attached to it. As the device was moved up or down, the weights would "sense" the forces acting upon them, and the rotation of the disc would record the distance moved. We had planned to test the gadget on one of the deeper lifts of the London Underground, but, you will not be surprised to learn, it never got as far as that. The theory of the device was perfectly sound, and something similar steers every satellite into orbit today. But the engineering precision demanded was utterly beyond our means, and Mrs. Edwards put her foot down on hearing of our intention to cast lead weights in her best saucepan.

Balked on the speedometer front, we tried our luck with the rear-view mirror. To keep it on course during take off, and to provide the crew with artificial gravity, we had proposed to spin our spaceship like a rifle bullet. (The spin would be imparted by water jets, as the ship floated in a kind of raft before launching.) Even though the rate of rotation was quite low, it would obviously be impossible to take observations of the stars from our cosmic carousel, so we had to invent an optical system to unscramble the ship's spin.

This required no great originality, for the astronomers (who also look out at the stars from a spinning vehicle, the planet Earth) had solved the problem years before. Their answer is an instrument called a coelostat, which however has to cope with only one revolution every twenty-four hours. We built a similar arrangement of four mirrors—two fixed, two spinning—and I sacrificed the spring motor of my gramophone to provide the motive power.

The coelostat worked; it was the only thing we ever made that did. Its public demonstration took place in most auspicious surroundings, the hallowed halls of the South Kensington Science Museum, whose director deserves much credit for providing hospitality to such a far-out organization as ours. Next to the room where we held our meeting was the original Wright biplane, still in exile from the United States; on the floor above was an even more momentous piece of machinery—the "atom smasher" with which Cockroft and Walton had produced the first artificial nuclear reaction in 1932.

Our setup was simple, but effective. At one side of the room was a disc with lettering on it, spinning too rapidly for the words to be read. At the other was the coelostat—a wooden box about a foot on a side, looking rather like the result of a misalliance between a periscope and an alarm clock. When you peered through the coelostat at the spinning disc, the latter appeared to be quite stationary and you could read the inscription "BIS" painted on it. If you looked at the rest of the room, however, it appeared to be revolving rapidly; this was not recommended for any length of time.

Though our experimental efforts were unimpressive, we made ourselves known through countless lectures, newspaper interviews, and argumentative letters to any publication that would grant us hospitality. One controversy ran for months in the correspondence columns of the BBC's weekly the *Listener;* if we could not convince our critics, we usually routed them.

Looking back on it, I am amazed at the half-baked logic that was used to attack the idea of space flight; even scientists who should have known better employed completely fallacious arguments to dispose of us. They were so certain that we were talking nonsense that they couldn't be bothered to waste sound criticism on our ideas.

My favourite example of this is a paper which an eminent chemist presented to the British Association for the Advancement of Science. He calculated the energy that a rocket would need to escape from the earth, made a schoolboy howler in the second line, and concluded, "Hence the proposition appears to be basically impossible." But that was not enough; he could not resist adding, "This foolish idea of shooting at the moon is an example of the absurd lengths to which vicious specialization will carry scientists working in thought-tight compartments." I cannot help feeling that the good professor's compartment was not merely thought-tight; it was thought-proof.

As another example of the sort of stick that was used to beat us, I might mention an article that appeared under the eye-catching title "We Are Prisoners of Fire." This was based on the fact, deduced from radio measurements, that there are layers in the upper atmosphere where the temperature reaches a couple of thousand degrees Fahrenheit. Therefore, the writer announced, any space vehicle would melt before it got more than a few hundred miles from Earth. He had overlooked the point that, at the altitudes concerned, the air is so tenuous that the normal concept of temperature has no meaning, and one could freeze to death for all the heat that the few 2,000-degree molecules of nitrogen and oxygen could provide.

I must admit that we thoroughly enjoyed our paper battles. We knew that we were riding the wave of the future; as T. E. Lawrence said in *The Seven Pillars of Wisdom*, "It felt like morning, and the freshness of the world-to-be intoxicated us." But the world-to-be was moving inexorably, unmistakably toward war. I remember sending out, from the fourth-floor flat in Gray's Inn Road that was both my residence and the BIS headquarters, an emotional farewell to all our hundred members, and then descending to the shelters as the sirens gave their warning.

But it was a false alarm; nothing happened then, or for a long time afterwards. Finding to our surprise that we had not all been blown to pieces, we resumed contact and continued our discussions, by means of correspondence and occasional private meetings. As an RAF instructor, I was in a position to indoctrinate hundreds of hapless airmen, and made the most of the opportunity. For some odd reason, my service nickname was "Spaceship."

At last it was winter 1944. The European conflict was clearly drawing to an end—but though there was nothing about it in the papers, for several weeks large holes had been suddenly appearing in southern England. Despite this, we were holding a meeting in London to plan our post-war activities. The speaker had just returned from a mission in the United States, where a well-known authority had assured him that tales of large German war rockets were pure propaganda. We were still laughing at this when—*crash!*—the building shook slightly, and we heard that curious, unmistakable rumble of an explosion climbing backwards up the sky, from an object that had arrived faster than the sound of its own passage. . . . A few months later, when we knew his address, we hastened to confer the honorary fellowship of the society on Dr. Wernher von Braun.

That distant rumble was the only V2 I ever heard, and I have just remembered that many years earlier I had written in *Against the Fall of Night:* "Presently there echoed down from the heavens the most awe-inspiring of all the sounds that Man had ever made—the long-drawn thunder of air falling, mile after mile, into a tunnel drilled suddenly across the sky." I never imagined that one day I would be riding down such a tunnel myself, aboard *Concorde.*

Now that all the principals are dead I can expand a little on the above story. The American "authority" I didn't name then, for fear of hurting his feelings, was good old Willy Ley. He had argued that long-range (200-mile!) military rockets were simply not cost-effective—especially as liquid fuels would be needed, and who could imagine handling thousands of tons of LOX in wartime?

He had made these points to my friend the aeronautical engineer A. V. Cleaver, when he was visiting the United States on a mission for the Ministry of Defense in late 1944. Val listened patiently, knowing full well that V2s were dropping on London at that very moment, but being unable to say a word about it to anyone without a Secret clearance. All he could do was to grit his teeth and say, "Well, Willy"—or, more likely, "Vell, Villy"—it was catching—"If I were you, I wouldn't be *quite* so sure."

Yet Willy's logic was very reasonable: in England, Lord Cherwell, Churchill's science advisor, had used similar arguments to pooh-pooh the existence of large rockets. He had overlooked the role of the irrational in human affairs; and he had underestimated the ingenuity and determination of his ex-countrymen—even though he had been there at the beginning, when the first explosions shook the optimistically named *Raketenflugplatz* in the suburbs of Berlin.

It was a story he had just begun to tell in the pages of *Astounding,* and—as we'll see later—would be expanding and updating it for the rest of his life.

2 7

"REQUIEM"

In the very month that war broke out in Europe, John Campbell printed an inconspicuous little story called "Life-Line." The blurb reads "A new author suggests a means of determining the day a man must die—a startlingly plausible method!"

Plausible or not, "Life-Line" is still a good read. One Dr. Pinero invents an electrical device that can measure the extension of an individual's track in four-dimensional spacetime, by detecting the discontinuities at each end, much as engineers can pinpoint a break in an undersea cable. He can thus locate the moments of birth—and of death.

The impact on the life insurance companies is, of course, shattering, and they Take Steps to put Dr. Pinero out of business. He sits down to a good meal and calmly awaits the arrival of their enforcers; having already consulted his own machine, he knows that there is nothing else to be done. . . .

The story is smoothly written, and packs quite a number of punches. During the next three years Campbell's "new author" contributed an astounding (sorry about that) *twenty* stories to the magazine, including three serials. His name: Robert A. Heinlein.*

---

*I have made no changes to this chapter, written before Robert Heinlein's death on May 8, 1988, and deeply regret that he never had a chance of reading it.

"Life-Line," short though it is, already hints at some of the preoccupations which would provide Heinlein with themes for the rest of his career—e.g. mortality, and big business versus the individual. Others were developed during the next two years in a creative debut unmatched since the advent of Stanley Weinbaum. And, unlike that brief nova, Heinlein was to dominate the science fiction sky for the next half century, and effect a permanent change upon the pattern of its constellations.

Four months later (January 1940) he was back with a story which remains one of his best-loved—"Requiem." Now that we have watched whole armies of technicians working round the clock at Cape Canaveral, the idea of a couple of barnstorming rocket pilots giving $25 rides in a secondhand spaceship at a country fair is more than a little comic. (Come to think of it, when did you last see a barnstorming *airplane*? I haven't, since I made my maiden flight from a field outside Taunton at the age of ten.)

Heinlein's protagonist is D. D. Harriman, an aging millionaire who has made his fortune in the space business—but is not allowed to leave earth because of his heart condition. So he hires the two owners of a beat-up, mortgaged rocketship to take him as a passenger (one jump ahead of the bailiffs—just as in *Destination Moon*) and dies happily in the dust of the Mare Imbrium, the most magnificent of the lunar "seas." Over his grave are inscribed the lines that R. L. Stevenson wrote for his own epitaph, ending with:

> Here he lies where he longed to be
> Home is the sailor, home from the sea,
> And the hunter home from the hill.†

His final novel bears the perfect valedictory title *To Sail Beyond the Sunset,* and I suspect that this is no coincidence. Yet though published in his eightieth year, it is so full of vigor and the sheer joy of life that it reminds me (in more ways than one) of Picasso's last works.

†Bob, like everyone, misquotes the second line; Stevenson actually wrote "home from sea." Posterity has outvoted him.

"Requiem," dated though it may be, is a moving story. And, on re-reading it after many years, I have just discovered something that has given me quite a shock. The first "D" in D. D. Harriman stands for—*Delos*. Bob Heinlein chose better than he knew, when he selected that magic name; for, as I have good reason to remember, the Greek island of Delos is the reputed birthplace of Apollo. . . .

In 1965, as the Apollo Project was gathering momentum for the leap to the moon, I visited the island with Dr. Wernher von Braun and a handful of other delegates to the International Astronautical Federation Congress, then taking place in Athens. (As I type these words, the IAF is meeting again in Brighton, England, less than a month after the World Science Fiction Convention. I hope the town survives this double assault.)*

We were wandering among the impressive ruins of what was once the heart of Greek culture when I noticed a striking pattern in a mosaic floor—a trident with two "S"s between its prongs. It was instantly familiar, because I had just read Jacques Cousteau's *The Living Sea*. This was the villa of Markos Sestios, the wealthy shipowner whose thousands of amphorae *Calypso*'s divers had salvaged near Marseilles in one of the first great marine archaeological projects.

Just two years earlier I had been helping to bring up smaller but very similar bottles from a reef ten kilometers off the south coast of Ceylon.† These were only about a century old, and had contained not wine but soda water, manufactured in Colombo; I still cannot quite get over the fact that they bore the name CLARKE. And would you also believe that the last time I saw the Great Basses Reef was with Bob and Ginny Heinlein, from the plane I'd chartered to show them Sri Lanka in a single morning?

This chapter seems to be turning into an exercise in applied

---

*It did—barely. The worst hurricane in two hundred years chose this occasion to hit the south coast of England, and many functions had to be canceled.

†See *The Treasure of the Great Reef* (Ballantine, 1974).

solipsism—another of Bob's interests: his chilling story "They" (*Unknown*, 1941) remains the definitive work on the subject. And I'm afraid I've not finished yet.

Just fifteen minutes ago a cheerful but slightly disheveled multiple mailing arrived from Ginny Heinlein, typed on one of the unopened packing cases in their new home. (Yes—*typed*—she can't find the cable linking computer and printer. Personally, I don't believe I could ever use a typewriter again.) They are both fine, and Bob is campaigning furiously for Jeanne Kirkpatrick as next President of the U.S. . . .

Obviously I am imagining the universe: and, looking at the newspaper headlines, not doing a very good job of it.

But to return, for a moment, to Delos (if it exists). I took a photo of Wernher at the spot where we were assured Apollo had been born, and when he got back to Washington he was rash enough to mention that he'd sought the god's blessings for the project named after him.

Needless to say, there were protests from the Bible Belt. But NASA Administrator, Tom Paine, knew how to handle the situation.

"We're covering all bases," he said solemnly.

As we know, it paid off handsomely—especially when Apollo 13 suffered a near-catastrophic explosion while it was still outward-bound towards the moon.

And perhaps if NASA had remained faithful to the Greek pantheon, its luck would not have run out on January 28, 1986.

2 8

"THE END OF THE ROCKET SOCIETY"

Throughout its career, *Astounding* printed many excellent science articles, often containing material that was simply not available elsewhere. It also printed a good many non-fact articles, not all of them clearly labeled as such.

There are excellent examples of both types in the September 1943 issue. The previous year, Campbell had initiated a feature called "Probability Zero," which allowed authors to spin yarns too farfetched even to be classed as science fiction. (My own *Tales from the White Hart* continues this noble tradition.)

There is quite a surprise in the September "Probability Zero"—a little squib by a promising young (23) writer named Ray Bradbury. Even more surprising, he has another story in the same issue! You could win bets at most science fiction conventions from people who were quite certain that the famous fabulist had never appeared in *Astounding*'s hard-core pages—let alone *twice* in a single issue.

The item that follows Ray's "Doodad"* could hardly have presented a greater contrast. It is the conclusion of a two-part series by Willy Ley describing the origin and checkered history of the "Society for Space Travel" (*Verein fur Raumschiffahrt*)

*"Doodad" also deals with Thingumbobs, Watchamacallits, Hinkies, Formodaldafrays, Hootinannies, Doohingies—and, of course, Gadgets.

from its founding in 1927 to its dissolution half a decade later.

As Willy himself had, very wisely, left Germany in 1934, and his former colleagues were now enemy aliens, the story he was telling had many gaps. Some were deliberate; as he explained, the Gestapo would be most interested to see what he had to say about a subject the very mention of which was now forbidden in Germany.

A year later, Willy used these two articles as the basis for *Rockets: The Future of Travel Beyond the Stratosphere* (Viking, 1944), an invaluable book which went through many transformations and printings during the next quarter century. The last edition, *Rockets, Missiles, and Men in Space* was published in 1968, the year before Willy's death. It runs to 557 closely printed pages, and he had complained to me that the whole subject had now got so much out of hand that it could no longer be covered in a single book—or by a single author.

But back in 1943 Willy was *the* world authority on the history of rockets, even if he did not always guess right about their future. I have already mentioned his skepticism about the existence of the V2, even when it was actually dropping on London, and he really went out on a limb in his September 1943 article: "There is no future for war rockets, except for minor applications, like sending trailing wires to tangle dive bombers, or firing a dozen shells at very close range to confuse tank commanders. . . . At ranges which can be attained by guns as well as rockets, the gun is immensely superior in accuracy and at ranges beyond gun range the bombing airplane can carry an immensely superior load." No wonder that Willy had to hastily revise the second edition of *Rockets*. (I had to do exactly the same thing with *The Making of a Moon*, which was largely devoted to the United States's Vanguard satellite. The month after it was published—September 1957—*Sputnik 1* went into orbit. Fortunately, it wasn't a case of instant obsolescence, since the basic theory remains the same for space missions of any nationality.)

Despite that momentary failure of his crystal ball, Willy's two articles are a fascinating slice of history at the very moment it was being made. And his general conclusions were completely sound; he was quite right in thinking that the time had passed when any group of enthusiastic amateurs could do useful rocket experimentation. As he said: "At present the problem has to rest until Hitler is dead—after the war we'll see. In any event I believe as firmly as ever in the feasibility of the first practical step, the instrument-carrying high-altitude rocket. And I have never for a moment stopped believing in the ultimate goal: the spaceship."

It would be a little while yet before Willy—and the rest of the world—learned that the spaceship was already one year old; it had been born on October 3, 1942, at Peenemünde.

2 9
WERNHER

In his second article, Willy referred in passing to "Count von Braun, the youngest member of the (VfR's) board of directors," who had been "made to accept a commission" when the German Army started to take an interest in the noisy goings-on at the *Raketenflugplatz*. What happened after that has been told many times, from many points of view, perhaps best of all by Walter Dornberger in *V.2* (Viking, 1954).

It was General Dornberger who remarked to von Braun, after that first successful flight: "Today the spaceship was born." And it was Dornberger who, at considerable risk, got his brilliant young engineer out of prison when he had been arrested by Himmler on the not totally unfounded charge that he was more interested in designing spaceships than in perfecting war rockets.

This is a good place for my favorite Dornberger story, which Walter himself told to me more in amusement than in anger. Sometime in the mid-1950s, the ex-German general took a trip round the world, and visited Ceylon. He was walking along a Colombo street when some unfriendly local called out at him: "Yankee, go home!"

Well, by that time he *was* a director of Bell Aircraft—and Wernher von Braun and Willy Ley had joined forces again, to promote the cause of spaceflight—notably with such very influential books as *Across the Space Frontier* (Viking, 1952).

It would have been interesting to have been present at their first meeting after the war; before that event, Willy had written to me, "Well, I suppose I'll offer him a cup of tea." And he contributed a long letter to the June 1947 issue of the *Journal of the British Interplanetary Society* that, with the hindsight of history, makes amusing reading. Here are a few extracts:

> I have to admit that I did not pay more attention to him (Wernher von Braun) then than to any other active member of the VfR, at any event not as much as I surely would have done had I been able to look into the future . . . but I do remember that he visited me in my home one day, during the summer of 1929. He told me that he was greatly impressed with the possibilities of liquid fuel rockets and had decided to devote his life to that problem. . . . He was about 18 then and one of my female relatives compared him to the famous photograph of Lord Alfred Douglas. His manners were perfect and I remember he spoke rather good French. One day he came in while I was struggling with a Sarabande by Handel; after I had finished he sat down and played Beethoven's *Moonlight Sonata* from memory.
>
> Did we discuss politics? Hardly; our minds were always far out in space. But I remember a few chance remarks which might be condensed into saying that the German Republic was no good and the Nazis ridiculous. . . .

My own first contact with Wernher was in the summer of 1951, when, as Chairman of the British Interplanetary Society, I wrote to him appealing for support in a dispute we were having with the influential magazine *Picture Post*—Britain's answer to *Life*. It had just published an article about space travel by its science expert (an authority on ants!) full of the most incredible nonsense—among other things, the statement that "multi-stage rockets have no relevance to interplanetary travel." One day, I hope, this will be true; but we are still a long way from single-stage vehicles even to earth orbit, let alone to the planets.

When we pointed out all his errors, the "expert" (doubtless feeling that his job was at stake) simply answered that we didn't know what we were talking about; hence my appeal to Wernher, who promptly replied with a three-page, single-spaced letter which began: "You called on me as a brother-in-arms in your war with the *Picture Post* and I can only hope that I shall not disappoint you." He certainly did not, quoting official sources at length and adding his own "personal if angry reply to your opponent . . . I hope that will help you to give your obstinate zoologist* hell! Good luck, and let me know how many rounds it took you to knock him out." I think the answer was 1, or at most 2.

When we finally met in my New York hotel in 1953, we discovered that a movie we both wanted to see was being screened in Brooklyn and, greatly daring, we took the subway into that unknown territory. We never found the cinema, but managed to get safely back to Manhattan.

The next year I visited Wernher at Huntsville, and there occurred a little incident that (a) convinced me of his mechanical genius and (b) instantly de-convinced me. His wife Maria sent us to get ice for the drinks, and Wernher drove me to a store equipped with a machine that dispensed it in large blocks.

He inserted some quarters, and nothing happened.

He gave the machine a couple of kicks—and there was an avalanche as it disgorged its entire contents. We stood surrounded by small icebergs, and loaded the car with as many as it could carry.

But back home, when he used a pick to break up the ice into drink-sized lumps, Wernher made such a hash of it that Maria threw him out of the kitchen and did the job herself. I was bitterly disillusioned.

Those who knew him only from TV appearances, or identi-

---

*Willy Ley was primarily a zoologist, and wrote widely on the subject. So one speciality need not exclude the other.

fied him with Dr. Strangelove,* may be surprised to know that he was full of fun and had a great sense of humor—though it was once tested to the breaking point at a party where some tactless person played Tom Lehrer's brilliant song, with its satirical refrain:

> If the rocket goes up, who cares vhere it comes down?
> That's not *my* department, says Wernher von Braun. . . .

Well, there was one occasion when he cared very much indeed, as he wryly told me himself. During a test firing to a target in Poland, he was walking away from the tracking station (situated at the actual bull's-eye, because Dornberger said, "That's one place we'll *never* hit") when he noticed that the red warning flag was flying. By one of those communications lapses even more common in war than in peace, the "All Clear" had been given too soon: another rocket was on the way.

"I looked up," said Wernher, "and there it was, clearly visible. So clear that I could see *all four fins.*"

The chilling implications of that made him hit the ground a few seconds before the rocket did, only a hundred meters away. It was, of course, carrying no warhead, but the shock was considerable; and for a moment the engineer was, almost literally, "hoist with his own petard."

Our last meeting was at his home outside Washington, in late 1976. He knew he did not have much time, and was very anxious about the future of the National Space Institute,† which he had just founded. I was both flattered and moved when he suggested that I might head the infant organization, but for many reasons that was quite out of the question. Fortunately, it has flourished under the leadership of three

---

*Stanley Kubrick once said to me, "Tell Werner I wasn't getting at him." I never did, because (a) I didn't believe it (b) even if Stanley wasn't, Peter Sellers certainly was.

†Now the National Space Society, 922 Pennsylvania Avenue, Washington, DC 20003.

other old friends—Chairmen Dr. Arthur Kantrowitz and Hugh Downs, and President Ben Bova (Editor of *Astounding/Analog,* 1972–78).

Finally, although it is a painful subject (recently reopened by the declassification of the "Paperclip" files) I do not believe I am doing a disservice to the memory of a good friend, if I close this chapter with words which, for the sake of Truth and History, I believe he would have wished to have on record:

"No—I never knew what was happening in the concentration camps. But I suspected it, and in my position I could have found out. I didn't, and I despise myself for it."

30

"VAULT OF
THE BEAST"

Almost every issue of the early 1940s is dominated by Robert Heinlein or his alter ego Anson MacDonald, often with stories that have now become classics—e.g. "Universe," "By His Bootstraps," *Sixth Column, Methuselah's Children, Beyond This Horizon, Coventry, The Roads Must Roll* . . . I could go on for quite a while but won't, because all Bob's fiction is readily available in various collections.

But I must salute one of my favorites, the hilarious "—And He Built a Crooked House," a fourth-dimensional fantasy set (where else?) in the wilder enclaves of Los Angeles. As you will already have gathered, I have a soft spot for the Fourth Dimension; and, for that matter, for Los Angeles.

At the same time, other distinctive voices were beginning to emerge, one of the most notable being the Canadian A. E. van Vogt. I can still recall the impact of his "Weapon Shop" series, enhanced by the fact that many of them appeared in the splendid large-format edition of the magazine—soon, alas, a casualty of wartime paper shortages.

The first of the Weapon Shop stories, "The Seesaw" (July 1941) ends with what must surely be one of the most awe-inspiring sentences in *any* work of fiction. Van Vogt had an unmatched ability to get his heroes into appalling predicaments (often by page two) and then extricating them at the last moment, sometimes so deftly that the bemused reader was not quite sure what had happened.

The protagonist of "The Seesaw," however, was not permitted the luxury of a happy ending. He was set swinging back and forth in Time, in wider and wider oscillations, gathering more energy on every cycle until:

> Quite suddenly it came to him that he knew where the seesaw would stop. It would end in the very remote past, with the release of the stupendous temporal energy he had been accumulating with each of those monstrous swings.
>
> He would not witness, but he would cause, the formation of the planets.

Si monumentum requiris, circumspice indeed! I defy anyone to find a more awesome last line in the whole of fiction.

It is usually impossible to identify the inventor of any major idea in science fiction, because some ink-stained scholar can be relied upon to exhume an earlier example. In my opinion, however, van Vogt is the rightful holder of the "Alien"* patent, with a string of stories in which spaceships are threatened by monsters of ever-increasing nastiness and capability. True, this was also the theme of Campbell's "Who Goes There?" (see Chapter 25) and that classic story was indeed the direct inspiration of "Vault of the Beast" (August 1940).

Colin Wilson considers this tale "probably the most remarkable first science fiction story ever written, at least as exceptional as Stanley Weinbaum's 'A Martian Odyssey'."† Like most of van Vogt's shorter pieces, it is so action-packed that any summary is likely to be longer than the original. "Vault of the

---

*I have just realized that I must have known the durable "Ms. Ripley" as a very young girl: in the 1950s, when he was head of NBC, I frequently visited Sylvester "Pat" Weaver's apartment on the Upper East Side. Little did any of us guess at Sigourney's future contributions to interstellar friendship.

†In *Science Fiction Writers* (Scribner's). Weinbaum, however, had written several novels before "A Martian Odyssey."

Beast" 's sustained tension is all the more astonishing when one considers that its central idea is based on a subject not noted for excitement—the foundation of pure mathematics known as the Theory of Numbers.

As I did with Captain S. P. Meek (Chapter 6) I must now gently castigate van Vogt for peddling fictitious science. The challenge confronting his hero—the world's most brilliant mathematician—was that of opening a time lock "geared to the Ultimate Prime." (For good measure, the Vault was also constructed of the "ultimate metal." Van seldom did anything by halves.)

The Ultimate Prime! It certainly sounds impressive. Unfortunately, it's easy to prove that no such beast can possibly exist, even in Martian time vaults. The proof is one of the simplest and most elegant in the whole of mathematics, and has been known since the time of Euclid (*c*. 300 BC), to whom it is usually attributed.

If van Vogt had talked about an "ultimate"—i.e. final—*number*, everyone would have known that the concept was ridiculous. No matter how large a number is, you can always add 1 to it, and so on forever. The sequence of (integral) numbers is endless—and so is the sequence of primes. (With this hint, you can prove Euclid's theorem in five lines. If you can't, please go to the bottom of the class, and look up the entry "Number Theory" in the *Encyclopaedia Britannica*.)

It is quite obvious that van Vogt knew this perfectly well, because his story shows a wide familiarity with mathematics; the young magician was simply deceiving the reader by the swiftness of his pen, and extricates his hero in a typical "with one bound he reached freedom" ploy. In just four lines, he gets from Mars into the arms of his girlfriend on earth, but by this time the reader is so breathless that such absurdities pass unnoticed.

These old *Astoundings* are full of surprises. Next to "Vault of the Beast," is one of the eight stories contributed to the magazine by the major American poet John Berryman. Anyone who thinks that a poet would be incapable of writing "hard" science fiction should read "The Trouble with Telstar," a highly technical piece about repairing a satellite belonging to COMCORP. The story appeared in June 1963—the very year that COMSAT was incorporated. However, it was another two decades before the first satellite was repaired in orbit, almost exactly as in Berryman's story, and he never lived to see it become reality. Perhaps the strain of bridging the gap between the Two Cultures proved more than he could handle. He jumped to his death in 1972.

31

"FAREWELL TO THE MASTER"

If a spaceship landed in front of the White House today, its occupants might have some difficulty in convincing the other tourists that they were not on location from Hollywood. This well-established cliché was started, as far as I know, by Harry Bates's novelette in the October 1940 *Astounding*, later made into one of the most famous of science fiction movies, *The Day the Earth Stood Still* (1951).

Director Robert Wise was to go on to far more ambitious projects, in and out of science fiction, but *The Day the Earth Stood Still* retains its classic quality. Bernard Herrmann's eerie space music is running through my brain even at this moment, and Michael Rennie made "Klaatu" the most convincing *humanoid* alien until David Bowie. However, it was the massive robot, Gort ("Gnut" in the original) who really stole the show, with its combination of power and potential menace.

As also happened with "Who Goes There?", the most striking element of the story was abandoned in the film version— though in this case with better reason, for concepts which work well on paper cannot always be transferred to the screen. Bates's story ends with a punchline almost as stunning as van Vogt's "Seesaw," though in a very different way.

In a tragic accident, the emissary from the stars has been killed, and his body is handed back to the robot.

"Tell your master—the master yet to come," says the grieving Earthman, "that what happened to the first Klaatu was an accident, for which all Earth is immeasurably sorry."

"You misunderstand," the robot answers gently. "I am the Master."

To the general public, science fiction is almost identified with the theme of human–alien contact—and usually conflict, even when there is good will on both sides. By this time, all the obvious scenarios must have been worked out, but there is still scope for ingenious surprises.

A. E. van Vogt conceived one of the most unsettling—and thought-provoking—in his novelette "Asylum" (May 1942). On the contents page, Campbell spells out the famous question "Where's everybody?" which Fermi had asked at a brainstorming session in Los Alamos two years earlier. It is not impossible that Fermi's remark had somehow reached Campbell, though the so-called Fermi Paradox must have struck any imaginative observer of the night sky: "Among the thousands of stars, in the ages of time, somewhere, some race must have developed interstellar travel. Why haven't they visited us?"*

Van Vogt's answer is half-revealed by the story's title. He must have been furious with Campbell (I would certainly have been) when the editorial blurb gave the rest away: "Wherein is presented a lovely notion—that we live on a reservation, watched over by morons, since meeting normal members of the Watcher's race would be fatal."

I might add that van Vogt's "morons" had IQs of around 400, which is probably adequate for such an unexacting job as keeping the human race from becoming too much of a nuisance.

This idea—the "Zoo" or "Quarantine" Hypothesis—is now taken very seriously indeed among those engaged in the Search for Extra-Terrestrial Intelligence (SETI). It explains many

---

*Leo Szilard, who was in a good position to know, had promptly replied, "They are among us, but they call themselves Hungarians." (My Wordstar 4 spelling-checker has just chewed up "Szilard" and asked if I mean "salaried." Nice try, but no cigar.)

things—perhaps too many—and though it is not altogether flattering, there are worse possibilities. Such as—

Damon Knight's chilling little squib "To Serve Man" did not appear in *Astounding,* but in its rival *Galaxy* (November 1950) and I don't seem to have a copy on my shelves. No matter; it's not the sort of story one is likely to forget.

Benevolent aliens land on Earth and proclaim that their only intention is to serve the human race. They seem too good to be true, and finally someone steals their secret manual of operations.

It's a cookbook.

3 2

ATOMIC

POWER

John Campbell's editorial in the August 1941 issue must have caused considerable alarm—though not as much as he produced later—among the people responsible for security in the Manhattan Project. Here he was, in the open literature—and you couldn't get much more open than a pulp magazine—discussing the possibility of energy from the atom being cheaper than from coal. And this at a time when Fermi's first self-sustaining reactor was still more than a year in the future!

Campbell made the very valid point that, however cheap atomic power might be, "coal will remain for unguessable ages as man's prime source of the chemical substance carbon, and a whole raft of immensely valuable and important carbon compounds." I have often summed this up myself in the statement, "Coal is much too valuable to burn."

He was wrong, however—and this must really have upset them at Los Alamos—when he remarked casually: "Atomic explosives won't be usable for such purposes as quarrying, mining, tunneling, etc. They're too intense. . . ." How did he know, anyway, four years before Trinity?

The story that brought Security running to Street and Smith appeared in the March 1944 issue. The author of "Deadline," Cleve Cartmill, later called it "that stinker," and it would certainly have been forgotten today if it hadn't contained passages like:

And the fuse—a tiny can of cadmium alloy containing a speck of radium in a beryllium holder. Then—correct me if I'm wrong, will you?—the powdered uranium oxide runs together in the central cavity. The radium shoots neutrons into this mass—and the U-235 takes over from there. Right?

Wrong. Uranium oxide can't explode: only the metal will do that. But this paragraph must have screamed "Leak!" to any security man who didn't read science fiction, and John Campbell had to do some fast talking to clear himself. Luckily he was very good at that—few better, in fact.

Curiously enough, the very latest issue of the magazine to come into my hands (Mid-December 1987—more about that anon) prints a common error on the same grim subject. In "Hardening Humans," a stimulating essay about protection against ionizing radiation, Harry Stine* writes that: "Nuclear explosives are extremely difficult to initiate because a series of events must take place on a microsecond basis."

That's just what I thought as well—but listen to this chilling piece of information from Luis Alvarez's autobiography (Alvarez: Adventures of a Physicist):

With modern weapons-grade uranium, the background neutron count is so low that terrorists, if they had such material, would have a good chance of setting off a high-yield explosion simply by dropping one half of the material onto the other half. . . . If separated U-235 is at hand it is a trivial job to set off a nuclear explosion, whereas if only plutonium is available, making it explode is the most difficult technical job I know. . . . Given a supply of U-235, however, even a high school kid could make a bomb in short order.

Another story which, had it been published a few months later, might have got John Campbell into trouble appeared in

*I'd like to take this belated opportunity of thanking Harry and his fellow conspirators for smuggling me into the White Sands Proving Ground in 1952—though at the time they didn't tell me just *what* it was I saw heading skywards in a cloud of smoke.

the August 1941 issue, shortly before the United States entered the war. William Corson—if that was his real name—never appeared again, and was obviously an electronics engineer, probably with the Navy. "Klystron Fort" is about an undersea detection system and its problems with whales—problems which are even more acute in today's world of missile-carrying submarines.

The klystron was not secret in 1941; in fact that very year the February *Astounding* carried an excellent article describing exactly how it worked. It had been invented several years earlier, as a generator of extremely high microwave frequencies, but no one in the radar business was supposed to talk about it. I can vividly remember, around 1944, having to carry some 3-centimeter (K-band, as we would say now) klystrons from our GCA unit to an RAF Stores several miles away. I was given an armed guard—and issued with a revolver of my own, in case the news reached any local German agents that Flying Officer Clarke was traveling through the Cornish countryside with top secret equipment. (I was also carrying something far more important than the low-powered klystron—several specimens of the device which *really* won the war by producing microwaves by the megawatt—the 10-centimeter cavity magnetron.)

It must have been just around this time that I myself encountered a genuine leak from the Manhattan Project, though I didn't realize it until several years later. Luis Alvarez had already left us, to lead the team designing the implosion mechanism for the plutonium bomb, but some of his colleagues may have guessed what he was up to. And one of them told me a very curious rumor—that a section of the Columbia River in the western United States had started to boil. . . .

I didn't believe him, and indeed the story was exaggerated—by about eighty degrees Centigrade. However, the great reactors of the Hanford Engineer Works had indeed started to warm the Columbia River in September 1944*, and I had received the first hint of the greatest secret of the war.

---

*According to *Atomic Energy for Military Purposes* (the "Smyth Report"): "The actual rise in temperature was so tiny that no effect on fish life could be expected." In fact, it might have been beneficial, as has proved to be the case elsewhere.

Twenty years later, on one of the lecture tours which took me all over the United States during the 1960s, I was invited to Hanford. In contrast to affairs at White Sands, there was a momentary panic when my hosts belatedly discovered that I was a Brit, and there was a lot of phoning to the Pentagon before I could be admitted. (I wish I could have overheard the conversation.)

After a quarter of a century, I still have one vivid memory of Hanford. I was given a fuel element to hold—it was about the size and shape of a can of beer, but considerably heavier. *And it was warm;* the continual explosion of dying uranium atoms kept it well above room temperature.

Flowing into the palm of my hand, easily detectable even to crude human senses, was the power that would run our world, or destroy it. That flux of heat would remain virtually unchanged for centuries; long after I was gone, that little cylinder would still be pouring forth energy into the universe around it.

And this has reminded me that I saw my first atomic explosions when I was about fifteen years old. It was in my own bedroom, and as only one atom at a time was involved, damage was minimal.

I'd been reading how the great Rutherford had studied the disintegration of the nucleus, in the days long before Geiger-Muller counters, by counting the scintillations produced by alpha particles on a fluorescent screen.* "Why, I can do *that*!" I realized. "I've got a source of radioactivity on my wrist."

So late that night I burrowed under the bedclothes and waited ten minutes or so until my eyes were completely dark-adapted. Then I took a low-powered magnifying lens and stared at the glowing numbers on the dial of my watch.

---

*Dr. Bernard Crowther, my editor at *Physics Abstracts,* who was one of Rutherford's pupils, told me this story of the great man. He had been sitting in total darkness for twenty minutes, waiting for his eyes to become dark-adapted. . . .

Rutherford: "How many cups of tea did I have this afternoon?"
Lab Assistant: "Three, sir."
Rutherford: "I thought so. Where's the sink?"

It was true; the faint glow was not continuous. It was made up of myriads of tiny flashes, and I knew that each one marked the impact of an alpha particle on the phosphor. How amazing that a *single* helium nucleus could carry enough energy to be detected by the unaided eye!

That simple experiment—which anyone can carry out—made a great impression on me. A couple of decades later it inspired the passage in *The City and the Stars* describing the ancient fortress of Shalmirane—a huge bowl lying among the mountains, from which awesome energies had once been directed into the sky in the defense of earth:

> As their eyes grew accustomed to the scene, they realized that the blackness of the bowl was not as absolute as they had thought. Here and there, so fugitive that they could only see them indirectly, tiny explosions of light were flickering in the ebon walls. They came at random, vanishing as soon as they were born, like the reflections of stars on a broken sea. . . .

Years later, I found myself standing on the edge of such a giant bowl in reality. Though the scintillations were lacking, and the enormous dish was made not of rock, but of aluminium, it too had been used to beam radiations at the sky.

Long before it was built, I had seen the thousand-foot radio telescope at Arecibo.

33

VENUS EQUILATERAL

The October 1942 *Astounding* featured one of those "hard science" stories for which the magazine was now justly famous. The author, George O. Smith, was an electronics engineer; and you had to be in the same line of business to enjoy "QRM—Interplanetary"—or even to understand the meaning of the title. ("QRM" is radio amateur slang for reporting interference.)

Over the next few years Smith published ten stories in this series, later collected under the title *The Complete Venus Equilateral* (Ballantine, 1976). This was a remarkable feat, when one considers that he was heavily engaged in war work; he also managed to produce a three-part serial and several novelettes during this period!

The last "Venus Equilateral" story ("Interlude," a.k.a. "The External Triangle,") did not appear in the magazine, but in the John Campbell Memorial Volume *Astounding*, 1973. George Smith, who himself died in 1981, must have written it with mixed feelings, for his wife had previously been Dona Campbell (hence the "Don" in Don A. Stuart). Campbell, however, was too good an editor to let this domestic convulsion prevent him publishing later stories of Smith's.

When the Venus Equilateral stories were collected, I was asked to write an introduction—and, as you will see, I felt it was one way of discharging a debt of honor. Here it is:

Like all science and science fiction writers, I am used to talking glibly in millions of years—but it's very hard to accept the fact that I started reading these stories a quarter of a century ago. It seems only yesterday, and I can remember exactly how it happened.

Owing to the war, normal supplies of *Astounding Stories* (*Analog*'s precursor) had been cut off by the British authorities, who foolishly imagined that there were better uses for shipping space and hard-earned dollars. Luckily, before withdrawal symptoms had become too serious, my good friend Willy Ley came to the rescue. He conscientiously mailed me every issue until I was able to renew my subscription on the outbreak of peace.

So I read George O. Smith's "Venus Equilateral" stories within a few weeks of their appearance, and greatly enjoyed them because I was obviously in the same line of business as the author. We were both working on radar, though that name had yet to enter the public domain. There was, however, a slight difference in the size of our hardware. My gear weighed about thirty tons and occupied two large trucks—and was the only sample of its kind ever built. (You'll find the details, more or less, in the novel *Glide Path*.) George's contraptions weighed a few ounces, were a couple of inches long, and were manufactured in tens of thousands. Even more remarkable, they were built to be shot from anti-aircraft guns—not a procedure usually recommended for delicate electronic equipment. (Especially vacuum tubes, which were all we had in those pre-transistor days.) I can still hardly believe in the Radio Proximity Fuse, and have often wondered what crackpot invented it. He probably read science fiction.

I imagined that George wrote these stories as relaxation from the serious business of winning the war, and I momentarily expected him to run into trouble with Security. From time to time he skated on pretty thin ice, and in this he was in good company. Everyone knows how John W. Campbell, Jr. (then, as now, Editor of *Astounding/Analog)* was once visited by the FBI, and asked if he would kindly desist from publishing stories about the military uses of uranium. . . .

Though there had been many tales about "space stations" long before the Venus Equilateral series (Murray Leinster's "Power Planet" is a classic example from the early 1930s), George Smith was probably the first writer—certainly the first technically qualified writer—to spell out their uses for space communications. It is therefore quite possible that these stories influenced me subconsciously when, at Stratford-on-Avon during the closing months of the war, I worked out the principles of synchronous communications satellites now embodied in Syncom, Early Bird and their successors. Appropriately enough, the person who pointed this out to me is another long-time science fiction fan—Dr. John Pierce, instigator of the Bell Laboratories program that led to ECHO and TELSTAR.

It is interesting to see how George and I, who consider ourselves imaginative characters, both failed to anticipate the truly fantastic technical advances of the last few decades. We both thought that our "extraterrestrial relays" would be large, manned structures carrying armies of engineers—as, indeed, will one day be the case. Neither of us dreamed that most of the things we described would be done—within twenty years!—by a few pounds of incredibly miniaturized electronic equipment. And neither of us could possibly have foreseen the maser, that wonderful amplifying device which has made communication over "merely" planetary distances almost laughably simple.

Nevertheless, the problem which George Smith set out to solve remains, and will probably always remain. For short but annoying—and therefore intolerable—periods of time the sun will block communications between planets and spacecraft. Some kind of repeater station will therefore be necessary to bypass signals around this million-mile-diameter obstacle.

Perhaps it will not be where George placed it, equidistant

from Venus and the sun; for numerous reasons, a relay in Earth orbit, leading or trailing our planet by a constant few million miles, might be preferable. It is true that such a position would not be dynamically stable, but then I have always had doubts concerning the long-term stability of Venus Equilateral. Even mighty Jupiter cannot stop his "Trojan" asteroids from drifting back and forth over hundreds of millions of miles of orbit, and anything that approached Earth as closely as Venus Equilateral would be violently perturbed by our planet's gravitational field. However, such wanderings would be of little practical importance, and if necessary could be corrected rather easily by modest amounts of rocket power. Witness the ease with which today's synchronous satellites are kept on station over fixed lines of longitude, at the cost of a few pounds of fuel per year.

There is another respect in which George Smith, I am sure, correctly anticipates the future. Large, manned space stations will certainly not be used merely for communication. They will open up unlimited—literally—vistas for scientific research, technology, medicine, tourism, manufacturing and even sport. Though not all the eventful happenings of the following space opera will actually materialize, you can be sure that still more surprising ones will.

And I hope that George and I are still around, another quarter of a century from now, to see how unimaginative we both were.

May 1967

Well, that hope of seeing 1992 will not be fulfilled, as far as George is concerned; he missed it by more than ten years. But I still hope to welcome it, from my hi-tech, computer-controlled wheelchair with its two-way K-band satellite video, audio, and teletext facilities.

3 4

"THE WEAPON SHOP"

It was very bad luck for John Campbell that the first issue—January, 1942—of his magazine in a handsome, large-size format appeared on the stands just a week after Pearl Harbor. Despite the price increase—all the way from 20 to 25 cents—it might well have continued in that size until replaced by the electronic, satellite-distributed edition. However, paper shortages doomed the brave experiment after only sixteen issues; by May 1943 it was back to the regular pulp size, and before the end of the year it had shrunk yet again to the still smaller digest format, which it still retains.*

I still look back on those sixteen issues with a special affection; they had some of the magazine's best covers and most memorable stories. The July 1942 cover was an historic exception; that month every American magazine, as a gesture to the war effort, had the same cover illustration—the Stars and Stripes waving in the breeze. Campbell missed an opportunity here; he should have shown it on the moon, where it would be erected—unfurled is not the right word—twenty-seven years later to the very month.

I have already mentioned A. E. van Vogt's "Asylum" (May

---

*The magazine did return to the large (8″ x 11″) size in March 1963, but only for two years.

1942) but his story "The Weapon Shop" in the December issue had a much greater impact on me at the time. It was full of brilliant and crazy ideas—just like Campbell's Editorials. Immediately preceding "The Weapon Shop" is another Security-defying specimen with the innocuous title "Power Supply."

On December 2, 1942, Enrico Fermi and his colleagues had started the world's first self-sustaining nuclear reaction in a University of Chicago squash court (without, of course, informing President Robert Hutchins; a mere lawyer could not be expected to understand that there was really very little risk of blowing up Chicago). Because *Astounding* was—and is—favorite reading material of scientists, some of the group must already have seen the editorial in the issue on the stands at that very moment. It opened:

> Burning atoms for fuel is considerably closer to reality now than it appeared to be even four years ago ... present knowledge indicates that U-235 could be made to release atomic energy which in turn could be trapped in the form of high-intensity heat, and the heat made to boil water, the steam to turn an engine. . . .

How right Campbell was; he was also correct in saying that this would be an inefficient way of generating electricity, and that there was no means in sight that could make electricity directly. (This is still true; though some still highly theoretical fusion reactors might do the trick—if we can get them to work at all.)

There was one exception, even then, and it sparked a truly Campbellian proposal. He pointed out that you need tens of thousands of volts—but an infinitesimal current—to operate a television picture tube. One way of providing this would be by a suitable radioisotope—synthesized by atomic power—which could be sealed up to make a tiny 150,000 volt battery.

The concept is perfectly sound, and has been used in certain specialized applications. But I don't think TV would have made much headway, at the cost of putting a little capsule of radioactivity into every home.

Yet the editorial, as a whole, is stunningly accurate, and even more relevant now than it was forty-five years ago. After pointing out that atomic energy can't do everything, he discusses alternatives. Solar power? Too dilute: "the area that must be covered to gather enough horsepower is too great." But read on:

> Solar energy is so vast in total amount that any drains man might put on it would be completely undetectable; the trick we lack now is a method of using the already existent immense area of sun-energy absorber that also acts as a reservoir during the night. . . . *Figure a way to turn the thermal energy of the Earth's atmosphere, and of its seas, into electric power directly, and there won't be any real need for atomic power plants here on Earth.* (My italics.)

Here, I suspect, Campbell was right on target, the key phrase being "of its seas." Many years ago, my own story "The Shining Ones"* made a case for the already century-old concept of Ocean Thermal Energy Conversion (OTEC)— using some kind of heat engine to tap the thermal gradient between the warm surface layers and the near-freezing waters of the abyss. As I dislike any machine with moving parts, I suggested direct electrical generation by the use of thermocouples.

At the time, I didn't really believe that this would be practicable; over such a small temperature difference, the efficiency would be too low. Today, I am more optimistic; even though you can't fight the Second Law of Thermodynamics, the superconductivity revolution suggests that we may be able to bend it, and now all bets are off.

We may be able to get unlimited amounts of electricity *directly* from the sea, without huge masses of spinning hardware.

Or the idea may be as crazy as John Campbell's atomic-powered TV sets.

*Reprinted in *The Wind from the Sun*.

* * *

Van Vogt's "The Weapon Shop" (December 1942) and its novel-length sequel *The Weapon Makers* (February–April 1943) is based on the thesis, set out in capital letters:

THE RIGHT TO BUY WEAPONS IS THE RIGHT TO BE FREE

Although I was in the middle of the war against Hitler, I remember thinking at the time that this was pernicious—or at best romantic—nonsense. An American (yes, yes—I know Van was born in Canada) writer of science fiction was the last person who should have nostalgic hang-ups about George III and Minutemen.

One of the greatest values of sf is the way it can challenge long-held beliefs, and make the reader appreciate, after he has stopped foaming at the mouth, that the external world need not always conform to his hopes or expectations. It forces one to think—which is why so many people dislike it. Van Vogt was very good at this kind of provocation; Campbell was better (when he didn't overdo it)—and Robert Heinlein was best of all.

In "The Weapon Shop" van Vogt invented a fascinating future society where his slogan was indeed applicable, and "free men" needed tools to defend themselves against dictatorship. And what is a weapon but a tool?

I have just remembered that famous bone, spinning over and over in the air, and three million years later turning into an orbiting bomb. I can still see Stanley throwing it into the air, while I worried that it might fall back on his head and make an abrupt end to our little movie.

Nevertheless, I hate guns, and think there is something wrong with people who don't share that emotion. But it is necessary to draw a distinction between those who *need* guns (soldiers, policemen, game wardens, farmers protecting their crops) and those who *want* them. To the latter I dedicate a phrase I concocted many years ago: "Guns are the crutches of the impotent."

However, it is very bad manners to make fun of those who

need crutches, and fortunately there is now a vastly superior alternative to guns. Video war games are much more fun; and nothing like so hard on the environment.

I had just finished—so I thought—this chapter when the latest issue of *Astounding/Analog* arrived. (Yes, I am happy to see it still has the first name on the cover. But the price has gone up exactly tenfold, to $2.00—not at all unreasonable after almost sixty years, especially in view of the much improved quality.)

I had not seen a copy of the magazine for several years, and the Mid-December 1987 issue arrived only because I have a short piece in it. This was originally intended as my commentary on T. A. Heppenheimer's essay "War" in *Arthur C. Clarke's July 20, 2019* (Grafton, 1987) but some Higher Power decided otherwise. (This was not the only time when my editorial role in this book was negated, and as I was never sent the final proofs it contains some stupid captioning errors. But it's a handsome volume and well worth getting.)

So the essay ended up in *Astounding*, and makes a perfect finale to this chapter—and, perhaps, to my own long association with the magazine. As I opened my career there with the planetary genocide of "Loophole," based on the popular idea that the only good Martian is a dead Martian, I should be very happy to retire on a more humane note.

ON WEAPONRY

The subject of war disgusts me, and I am deeply suspicious of anyone who appears to be fascinated by it. But men I greatly admire have done so; by a quite startling coincidence, I came across this very relevant quotation just as I was beginning this essay:

Before 1914, Wells, like many of his generation, had been interested and excited by war. He had written on it at length, demanded the application of science and technology to military preparation and fought his "little wars" with toy soldiers.

... The Great War changed his attitude to war, like those of so many others, to revulsion. He never again wrote of war with his pre-1914 enthusiasm or his pre-1914 detail and length. He ended his "little wars." After 1918, he wrote against war, repeatedly. He warned against the fascination he had formerly felt. He condemned the application of science and technology to war. (Stern, R. T., "The Temper of an Age: H. G. Wells' Message on War, 1914 to 1936", *The Wellsian*, 1985, 8:9–27.)

I appear—quite unconsciously—to have followed in Wells's footsteps (not for the first time . . .). In 1946, my *Royal Air Force Quarterly* essay "The Rocket and the Future of Warfare" explored all the possibilities opened up by the advent of the V2 and the atomic bomb. It ended with the paragraph:

One returns to the conclusion that the only defense against the weapons of the future is to prevent them ever being used. In other words, the problem is political and not military at all. *A country's armed forces can no longer defend it: the most they can promise is the destruction of the attacker*.

Science writer Thomas Heppenheimer recently reviewed this now forty-year-old essay and commented: "It was over fifteen years before the doctrine of Mutual Assured Destruction became U.S. policy; yet its essential concept is not only set forth in this article, but emphasized."

To have invented MAD is not one of my prouder achievements (an example of British understatement). Perhaps my "technoporn" speech to the MIT Club of Washington (Chapter 15) may do something to redress the balance—and help to put the Weapon Shops out of business.

3 5

THE
THIRD LAW

Law 1. When a distinguished but elderly scientist says that something is possible, he is almost certainly right. When he says it is impossible, he is very probably wrong.

Law 2. The only way of finding the limits of the possible is by going beyond them into the impossible.

Law 3. Any sufficiently advanced technology is indistinguishable from magic.*

It is now almost thirty years since I formulated the First Law (in *Profiles of the Future*), and during that time it has often been thrown back at me, when I have ventured a negative forecast. Nowadays, however, the Third and much later Law is the one most frequently quoted, perhaps because its truth has been demonstrated so often during the last decade. I suspect it is also the most important of the Laws, because it reminds us that the future is essentially unpredictable. It may also explain why no one has ever been able to define "science fiction"; the boundaries are continually moving. Let me give an example.

Suppose that, in 1930, someone had written a story in which two golf-ball-size hemispheres of metal were banged together—

*As I've frequently said, if three laws were good enough for both the Isaacs, they're good enough for me.

and the result was an explosion equivalent to twenty thousand tons of TNT. At that date, such a story would not have been science fiction, but pure fantasy—and few scientists would have doubted that it could ever be anything else.

Yet ten years later, after the discovery of uranium fission, it was very plausible science fiction—as Cleve Cartmill demonstrated. And only five years after *that*, it was terrifying reality.

Less terrifying, but just as magical, is the machine which is storing these words. Though computers had been around for a century, who would have dreamed, a generation ago, that we would be able to squeeze the equivalent of a million vacuum tubes into a thumbnail-sized chip of silicon? What absurdity!

There are plenty of examples of my Third Law in *Astounding*, when the author tiptoes on the borderline between science and magic. Robert Heinlein's "Waldo" (August 1942, under the name Anson MacDonald) is a prime specimen, because it involves high technology as well as Pennsylvania Dutch "hexes." It also introduced, possibly for the first time, the concept of remote-controlled manipulators which could magnify a man's physical strength, or allow him to work vicariously in dangerous places. Such devices are now, of course, familiar in underwater and space environments.

Yet the story which, in my mind, most perfectly demonstrates the principle is Lewis Padgett's "Mimsy Were the Borogoves" (February 1943); it is also one of the finest—and most chilling—pieces of fiction ever to appear in the magazine. I do not recommend it for parents of small children.

"Lewis Padgett" was the husband-and-wife team of Henry Kuttner and C. L. Moore, both superb writers who were able to combine their talents synergistically. "Mimsy" is about some children's toys which an irresponsible experimenter dumps in the very remote past—viz. modern America and Victorian England. As all toys are to some extent, they are also teaching machines; and the things they are designed to teach the children of a million years hence are—well, magic. A child of our time who masters them will no longer be human, but superhuman.

If "Lewis Padgett" had lived a few years longer he would have seen his fantasy starting to materialize. Any baffled adult who has watched an intent four-year-old plugged into a computer will know exactly what "Mimsy Were the Borogoves" is all about.

John Campbell was always fascinated with what is loosely called the paranormal; his brief stint as one of Rhine's subjects has already been mentioned. In later years it became almost an obsession, and the magazine was so full of stories and articles about "Psi" that many readers (including this one) became restive. But, as the Second Law clearly states, Campbell had a right—even an obligation—to explore this frontier region; unfortunately, he was not the sort of man who did things by halves.

Lewis Padgett's most ambitious treatment of psi phenomena and what he called "variable truth" was the two-part serial, *The Fairy Chessmen* (January–February 1946). Many stories (as already demonstrated) have memorable last lines; few have had such an unforgettable first one: "The doorknob opened a blue eye and looked at him."

In "Fairy chess," to quote Padgett:

". . . you may have men of different powers and boards of different types. Modified space compositions—here's one."
He showed DuBrose an oblong board, eight squares by four.
"Here's another, nine by five; here's a larger one, sixteen by sixteen. And here are fairy chessmen. . . . The grasshopper. The nightrider—the blocker, which can block but never capture. Here's an imitator . . . when any man moves, the imitator must move for the same number of squares in a parallel direction . . ."

In 1951 I had the privilege, though it was completely wasted on me, of watching a game between Lord Dunsany (one-time chess champion of Ireland) and Dr. Dawson, who if I remember correctly was the editor of *The Fairy Chess Review*. Dawson told me that he had also played many games of three-dimensional chess—and one in four dimensions, though not on a full 8 × 8 board.

This way, I decided, lay madness, and it confirmed my

resolution never to learn the rules even of old-fashioned two-dimensional chess. It was a good thing that I stuck to this policy, otherwise *2001* might never have been made. I am not a good loser, and if you want to learn how Stanley Kubrick once earned a modest living as a chess hustler in Washington Square, and still tries to dominate his associates by the exercise of his skills, read Jeremy Bernstein's "How About a Little Game?"*

The only other chess game I have ever watched, again out of politeness, was between Norbert Wiener and Claud Shannon, at MIT. I don't recall who won, but I do remember Wiener's ambiguous parting words. "I don't suppose," he said, "that we'll ever meet again." To this day I'm not sure whether he was expressing hope or regret; in any event, his prediction was perfectly correct.

The point that Lewis Padgett was making in both "Mimsy Were the Borogoves" and *The Fairy Chessmen* was really summed up by J. B. S. Haldane at least half a century ago in his famous dictum: "The universe is not only stranger than we imagine—it is stranger than we *can* imagine."† My own attitude towards the paranormal and fringe sciences generally has changed over the years from tentative acceptance to disillusioned skepticism. When I wrote *Childhood's End* (1953) and "Second Dawn" (1951, reprinted in *Expedition to Earth,* 1953) I was a semi-believer; my present position is given at some length in *Arthur C. Clarke's World of Strange Powers* (1984) but may be summed up as follows: if there was *really* something in telepathy, ESP, etc., it would have been proved by now without doubt. We wouldn't still be arguing and waving our hands after centuries of investigation; scientific controversies seldom take more than a decade to settle, one way or the other.

Yet there are things in this universe which I would never have believed, without incontrovertible evidence. A few paragraphs ago I mentioned Jeremy Bernstein; in his book *The*

*In *A Comprehensible World* (Random House, 1967).

†J.B.S. actually said "queerer," but I've always changed the adjective to avoid unfortunate misunderstandings.

Analytical Engine he quotes the case of a man who was able to calculate mentally the seventy-third root of a five hundred digit number—in just over two minutes!

How could such a truly fantastic—and really quite pointless, since it has no real survival value—ability have evolved in the human brain? Is it not almost less incredible to suggest that the calculator had somehow tapped a source of pre-existing knowledge?

And consider the case of Srinivasa Ramanujan, whose 1987 centennial has just been celebrated. Here was a poor Hindu, with virtually no access to the body of western mathematics, who in his short life produced a torrent of amazing theorems which, as his collaborator G. H. Hardy remarked, *must* be true because no one could possibly have imagined them.*

I am tempted to link these mysteries with the theory that some kind of universal field of information may exist, and that a part of what we think is memory is not in the brain at all, but somehow outside it. Sheldrake's controversial "morphogenetic field hypothesis." if I understand it, is based on a similar idea, and it seems a pity that we have just missed an ideal chance of testing it.

In 1979, something new came into the world—in exactly 43,252,003,274,489,856,000 varieties; the problem was to find just *one* of them. I refer, of course, to Erno Rubik's diabolical cube.

I never succeeded in unscrambling it, during a few months of desultory twisting, but would have predicted that it might be solved in a few hours by someone who really put his mind to it and made careful notes of the key transformations. Yet—and I can still hardly believe my eyes—I've seen an ordinary small boy sort out a randomly scrambled cube in a couple of minutes. When I last heard, the world record was under thirty seconds; it would surely be impossible merely to move the

---

*But Ramanujan wasn't always right. As the *Britannica* rather quaintly puts it: "Though brilliant, many of his theorems on prime numbers were completely wrong." This reminds me of the critic who remarked that Wagner's music is better than it sounds.

components around in much less time than this, even if no time at all was required for thought.

And I don't think there is; a Rubik racer seems to be acting purely automatically. He's plugged in.

Into what? Why, of course, the global "Rubik field" created by the mental efforts of frustrated millions—most of whom never did reach their goal. Don't ask me how it works, or how the successful operators get tuned into it. . . .

Anyway, do *you* have a better explanation?

3 6

A
VERY PEACEFUL
WAR

If I had planned it deliberately, I could not have done a better job of avoiding World War II; at its worst, it was never more than a background inconvenience. My department in the Civil Service—the Ministry of Food—was evacuated from London just before the Blitz, to the safety of North Wales. By the time I had volunteered (one jump ahead of the draft) and received my initial Royal Air Force technical training in the east end of London, the air raids on the city had just stopped.

Number 9 Radio School, Yatesbury, Wiltshire, where I was first a radar mechanic and later an instructor, was never attacked, though it should have been a prime target. I recall only one alert, when a reconnaissance plane passed over at a very high altitude; I could just see it, a tiny silver toy glittering against the stratosphere.

Typically, much of my training was irrelevant, because it was devoted to the already obsolete meter-band radar—and my first posting, when I received my commission, was to a microwave (ten centimeter) coast defense installation. I had not been there for long when I received a summons to Group Headquarters, and, after an interview with a Wing Commander, was selected for a mysterious job in the remoter wilds of Cornwall. What it would be, I had no idea.

It turned out to be the one and only GCA Mark I, which

Luis Alvarez and his students had built at MIT's Radiation Lab to demonstrate the now familiar radar "talk down" principle. At first, it had not always been easy to sell the idea, the reaction of many pilots being that they'd be damned if they'd let some clown in a box full of vacuum tubes tell them what to do. In the early days, such skepticism was often well-founded; see my essay "You're on the glidepath—I think . . ." (in *Ascent to Orbit*).

Having convinced the USAF that GCA actually worked, Luie soon found an even more eager customer in the RAF's Bomber Command, then losing more aircraft to the English weather than to the Luftwaffe. The Mark 1—which had only been built for demonstration purposes, not for operations—was packed up and carried across the Atlantic aboard a British battleship under day-and-night guard. (Very necessary, as it was stuffed with whiskey, nylons, and similar treasures.) In July 1943 it was installed at Elsham Wolds, a Bomber Command airfield in the Midlands; a few months later it moved to St. Eval, near the southwest tip of England, and this was where I joined it in the autumn of 1943.

It would not have been possible to design a more stimulating environment for a would-be science fiction writer. I was *living* what would have been sf only a decade earlier; moreover, for the first time in my life, I was working with real scientist-engineers. Although Alvarez and Larry Johnson (the co-inventor of GCA and the only man in the world to be at Trinity, Hiroshima, *and* Nagasaki) had already left to design the implosion trigger of the plutonium bomb, they had handed over the Mark 1 to the men who had built it, and so could best keep it running. My job was to train RAF radar mechanics to take over from them, and to prepare for the arrival of the operational units, the GCA Mark 2s, now being rushed into production in the United States. These differed from the handmade prototype in almost every detail, so there was much to be learned.

How I ever found time to do any writing in these circumstances, I can no longer imagine. It may have helped, from the inspirational point of view, that the unit eventually moved to an airfield just outside Stratford-on-Avon; my short story "The

Curse" (reprinted in *Reach for Tomorrow*) was certainly the result of a visit to Shakespeare's grave.

In any event, during my GCA incarnation I wrote more than twenty short stories and articles—and made my first sale to John Campbell, with the 12,000-word novella "Rescue Party." What fixes this indelibly in my mind is not the $180 (big money in those days) but the fact that before Street and Smith's cashier would release it I had to cycle into Stratford and find a Commissioner of Oaths who would certify that I was indeed Arthur C. Clarke, and not someone else of the same name.*

"Rescue Party" was written in March 1945—roughly midway between the V2 rocket and the atomic bomb. It is time once again to look at their impact on the magazine.

---

*There are quite a number of us—and one is a senior engineer at the Goddard Spaceflight Center! But I regret to say that many American branches of the family have been careless enough to lose the final letter of their name. We treat these unfortunates politely, but do not invite them to stay for tea.

37

THE
FIRST
SPACESHIP

While I was supervising my radar mechanics' battle to keep the GCA Mark 1 operational, another battle was going on in Whitehall. British Intelligence had finally decided that the V2 rocket was not a propaganda myth. Though there were a few skeptics (Lord Cherwell hung on to the bitter end) some had gone to the other extreme and believed that the Germans had built a rocket with a *ten-ton* warhead. The moderate faction believed it was "only" one ton, which in itself was an enormous advance over anything in the past.

To settle the matter, a debate was conducted in an Air Ministry basement, presided over by a (it was hoped) neutral American. In Walt Rostow's own words:*

> I had acquired some experience with both academic and government bureaucratic structures and their capacity for bloodless tribal warfare. But I had never been present at a meeting with more emotional tension than that centered on the size of the V2 warhead.
>
> What emerged was a reasonably solid intelligence case for a 1-ton warhead against a deeply emotional conviction among

*Quoted from *The Rocket Team* by Frederick I. Ordway and Mitchell R. Sharpe (Crowell, 1979).

the British rocketeers that if they had been backed by their government, they could have produced a rocket with a 10-ton warhead. . . . After some exchange on the curious way that essentially rational problems of intelligence and science could generate emotional attachments of great strength, I departed.

Professor Rostow has now had endless opportunities of watching the same phenomenon at work in the SDI debate. Back in the Early Paleotechnic 1940s, the warhead argument was finally settled when a stray V2 landed in Sweden, and the bits were promptly flown to England. It was then obvious that the payload was just one ton, and the ten-tonner advocates were routed.

I have already quoted Willy Ley on this subject, and poor Willy must have been horribly embarrassed by his article "Rocket Artillery" in the April 1944 *Astounding*. This badly timed piece concluded that liquid-fueled rockets had no military value, as they lacked storability. The alternative—the powder rocket— could not provide the range, even if it could be made large enough to carry a useful warhead. And Willy stated categorically that it was impossible to make powder rockets weighing more than two thousand pounds; they'd blow up on ignition. He concluded triumphantly: "End of chapter."

Of course, it wasn't—though Willy's point on storability was well taken. This was the reason for the eventual switch to solid propellants, first for submarine-launched missiles, later for landbased ICBMs like Minuteman. In a few decades, solid rockets grew from an "impossible" two thousand pounds to several hundred *tons*.

In his history of the Jet Propulsion Laboratory,* Frank J. Malina described how this happened:

Von Karman, in the spring of 1940, after listening to the opinion of the experts and to the repeated explosions on the

*"The Jet Propulsion Laboratory": in *The Coming of the Space Age* (Gollancz, 1967).

test stand, one evening at his home wrote down four differential equations, which he asked me to solve. He said to me: "Let us work out the implications of these equations; if they show that the process of a restricted burning powder rocket is unstable, we will give up, but if they show that the process is stable, then we will keep trying."

Malina solved the equations; all today's giant solid rockets are linear descendants of that early JPL work. (It was called the Jet Propulsion Lab because, in those days, rockets could not be mentioned in polite scientific society.)

This short extract from Frank Malina's memoir has triggered an avalanche of my own memories; I will attempt to put them in a logical order.

First—the great Theodore von Karman, founder of high-speed aerodynamical theory and much else. He was another of those Hungarian (or extraterrestrial—see Szilard's assertion) geniuses who made such an impact on the modern world. And on anyone who ever met him.

Though he never married, his interest in the other sex was notorious, and I have heard strange tales from lady scientists who sat next to him at conferences or official dinners. Having seen him in action, I can well believe them.

It was at the 1953 Congress of the IAF—the International Astronautical Federation. Von Karman was lecturing trilingually, repeating everything in English, German, and French—all with a strong Hungarian accent. I was seated in the first row, almost directly in front of him, and after a while it became obvious that the focus of his attention had shifted from his subject to the rather striking lady immediately on my left. He couldn't take his eyes off her, and the lecture began to sound like a gramophone record running down.

It was getting a little embarrassing when the lady concerned—who happened to be my wife—leaned over and whispered in my ear, "If I left the room, do you think that would help him finish his lecture?" Fortunately, we were able to get the distracted genius (then, incidentally, about 73) off the podium without using Marilyn as a decoy.

In the memoir I have just quoted, Frank Malina mentions a visit he paid in August 1936 to Professor Goddard's laboratory at Roswell, New Mexico, where the Goddards received him cordially, and showed him the machine shop, the test stand—and everything *except* an actual rocket.

Many years later, Mrs. Goddard gave me a hilarious account of this visit. On a trestle at the end of the laboratory was a long, torpedo-shaped object—completely shrouded with dust-sheets. His hosts did not offer to unveil it, though every few minutes young Frank's eyes strayed hopefully, and vainly, in its direction; rather like von Karman's on the occasion I have just mentioned.

Dr. Goddard's patents covered almost every aspect of rocket design, and after his death in 1945 (he lived just long enough to see a V2 rocket) Mrs. Goddard edited all his papers* and made a settlement with the U.S. Government for a round million dollars. Half of this she gave back to the Guggenheim Foundation, which (together with the Smithsonian) had financed her husband's work. And some of the rest she spent on a trip round the world—including a stop in Ceylon, where I had the privilege of entertaining her.

When it was time for her to go back to the hotel, we had a problem. For some reason a car wasn't available—and we couldn't find a taxi. However, my companion Hector Ekanayake volunteered to provide transport.

I bitterly regret my missed opportunity. How I wish I'd taken a photo of that great lady, Esther Goddard—then in her seventies—riding away on the back of Hector's motorbike. She never forgot the incident, and always reminded me of it when we met.

Frank Malina, after helping to get the U.S. rocket industry off the ground, later switched completely from engineering to

---

*With the assistance of G. Edward Pendray, one of the pioneers of American rocketry. As "Gawain Edwards" Pendray wrote a number of science fiction stories in the 1930s, one of which provided the cover illustration for the first sf magazine I ever saw (Chapter 1). I have just heard of his recent death, aged eighty-six.

art. This was partly, I suspect, as a reaction to the treatment of his brilliant fellow student Hsue Shen Tsien. After becoming the first Goddard Professor at Caltech, Tsien was arrested on trumped-up security charges, when he attempted to return to China during the McCarthy era. He later played an important role in his native country's space program; hence his appearance in *2010* and *2061*. . . .

Moving to Paris, Frank Malina became a Deputy Director General of UNESCO and a pioneer of "kinetic art"; he also founded a beautiful magazine, *Leonardo,* devoted to the sciences and the visual arts. After his death, his widow Marjorie donated his entire aeronautical library to the Arthur Clarke Center for Modern Technology, adjacent to the University of Moratuwa, where it is now being catalogued. I hope this cross-section of the moment in time when mankind was on the verge of entering space will be of value to future researchers.

But back to the historic summer of 1944. On September 8, just five months after Willy Ley had proved it didn't exist, the first V2 landed on London. After a suitable pause for reflection, Willy returned to the subject in the May 1945 *Astounding* with "V2—Rocket Cargo Ship"—and, I am sorry to say, again fell flat on his face. Though he was right in saying "Yes, we might as well admit it, V2 is the first spaceship," he then claimed that he could without question identify the designer—Hermann Oberth.

He might just as well have said Robert Goddard, who had described all the basic elements of the V2 in his patents. And as it turned out later, Oberth had nothing to do with the project, which was already far advanced when he arrived at Peenemünde in 1941; Wernher von Braun knew his old (and admired) mentor for the impractical genius he was, and kept him out of the way until he could do no harm.

Ironically, Oberth's greatest contribution to the V2 effort may have been on the night of August 17–18, 1943, when the RAF launched six hundred bombers against Peenemünde. He later received a medal for his heroism in saving valuable files and equipment from burning buildings.

One of the men who had planned that raid was Colonel

George Jones, USAF, then a target evaluator with Bomber Command. After the war, he was my good friend and editor at Harper's, starting with *Interplanetary Flight* in 1950 and continuing until his retirement twenty years later. When I told him that I was on the way to Huntsville (see Chapter 29) he said, "Tell Wernher I once did my best to kill him."

When I passed on the message, Wernher laughed and produced his portfolio of "morning after" photographs of the still-smoking ruins.

"Tell George," he said ruefully, "that he did a pretty good job."

I must program one of the macro keys to print out automatically "By a curious coincidence . . ." whenever I press it; I seem to require the phrase at least once per chapter.

Anyway, by a curious coincidence I've just noticed that the very next article to Willy's "V2—Rocket Cargo Ship" was the direct, and duly acknowledged, inspiration of my own short story "A Slight Case of Sunstroke" (reprinted in *Tales of Ten Worlds*). This is a tongue-in-cheek piece about a strange incident in a South American football stadium, when a few hundred thousand fans disposed of an unpopular referee, using only the silver-paper covers of their extra-sized programs.

The article, as you may have guessed, is about the problem of making a heat-ray. To quote J. J. Coupling's title, "It Isn't So Easy." In fact, the rules of optics make it downright impossible—*unless*—

Then follows what is, for 1945, a really stunning piece of prediction. Heat, the writer points out, is "disorganized energy—that is, energy of many wavelengths. . . . If heat rays are to be effective, they must presumably be single wavelength beams."

For 1945, I find this absolutely astonishing. At least four decades before they became practicable, J. J. Coupling had clearly outlined the basic principle of laser weapons!

Here we go again. By a *very* curious coincidence, I look forward to meeting "J. J. Coupling" again next month; as already mentioned, that was the nom de plume used by Dr. John Pierce for his early articles and short stories.

I bet he's forgotten all about "It Isn't So Easy," and will remind him of it when he arrives in Colombo next month, to deliver the Arthur Clarke Lecture on my seventieth birthday (see Chapter 22). John is seven years older than I am—and he's coming on his honeymoon, with his new wife Brenda. Reading (and writing) science fiction may not guarantee eternal youth: but it helps.

3 8

THE END
OF THE
GOLDEN AGE

During the period 1942 to 1945 many of *Astounding*'s best authors (and artists) had been caught up in the war effort, and disappeared temporarily from its pages. A surprising number, however, still managed to find time and opportunity to write, and there was certainly no falling off in the quality of the magazine. Indeed, so many classic stories appeared during this period that some readers consider it the Golden Age of science fiction.

I recently went on record as saying that what we *thought* was gold was only gilt—but the very best gilt: the real Golden Age is *now*. That is undoubtedly true from the crassly commercial viewpoint; even allowing for inflation, the half-cent-a-worders of the 1930s would have been stunned by today's market with its movie deals and its megabuck advances. But we creative artists don't concern ourselves with such sordid matters (except when we phone our agents to complain about the reversion of Lower Slobovian serial rights on page 47, para 5 . . .) and the real question is: has the quality of the product improved?

Of course it has, often beyond recognition. But just as there is a naive charm about primitive works of art that a more sophisticated age can never recapture, so the early pulps created a magic of their own—on occasion, potent enough to endure to this day.

Moreover, when something is done for the very first time—even if it is not done particularly well—that gives it an unique power and authority. For example, dated though they are, parts of *The Time Machine, First Men in the Moon,* and *The War of the Worlds* will never be surpassed.

In those last two years of the war, *Astounding* published A. E. van Vogt's "Far Centaurus" (January 1944), Clifford Simak's "City" (May 1944), Fredric Brown's "Arena" (June 1944), Theodore Sturgeon's "Killdozer!" (November 1944), C. L. Moore's "No Woman Born" (December 1944), Murray Leinster's "First Contact" (May 1945), Lester del Rey's "Into Thy Hands" (August 1945), Bertram Chandler's "Giant Killer" (October 1945) . . . I could go on for another page, but lists of titles quickly become boring. The point I wish to make is that every one of these tales is better known now than when it first appeared; and of how many stories of the 1940s is that true? The extraordinary durability of good sf has often been noted; every new generation discovers the classics all over again.

Although such a dividing line is purely arbitrary, to me the Golden Age—the first one, anyway—of *Astouding* came to an end with the November 1945 issue. As John Campbell remarked in his Editorial for that month, he did not publish a news magazine, and it took a few weeks for the contents page to reflect the dawn of the Atomic Age.

That first postwar Editorial now makes fascinating reading—especially to anyone (and we must now be a rapidly dwindling minority) who lived through those times. As Campbell remarked:

> The science-fictioneers were suddenly recognized by their neighbors as not quite such wild-eyed dreamers as they had been thought, and in many soul-satisfying cases became the neighborhood experts.

After that fully justified piece of self-congratulation, Campbell went on to take the wider view:

> People do not realize civilization, the civilization we have been born into, lived in, and indoctrinated with, died on July 16, 1945, and that the Death Notice was published to the world on August 6, 1945.
>
> The first atomic bomb ... was the death of an era, and the death of a cultural pattern based on a balance of military power.... Atomic war is as suicidal as a duel between two men armed with flame-throwers in a vestibule. Neither party can have the slightest hope of surviving.... The atomic bomb must, inevitably, force upon us an era of international good manners and tolerance—or vast and sudden death.

In the course of a single year, two of the main themes of science fiction—space travel, and the ultimate weapon—had ceased to be playthings of the mind. Dreams had turned into realities: perhaps into waking nightmares. Among writers, a new sense of responsibility—even guilt—was abroad, and from now on it would be reflected in all their work, whether they intended it or not.

In Oppenheimer's famous phrase, the physicists had known sin. And the science fiction writers had, at the very least, lost their innocence.

The best valediction I can pay to the old *Astounding* comes from an unexpected source. When I met Lord Dunsany in 1951, as mentioned in Chapter 35, I took the train from Charing Cross, got out somewhere in Kent, and walked to Dunstall Castle. I remember that I was carrying a novelty—one of the first truly portable radios, about the size of a large book. In those pre-transistor days it used miniature vacuum tubes, and ate batteries at an alarming rate.

I was also carrying the copy of *The Charwoman's Shadow* open before me at the moment. (I see I acquired it on February 20, 1947, twenty-one years after publication.) Lord Dunsany inscribed his name on the first page; it was the only time I have ever seen anyone use a quill pen. It stalled after two letters and he had to start again, so the book has one-and-a-third Dunsany signatures.

He also took the opportunity of correcting the text, on pages 388 and 389; even the greatest writers sometimes have second thoughts. He transferred "The Country Towards Moon's Rising" into another, and far stranger, universe, by changing it into "The Country Beyond Moon's Rising."

I am glad that he did so, and in my presence, because those two pages contain the most magical writing I know—the distilled essence of fantasy. They prove that—as Bates, and Tremaine, and Campbell all knew in their different ways—the search for wonder can sometimes be successful:

And there came upon him at last those mortal tremors that are about the end of all earthly journeys. He hastened then. And before the human destiny overtook him he saw one morning, clear where the dawn had been, the luminous rock of the bastions and glittering rampart that rose up sheer from the frontier of the Country Beyond Moon's Rising. This he saw though his eyes were dimming now with fatigue and his long sojourn on earth; yet if he saw dimly he heard with no degree of uncertainty the trumpets that rang out from those battlements to welcome him after his sojourn, and all that followed him gave back the greeting with such cries as once haunted valleys at certain times of the moon. Upon those battlements and by the opening gates were gathered the robed Masters that had trafficked with time and dwelt awhile on earth, and handed the mysteries on, and had walked round the back of the grave by the way that they knew, and were even beyond damnation. They raised their hands and blessed him.

And now for him, and the creatures that followed after,

the gates were wide that led through the earthward rampart
of the Country Beyond Moon's Rising. He limped towards it
with all his magical following. He went therein, and the
Golden Age was over.

IV

EPILOGUE
. . . ANALOG

39
METAMORPHOSIS

John Campbell continued to edit the magazine, with an increasingly dictatorial and eccentric hand, up to the day of his death in 1971. During the postwar years he published five of my own stories, all of which are available in book form (see Appendix). He also serialized some of the most famous science fiction novels of all time—notably Hal Clement's *Needle* (May–June 1949); Robert Heinlein's *Double Star* (February–April 1956); Isaac Asimov's *The Naked Sun* (October–December 1956); Frank Herbert's *Dune* (as *Dune World*, December 1963–February 1964 and *The Prophet of Dune*, January–May 1965) and many shorter classics: Lawrence O'Donnell (Kuttner and Moore's) "Vintage Season" (September 1946); Jack Williamson's "With Folded Hands—" (July 1947); Theodore Sturgeon's "Thunder and Roses" (November 1947); C. M. Kornbluth's "The Little Black Bag" (July 1950); Tom Godwin's "The Cold Equations" (August 1954); Bob Shaw's "Light of Other Days" (August 1966). . . .

But the magazine, though still generally considered the first in the field, faced increasing competition on several fronts. Two friendly rivals, *Galaxy* and *The Magazine of Fantasy and Science Fiction*, published stories of equal merit, and developed their own characteristic styles under a series of able editors. And even more important, there was a virtual explosion of sf books, both in paperback and hardcover. As I mentioned in Chapter 3, a genuine science fiction *book* was once a rare phenomenon indeed, and no one dreamed that a time would come when several would share the bestseller lists.*

Even if one abandoned all else (including sleeping) it became impossible to keep up with the entire field. In my own case, other interests also intruded and drastically cut down my reading time. The Great Barrier Reef of Australia, the Indian Ocean round Ceylon, the movie *2001*, the Apollo Project, all seduced me in turn; even if I wished to do so, it was not easy to keep up with *Astounding,* or its rivals, in my wanderings round the globe.

Sometime in the 1960s, I defected by not renewing my subscription—something that would once have been unthinkable. Both I and the magazine had changed so much that the old compulsion to read every issue had vanished. It was like the slow waning of a love affair; there was no definite breakoff point.

In 1960 Campbell had, quite deliberately, tried to bury the old *Astounding;* he felt—and I must reluctantly agree with him— that the time had come for a more dignified name. The pulp era had gone forever, and he wished to appeal to a more mature audience than the one that still secretly yearned for such titles as *Stupendous Stories* and *Flabbergasting Fiction.*†

So the last issue of *Astounding Science-Fiction* (note the hyphen) was dated January 1960. Campbell planned to change it

---

*A few years ago James Michener's *Space* sat for several weeks right on top of *2010: Odyssey Two* when they shared first and second place on the *New York Times* bestseller list. Next year, according to present plans, Michener and I will be shipmates on the *Queen Elizabeth II,* when she makes an appointment in the South China Sea with the solar eclipse of March 18, 1988. He'd better wear his life jacket during the two-minute blackout of totality. (Alas, health problems caused me to cancel this.)

†Confronted with some of the erotic covers of the late 1940s, my first collaborator Eric Frank Russell invented *Fantastic Fornications.* A lot of people might still salute if that was run up the flagpole. . . .

to *Analog Science Fact-Fiction*, but to minimize withdrawal symptoms among the most badly addicted of his readers he did it in stages. February 1960 was *Astounding/Analog Science Fact & Fiction;* the *Astounding* part of the title was printed more and more lightly, until it faded out, a process which was completed by October 1960.

However, *Analog Science Fact-Fiction* lasted only 14 issues before becoming *Analog Science Fact-Science Fiction;* that lasted 40 issues (are you still with me?) before switching to *Analog Science Fiction-Science Fact,* which it still is today. However, I note with amusement (and satisfaction) that across the top lefthand corner of the cover is a little insert that reads "Since 1930 ASTOUNDING." In its first fifty years, the magazine changed its name twice as often as its editors; since January 1930 there have been only five.

The last issue that bears Campbell's name is that of December 1971; Ben Bova took over in January 1972, and was editor for 83 issues, until November 1978. Ben is now President of the National Space Society (see Chapter 29) and was already involved in space when I first met him in 1956, while researching *The Making of a Moon.* At that time he was working in the publications department of the Martin Company of Baltimore, builders of the Vanguard rocket which, everyone in the West confidently assumed, would orbit the first satellite of earth. Things didn't quite work out that way, and Ben's editorial skills must have had plenty of exercise when Sputnik got there first.

After his stint with *Analog* Ben became Editorial Director of *Omni* Magazine, and in his spare time has produced a remarkable number of books, both science fact and science fiction. His *Assured Survival* (Houghton Mifflin, 1984) was a thoughtful but perhaps too idealistic attempt to show how SDI might succeed in preserving peace—not as a national, but as an international project. He had already written a political novel—*Millennium* (Random House, 1976)—on this subject, so had been thinking seriously about it long before President Reagan fell in love with the idea. And it's amusing to note that earlier still Ben had written the novel version of *THX 1138* in collaboration with its director George Lucas—the man who was to make "Star Wars" a household name years before it was taken over by the Pentagon, to his great annoyance.

From December 1978 to the present, *Analog*'s editor has been Stanley Schmidt; he has now passed his hundredth issue, and so is a quarter of the way towards Campbell's unbelievable 409. (Confusingly, there are now *13* issues a year—two in December. *Astounding*/*Analog* does seem to enjoy giving headaches to librarians and indexers.)

I have already quoted, in the "Weapon Shop" chapter, my own latest contribution to the magazine, and there have been two others during Stanley's regime. I am particularly proud of "The Steam-Powered Word-Processor," and hope it has made a contribution to the language. Recently the London *Sunday Times* columnist Godfrey Smith challenged his readers to find a more elegant name for the machine which has relegated the typewriter to the scrap heap; see the next chapter for my answer, which he says "won hands down." The prize—a magnum of Bollinger—was duly dispatched to the Clarkives, where it was consumed *today* (November 12, 1987) by the directors and accountants at the Annual General Meeting of the Rocket Publishing Company (i.e. Arthur C. Clarke, Esq.). Their slightly incoherent greetings have just been modemed to my office computer.

Yet *I* seem to have been the one who has not had his wits about him today. A few hours ago, I started to print out this chapter, which I could have sworn I had saved to disk and then copied not once, but *twice*. All versions had vanished into limbo.

After a brief interval for cardiac massage, I called the local computer firm, who immediately sent round a disk jockey with lots of fancy software, designed to deal with such catastrophes. He prowled around in the machine's memory, and salvaged a few vanished files—but *not* the vital ones. So it was back to the keyboard, cursing . . . and dredging the depths of my own random access protoplasmic memory to retrieve the vanished bytes.

My powers of concentration were not helped by a telex I

received just as I was starting the job: "Dear Arthur—When can I read *2061*? Best regards. Stanley Kubrick." But the fugitive files have not been replaced, and here are my last two pieces of fiction for *Astounding/Analog*—an old friend who, alas, like so many others, I now seldom see.

40

"THE STEAM-POWERED WORD-PROCESSOR: A FORGOTTEN EPIC OF VICTORIAN ENGINEERING."

Very little biographical material exists relating to the remarkable career of the now almost forgotten engineering genius, the Reverend Charles Cabbage (1815–188?), onetime Vicar of St. Simian's in the Parish of Far Tottering, Sussex. After several years of exhaustive research, however, I have discovered some new facts which, it seems to me, should be brought to a wider public.

I would like to express my thanks to Miss Drusilla Wollstonecraft Cabbage and the good ladies of the Far Tottering Historical Society, whose urgent wishes to disassociate themselves from many of my conclusions I fully understand.

As early as 1715 the *Spectator* refers to the Cabbage (or Cubage) family as a cadet branch of the de Coverleys (bar sinister, regrettably, though Sir Roger himself is not implicated). They quickly acquired great wealth, like many members of the British aristocracy, by judicious investment in the slave trade. By

1800 the Cabbages were the richest family in Sussex (some said in England) but as Charles was the youngest of eleven children he was forced to enter the Church and appeared unlikely to inherit much of the Cabbage wealth.

Before his thirtieth year, however, the incumbent of Far Tottering experienced a remarkable change of fortune, owing to the untimely demise of all his ten siblings in a series of tragic accidents. This turn of events, which contemporary writers were fond of calling "The Curse of the Cabbages," was closely connected with the Vicar's unique collection of medieval weapons, oriental poisons, and venomous reptiles. Naturally, these unfortunate mishaps gave rise to much malicious gossip, and may be the reason why the Reverend Cabbage preferred to retain the protection of Holy Orders, at least until his abrupt departure from England.*

It may well be asked why a man of great wealth and minimal public duties should devote the most productive years of his life to building a machine of incredible complexity, whose purpose and operations only he could understand. Fortunately, the recent discovery of the Faraday–Cabbage correspondence in the archives of the Royal Institution now throws some light on this matter. Reading between the lines, it appears that the reverend gentleman resented the weekly chore of producing a two-hour sermon on basically the same themes, one hundred and four times a year. (He was also incumbent of Tottering-in-the-Marsh, pop. 73.) In a moment of inspiration which must have occurred around 1851—possibly after a visit to the Great Exhibition, that marvelous showpiece of confident Victorian know-how—he conceived a machine which would *automatically* reassemble masses of text in any desired order. Thus he could create any number of sermons from the same basic material.

This crude initial concept was later greatly refined. Although—as we shall see—the Reverend Cabbage was never able to

---

*Ealing Studios deny the very plausible rumour that Alec Guinness's *Kind Hearts and Coronets* was inspired by these events. It is known, however, that at one time Peter Cushing was being considered for the role of the Reverend Cabbage.

complete the final version of his "Word Loom," he clearly envisaged a machine which would operate not only upon individual paragraphs but single lines of text. (The next stage—words and letters—he never attempted, though he mentions the possibility in his correspondence with Faraday, and recognized it as an ultimate objective.)

Once he had conceived the Word Loom, the inventive cleric immediately set out to build it. His unusual (some would say deplorable) mechanical ability had already been amply demonstrated through the ingenious mantraps which protected his vast estates, and which had eliminated at least two other claimants to the family fortune.

At this point, the Rev. Cabbage made a mistake which may well have changed the course of technology—if not history. With the advantage of hindsight, it now seems obvious to us that his problems could only have been solved by the use of electricity. The Wheatstone telegraph had already been operating for years, and he was in correspondence with the genius who had discovered the basic laws of electromagnetism. How strange that he ignored the answer that was staring him in the face!

We must remember, however, that the gentle Faraday was now entering the decade of senility preceding his death in 1867. Much of the surviving correspondence concerns his eccentric faith (the now extinct religion of "Sandemanism") with which Cabbage could have had little patience.

Moreover, the vicar was in daily (or at least weekly) contact with a very advanced technology with over a thousand years of development behind it. The Far Tottering church was blessed with an excellent twenty-one-stop organ manufactured by the same Henry Willis whose 1875 masterpiece at North London's Alexandra Palace was proclaimed by Marcel Dupré as the finest concert organ in Europe.* Cabbage was himself no mean

---

*Since the 1970s my indefatigable brother Fred Clarke, with the help of such distinguished musicians as Sir Yehudi Menuhin (who has already conducted three performances of Handel's *Messiah* for this purpose) has spearheaded a campaign for the restoration of this magnificent instrument.

performer on this instrument, and had a complete understanding of its intricate mechanism. He was convinced that an assembly of pneumatic tubes, valves and pumps could control all the operations of his projected Word Loom.

It was an understandable but fatal mistake. Cabbage had overlooked the fact that the sluggish velocity of sound—a miserable 330 meters a second—would reduce the machine's operating speed to a completely impracticable level. At best, the final version might have attained an information-handling rate of 0.1 baud—so that the preparation of a single sermon would have required about ten weeks!

It was some years before the Rev. Cabbage realized this fundamental limitation; at first he believed that by merely increasing the available power he could speed up his machine indefinitely. The final version absorbed the entire output of a large steam-driven threshing machine—the clumsy ancestor of today's farm tractors and combine harvesters.

At this point, it may be as well to summarize what little is known about the actual mechanics of the Word Loom. For this, we must rely on garbled accounts in the *Far Tottering Gazette* (no complete runs of which exist for the essential years 1860–80) and occasional notes and sketches in the Rev. Cabbage's surviving correspondence. Ironically, considerable portions of the final machine were in existence as late as 1942. They were destroyed when one of the Luftwaffe's stray incendiary bombs reduced the ancestral home of Tottering Towers to a pile of ashes.*

The machine's "memory" was based—indeed, there was no practical alternative at the time—on the punched cards of a

---

*A small portion—two or three gearwheels and what appears to be a pneumatic valve—are still in the possession of the local Historical Society. These pathetic relics reminded me irresistibly of another great technological might-have-been, the famous Anticythera Computer (see Derek de Solla Price, *Scientific American,* July 1959) which I last saw in 1965, ignominiously relegated to a cigar box in the basement of the Athens Museum. My suggestion that it was the Museum's most important exhibit was not well received.

modified Jacquard Loom; Cabbage was fond of saying that he would weave thoughts as Jacquard wove tapestries. Each line of output consisted of 20 (later 30) characters, displayed to the operator by letter wheels rotating behind small windows.

The principles of the machine's COS (Card Operating System) have not come down to us, and it appears—not surprisingly—that Cabbage's greatest problem involved the location, removal, and updating of the individual cards. Once text had been finalized, it was cast in type-metal; the amazing clergyman had built a primitive Linotype at least a decade before Mergenthaler's 1886 patent!

Before the machine could be used, Cabbage was faced with the laborious task of punching not only the Bible but the whole of Cruden's Concordance onto Jacquard cards. He arranged for this to be done, at negligible expense, by the aged ladies of the Far Tottering Home for Relicts of Decayed Gentlefolk— now the local Disco and Break-dancing Club. This was another astonishing First, anticipating by a dozen years Hollerith's famed mechanization of the 1890 U.S. Census.

But at this point, disaster struck. Hearing, yet again, strange rumors from the Parish of Far Tottering, no less a personage than the Archbishop of Canterbury descended upon the now obsessed vicar. Understandably appalled by discovering that the church organ had been unable to perform its original function for at least five years, Cantuar issued an ultimatum. Either the Word Loom must go—or the Rev. Cabbage must resign. (Preferably both: there were also hints of exorcism and reconsecration.)

This dilemma seems to have produced an emotional crisis in the already unbalanced clergyman. He attempted one final test of his enormous and unwieldy machine, which now occupied the entire western transept of Saint Simian's. Over the protests of the local farmers (for it was now harvest time) the huge steam engine, its brassware gleaming, was trundled up to the church, and the belt-drive connected (the stained-glass windows having long ago been removed to make this possible).

The Reverend took his seat at the now unrecognizable console (I cannot forbear wondering if he booted the system with a foot pedal) and started to type. The letter wheels rotated before his eyes as the sentences were slowly spelled out, one line at a time. In the vestry, the crucibles of molten lead awaited the commands that would be laboriously brought to them on puffs of air. . . .

"Faster, faster!" called the impatient vicar, as the workmen shoveled coal into the smoke-belching monster in the churchyard. The long belt, snaking through the narrow window, flapped furiously up and down, pumping horsepower upon horsepower into the straining mechanism of the Loom.

The result was inevitable. Somewhere, in the depths of the immense apparatus, something broke. Within seconds, the ill-fated machine tore itself into fragments. The vicar, according to eyewitnesses, was very lucky to escape with his life.

The next development was both abrupt and totally unexpected. Abandoning Church, wife, and thirteen children, the Reverend Cabbage eloped to Australia with his chief assistant, the village blacksmith.

To the class-conscious Victorians, such an association with a mere workman was beyond excuse (even an underfootman would have been more acceptable!).* The very name of Charles Cabbage was banished from polite society, and his ultimate fate is unknown, though there are reports that he later became Chaplain of Botany Bay. The legend that he died in the Outback when a sheep-shearing machine he had invented ran amok is surely apocryphal.

---

*How D.H. Lawrence ever heard of this affair is still a mystery. As is now well known, he had originally planned to make the protagonist of his most famous novel not Lady Chatterley, but her husband; however, discretion prevailed, and the Cabbage Connection was revealed only when Lawrence foolishly mentioned it, in confidence, to Frank Harris, who promptly published it in the *Saturday Review.* Lawrence never spoke to Harris again; but then, no one ever did.

AFTERWORD

The Rare Book section of the British Museum possesses the only known copy of the Rev. Cabbage's *Sermons in Steam*, long claimed by the family to have been manufactured by the Word Loom. Unfortunately, even a casual inspection reveals that this is not the case; with the exception of the last page (223–4), the volume was clearly printed on a normal flatbed press.

Page 223–4 however, is an obvious insert. The impression is very uneven, and the text is replete with spelling mistakes and typographical errors.

Is this indeed the only surviving production of perhaps the most remarkable—and misguided—technological effort of the Victorian Age? Or is it a deliberate fake, created to give the impression that the Word Loom actually operated at least once—however poorly?

We shall never know the truth, but as an Englishman I am proud of the fact that one of today's most important inventions was first conceived in the British Isles. Had matters turned out slightly differently, Charles Cabbage might now have been as famous as James Watt, George Stephenson—or even Isambard Kingdom Brunel.

41

FATHER
OF
FRANKENSTEIN

Although "The Steam-Powered Word-Processor" is what John Campell would have called a non-fact article, I can assure you that it was based on considerable research, and many of the references are perfectly genuine. And so, believe it or not, is everything in the following chapter. I'm not making *any* of this up.

The Rev. Charles Cabbage owes nothing more than his name to the eccentric patron saint of computers, Charles Babbage; his real prototype was an almost equally remarkable but now forgotten amateur scientist, Andrew Crosse. In 1836 Crosse created a sensation by reporting that minute insects ("acari") had apparently been produced in mineral salts through which he had been passing electric currents. He did not claim to have created life, but that was the implication. Although the great Faraday was sympathetic, the scientific community greeted his experiments with about as much skepticism as it now regards Fred Hoyle and Chandra Wickramasinghe's claim that Halley's Comet is covered with bacteria.

Nevertheless, Andrew Crosse's legacy to the whole world may be far greater than he could possibly have imagined, owing to the following sequence of events:

In 1806 the poet Robert Southey (1774–1843) was walking over the Somerset hills when he came across the little village of Broomfield, where Crosse was the local squire. They became good friends, Crosse told the poet about his electrical experiments—and Southey passed the information on to Percy and Mary Shelley, who were fascinated by science. When Crosse came to London in December 1814 to give a public lecture, Mary Shelley was in the audience. And three years later, she wrote *Frankenstein*—which, as Brian Aldiss has reminded us, marks the beginning of real science fiction.

The evidence, though purely circumstantial, is quite impressive. It is all set out by the anthologist of the occult Peter Haining, in a book of literary detection to which he gave the thought-provoking title *The Man Who Was Frankenstein.**

I first heard of Crosse in the late 1930s, when my friend William Temple worked him into one of his short stories. Yet, incredibly, not until two years ago did it dawn upon me that his residence (and laboratory) at Fyne Court was almost within sight of my own Somerset home—only four miles away, as the bat flies.

My brother Michael, who is a walking encyclopedia of local lore, took me to Broomfield when I visited England in 1985. Although a fire had destroyed the laboratory section (I cannot confirm that it was torched by fear-maddened peasants) some of the equipment and furniture still survive. Most remarkable of all, one of the conductors which Crosse used for ill-advised attempts to tap atmospheric electricity can still be seen, high up in the fork of an ancient tree on the estate. As I stared at this relic, I remembered how the lightning played around the hulking, soon-to-be-animated body of William Henry Pratt— a.k.a. Boris Karloff.

All this, only four miles away up in the rolling Quantock Hills over which I had often cycled in my boyhood! But there is more to come.

During World War II, there were numerous army camps in the vicinity, and the local soldiers often came to Ballifants Farm to hire our ponies for recreation. After checking that

*Frederick Muller, London, 1979.

they knew which end bit and which end kicked, Mother would send them off over the countryside. When I was on leave, I would sometimes act as a guide, so that they did not get hopelessly lost in the wilds of darkest Somerset. In those days, the bicycle and the horse were my preferred modes of transportation—at least for short distances, and in good weather. (I am still inordinately proud of being unable to drive a car; though I did get my driver's license in Sydney in 1955, that was the last time I ever sat behind a steering wheel.)

One of Mother's favorite customers in those wartime days was a young actor who, unlike most young actors, was later to become famous. I wonder if our ponies ever took him past Broomfield Churchyard, where—if Peter Haining's theory is correct—lies the man who would inspire his most famous role.

A couple of years ago I sent him my mother's reminiscences, and got a nice "Thank you" note, which ends:

"If you see Carrie Fisher again—please give her 'Grand Moff Tarkin's' best wishes!

"In all sincerity—Peter Cushing."

The most appropriate ending to this book—and, as you will see, to *anything*—is the shortest contribution I ever made to *Astounding/Analog*. It was originally only thirty-one carefully crafted words long; and would you believe that a vital one was misprinted on publication?

Here is the final version, and I hope the printer gets it right this time. Especially the title—which, I am sure you will agree, is the only possible one . . .

4 2

"SISENEG"

And God said: "Lines Aleph Zero to Aleph One—Delete."
  And the Universe ceased to exist.
Then She pondered for several eons, and sighed.
  "Cancel Program GENESIS," She ordered.
It never *had* existed.

APPENDIX

This, to the best of my knowledge (and thanks again to Mike Ashley's *Index)* is a complete listing of all my appearances in *Astounding/Analog*, 1938–87.

FICTION

1946 April: "Loophole" (1)
     May: "Rescue Party" (2)
1948 September: "Inheritance" (1)
1949 September: "Hide and Seek" (1)
1961 May: "Death and the Senator" (3)
1984 May: "siseneG"
1986 January: "The Steam-Powered Word-Processor"
(1) Reprinted in *Expedition to Earth*
(2) Reprinted in *Reach for Tomorrow*
(3) Reprinted in *Tales of Ten Worlds*

NON-FICTION

1976 July: "Man, Space and Destiny." (Address to the House of Representatives Committee on Space Science, July 24, 1975.)
     Reprinted in *The View from Serendip*.

LETTERS

(John W. Campbell usually made a brief comment at the head of each letter: these are printed *in italics*.)

May, December 1938

Not reprinted here as they are both largely mathematical: see Chapter 24, "Rocket Warfare." The first letter is photo-reproduced in *Ascent to Orbit* (Wiley, 1984); the second answers a critic and repeats the fundamental rocket equation. (My name is given as "Clark"! Grrr . . .)

October 1939

From the British Interplanetary Society

Dear Mr. Campbell,

I was very interested to see Schuyler Miller's letter concerning spaceship crews in the July *Astounding*. As you know, this Society has been working on the subject for several years and you have already seen our designs for a lunar ship, which were printed in our last *Journal*.

There's no need to have a large crew on an ordinary interplanetary voyage, apart from a fullblooded expedition out to take a planet to bits. Actually, one man could, as Miller suggested, do the job. It is only during the actual takeoffs and landings that there is anything much to do, and at these moments it's impossible for more than one pair of hands to be on the controls. At least, it's highly inadvisable!

During all the days of the voyage, apart from the few hectic minutes at the beginning and end there is practically nothing for the crew to do except take occasional observations and make the corresponding corrections. This would involve one man for only a small fraction of his time.

Moreover, spaceship machinery must be largely automatic, simply because things happen so quickly. Even in the first design for a lunar spaceship we have planned a practically automatic takeoff, as you will see by the article and circuits on robot control in the *Journal*. These circuits have been arranged so that by a selector system similar to that of an automatic telephone exchange, the correct tubes are picked out and fired in the right "staggered" sequence. Moreover, the arrangement will keep the ship on its course if it starts to "wobble"—linear stability is given to a large extent by the axial spin—and in addition we have incorporated the gyro-mechanism suggested by you some time back in a previous letter.

This "robot pilot" should take the ship safely away from the Earth without the interference of the crew. When free space is reached it will be necessary to take observations, reduce them—with luck, we could get the astronomers back on Earth to do this—and then make the navigational corrections. Then, for all the good it could do the crew might just as well go to sleep for the rest of the voyage. If anyone can think of a reason for keeping watch in space I'd be glad to hear it.

I'm sending a copy of this *Journal* to Miller, so that he and de Camp can fight it out between them. But I'm hoping that these remarks will be of general interest to your readers especially if anyone else joins in the scrap.

Arthur C. Clarke, British Interplanetary Society,
88 Gray's Inn Road, London, WCI, England.

March 1940

We hope they did get all the issues over there

Dear Mr. Campbell,

Many thanks for printing my letter regarding the control of spaceships: it has resulted in several inquiries from readers and no doubt more will come in as the mail trickles through. I have been able to deal with all letters received so far, but I would like to apologize in advance to any readers who may not receive replies to their communications. The BIS has now been carefully packed up in cold storage for the duration and until the war is over we have stopped all active work. Most of our officers have been scattered to the four winds or called up: I shall be going in a relatively short time now and so will not be in a position to answer any correspondence—even if it reached me safely.

When we get back again we will start the society going once more, and I'll drop you a line to that effect. Obviously a slight disturbance like the present civil war cannot be permitted to upset the conquest of space!

My best wishes for the future progress of *Astounding*. I sincerely hope that I can get hold of the rest of *Gray Lensman*!

Arthur C. Clarke, British Interplanetary Society,
88 Gray's Inn Road, London, WCI, England.

April 1946

Thanks—but we're just as glad it didn't develop. Besides, with atomic energy, chemical rockets seem unnecessary anyway.

Dear Campbell:

V2's erratic contrail is still a bit of a mystery. By now you'll have seen the newsreels which show that it goes up as sedately as an elevator, without any hunting or jerking at all. It seems possible that only the trail is irregular: quite obviously the rocket itself couldn't follow some of the right-angled bends the photos show.

There's a very common fallacy which I'm sorry to see you've repeated in your note on V2. A nose-drive rocket is no more stable than a tail-drive one. It's not like a pendulum hanging from a support which must be above the center of gravity for stability. If you consider a nose-drive rocket with the thrust making an angle with the center line, the rocket will keep turning indefinitely because the misalignment will always remain fixed. The result is exactly the same if the thrust is applied at the tail. So there's no point whatsoever in putting the motor ahead of the c.g.

Incidentally, the controlling vanes in the jet were made of wood in the later V2s! I spent an afternoon examining one the other day and sent some of the glass-wool insulation to Willy as a souvenir!

There was an historic gathering in London last month when the Chief Superintendent of Scientific Research at the Royal Aircraft Establishment gave a lecture to a packed audience of the Royal Aeronautical Society, the subject being German long-range rocket development. Handley Page was in the chair and looking at all the gold-braid around the hall I couldn't help thinking that the rocket had become respectable mighty fast. This was the first time that any information on the transatlantic projects had been released. In case you don't know what was coming to you, von Braun and his boys were going to put wings on a V2 and sit that on top of an 85-ton booster. The first two-step ship in fact. The bottom step would be dropped at 3,000 mph—and recovered by parachute—and the top one would go on to 8,000 mph. When it came down into the lower atmosphere it would go into a 2,000 mile glide, losing kinetic energy all the time. The total range would have been 3,000 miles, covered in 45 minutes. I won't make myself unpopular by saying it's a pity it never got past the project stage—but you know how the astronauts in this country felt about V2.

Flight Lieutenant A. C. Clarke, RAF

(Campbell's optimistic remark that we wouldn't need chemical propellants now that atomic energy had arrived reflects the feeling we all had, forty years ago. A nuclear-powered rocket was indeed successfully tested by the U.S.—then abandoned after more than a billion dollars had been spent. But some day . . .

And there's no mystery now about the V2's "erratic" trail, which prompted JWC to say that's just what you'd expect from a primitive rocket. Upper-atmosphere winds were merely zigzagging the vapor trail; you can often observe the same effect behind a high-flying jet.)

August 1948

Towards the end of the war, as much as ten megawatts was being generated on pulses!

Dear Campbell,

I was very interested in J. J. Coupling's article on the magnetron, the more so because Professor Randall—who with Dr. Boot invented the cavity magnetron—is my physics professor here at King's College. In the lab we have a fine selection of maggies with outputs up to 2½ megawatts. (I can't imagine any terrestrial application for the last one!)

There was nothing chancy or particularly spectacular about the evolution of the magnetron in Professor Oliphant's microwave group at Birmingham University—just the usual development once the original ideas have been worked out. Certainly no one stuck a cathode in a revolver chamber to see what happened. But I know how that story arose: a revolver barrel was used as a jig to make one maggie, as it happened to come out about the right size.

Oddly enough, the Russians were the first people to make cavity magnetrons, years before we did. There's a paper about it in the *Proc. IRE* in the early 1940s. Some of the designs were strikingly like the final Allied ones. But they were low-powered, c.w. jobs as far as I know and I don't think the Russians realized just what they'd got.

Arthur C. Clarke, King's College, University of London, Strand, London, WC1, England.

(How could I have dreamed that, almost forty years later, "J. J. Coupling", alias Dr. John Pierce, would be my guest here in Sri Lanka?)

December 1951

Radio reaching out 238,000 miles to finger moondust!

Dear Campbell,

I'd like to congratulate you on the "quantum jump" *Astounding* has made in the art and story departments in the last two months. I'd have written before but I was waiting to see if you could keep it up. You have.

A note on Daniel Whitton's "No Green Cheese": It is not generally agreed by astronomers that lunar craters are caused by meteors. I don't know any serious lunar observers in this country who believe it!

There's a sentence in this article that shows how dangerous it is to make negative predictions nowadays. Whitton remarks, re the lunar dust layer, "Our experimental limitations keep us, of course, from probing farther beneath." Actually, Australian radio physicists, working on 24,000 Mc/s, have already got about a meter inside the Moon! They have shown that the dust layer is probably only about 1 mm thick, with solid rock underneath. For full details, see "Microwave Thermal Radiation From the Moon," J. H. Piddington and H. C. Minnett. *(Aus. J. Sci. Res.* 2, 63–77—March 1949). Gold's theory did seem a little too ingenious to be true!

Arthur C. Clarke, London, N22, England.

(The anxious engineers at NASA seem to have overlooked this early disproof of Dr. Thomas Gold's theory that much of the lunar surface was covered with deep blankets of dust. And—luckily—it didn't prevent me writing *A Fall of Moondust* almost a decade later.)

September 1952

When we get there, and stake out our claims, maybe we'll find the British sector full of non-meteoric craters and the American sector covered with meteor splashes.

Dear Campbell,

My good friend Willy Ley has fallen smack into the trap I rather naughtily set—though I didn't bait it for him and am somewhat distressed by the result! When saying that I knew no British observer who believed in the meteor theory of lunar craters, I refrained from adding that I knew none who believed in the volcanic theory either. So Willy's demolition of this completely obsolete hypothesis is a little late in the day. . . .

Let me quote from a recent paper by the Secretary of the Lunar Section of the British Astronomical Association—with which is associated most of the world's leading practical observers, including Dr. Walter Haas's important group in the United States: "I do not know of any practical lunar observer who has any use for the meteoric theory today . . . it is as untenable as Nasmyth and Carpenter's volcanic fountain. We know a few meteor craters on Earth . . . but these objects are no more like lunar craters than are the cones of Vesuvius."

In the event that there's anyone besides Willy Ley who still believes in the meteor theory I'd like to make the following points:

1. The crater Wargentin has filled up to the brim—presumably with lava—forming a flat plateau fifty-six miles wide, standing high above the surrounding terrain. Clearly igneous forces are involved here—and if you have to bring them in, why bother about meteors?

2. Craters are not randomly distributed over the lunar surface; huge areas are relatively free from them. They also have a remarkable tendency to occur in bands running north-south. Turn a map of the moon sideways and see what I mean. It would take mighty intelligent meteors to produce these effects.

3. The existence of interlocked crater chains, clearly following some line of weakness, often not a straight one, is absolutely fatal to any impact hypothesis. The best example is the Hyginus cleft.

After all this, how were lunar craters formed? Don't ask me—I wasn't there. But I'd point out that the classic modern—and American!—book on the subject, Spurr's *Geology Applied to Selenology* gives a reasonably satisfactory explanation of all lunar formations from internal, igneous causes.

Finally, I'll backpedal a bit. There must be some meteor craters on the moon—perhaps quite a few of the smaller, shallow ones. And I must confess that I've a horrible feeling that when we're actually standing inside the wall of Plato, we'll still be arguing about what caused them.

Arthur C. Clarke

(This time, the American observers (and Willy Ley) were 90 percent right, and the British ones (and myself) 90 percent wrong; it now seems incredible that anyone doubted the meteoric explanation for the lunar craters. But my examples were well chosen; they did indeed prove that—as we now know—igneous forces were also at work.

The whole problem with this long debate—like even more protracted religious ones—is that each side insisted it was 100 percent right, and refused to admit any qualifications.)

October 1959

"Naughty but nice," maybe?

Dear John,

Urgent correction to Schuyler Miller's "Reference Library" for June. I never suggested sending some "nice girls" into space as astronauts' companions; the responsibility is Bob Richardson's.

You can quote me as recommending not nice girls, but naughty ones.

Arthur C. Clarke

(This exchange, which nowadays would be rightly condemned as blatant "sexism," was a response to a tongue-in-cheek article by Dr. Robert S. Richardson about some of the biological problems of space travel.

Bob Richardson was one of the first professional astronomers to take astronautics seriously, and wrote many articles for *Astounding/Analog* (as well as fiction under the name "Philip Latham"). I shall always be grateful to him for taking me around Mount Wilson Observatory on a sizzling day in 1952—

even though he terrified me by his technique for re-starting his stalled car on the way up the mountain. He simply cooled off the engine by pouring gasoline over it. . . .

For the reaction of my old sparring-partner C. S. Lewis to Bob's suggestion, see his farcical short story "Ministering Angels." (Originally published in *The Magazine of Fantasy and Science Fiction*, January 1958: reprinted in *Of Other Worlds* (1966) and *The Dark Tower* (1977). The "Mars" of this story is very different indeed from that of *Out of the Silent Planet*—more earthy, let's say. . . .)

March 1968

"Applied Science Fiction" applied to science fiction—completely appropriate!

Dear Mr. Campbell,

I was absolutely fascinated by Will Jenkins's story of his invention—because for the last two months Stanley Kubrick has been using it on the largest scale yet in *2001: A Space Odyssey*. When Stanley told me about "Front Projection" my immediate reaction was, "What crazy nut invented this?" I might have guessed it would be an sf writer. . . .

I gather that our use is the first time in Cinerama: the enormous screen of back-reflecting material cost about $15,000. The projector was specially built for 8–10 (I think) color transparencies shot in South West Africa. I've seen the results— they are completely convincing.

All this, incidentally, is for a very difficult sequence showing the origin of Homo sapiens, circa 3,000,000 BC. Sorry I can't show you any stills; there will never be any. Stanley won't allow this sequence to be photographed.

After my comsat contretemps, I also sympathize with Will over his patent problems. (It's no coincidence that another sf writer, Ted Thomas, has beaten the drum for both of us!) At least I can promise him a seat at the première around Easter. . . .

Arthur C. Clarke

(Ted Thomas is Theodore L(ockhard) Thomas, patent lawyer and author, who wrote a spoof article "The Lagging Profession" *(Analog,* January 1961) in which one Arthur C. Clarke tries to patent the communication satellite—and fails. Not that it would have mattered anyway, as the patent would have expired just before commercial operations started. . . .)

December 1971

My source—a respected British Journal—seems to have misled me. They evidently reported "deaths" where they should have said "cases."

Dear John:

As one who's been trying for the last few years to build up Ceylon tourism—despite recent discouragements from insurgents—I take an extremely dim view of your July editorial. Just how big do you think the country is? You've killed off half the population in two years! My friends often say I'm not very observant, but I'm sure I'd have noticed that. . . .

In 1966, when you say the malaria death toll was 2.8 million, the total number of deaths from all causes was actually about 95,000. (The population then was 11.4 million and the death rate 8.3 per thousand.) I don't have the later figures, but they're in the same ball park.

I can only assume that you've got hold of the sickness figures, though I find it hard to believe that they are that high. More likely the number of man-days lost. New York would sound a mighty unhealthy place if all 'flu cases were put down as deaths.

Nevertheless, there's some validity in your argument. Ceylon is the classic, textbook case of malaria control by DDT—in the late 1940s—followed by population explosion and its attendant problems. And a slackening of the spraying campaign did result in an upsurge in disease for a time.

Arthur C. Clarke

It would have been pleasant if my correspondence with the magazine could have ended on a happier note; alas, sixteen years later, both mosquitoes and insurgents are even more numerous in Sri Lanka.

But there is nowhere else on Earth that I wish to live, while I wait to see what *really* happens in 2001.

Colombo, January 15, 1988

ARTHUR C. CLARKE is perhaps the most famous science fiction writer of all time. In addition to *Rendevous with Rama*, he has written such million-copy bestsellers as *Childhood's End*, *2001: A Space Odyssey,* and *2010: Odyssey Two.* He cobroadcast the Apollo 11, 12, and 15 missions with Walter Cronkite and Captain Wally Schirra and shared an Oscar nomination with Stanley Kubrick for the film version of *2001: A Space Odyssey.* Mr. Clarke currently lives in the island country of Sri Lanka, where he is at work on the follow-up novel to his latest book, *RAMA II,* cowritten with NASA scientist Gentry Lee.